OUTLIVING · THE · SELF

Outliving the Self

GENERATIVITY AND THE INTERPRETATION OF LIVES

John N. Kotre

THE JOHNS HOPKINS UNIVERSITY PRESS

Baltimore and London

The Johns Hopkins University Press, Baltimore, Maryland 21218
The Johns Hopkins Press Ltd, London

The paper in this book is acid-free and meets the guidelines for permanence and durability of the Committee on Production Guidelines for Book Longevity of the Council on Library Resources.

LIBRARY OF CONGRESS CATALOGING IN PUBLICATION DATA

Kotre, John N.
  Outliving the self.
    Bibliography: p.
    Includes index.
    1. Adulthood—Case studies.   2. Self—Case studies.
3. Children and adults—Case studies.   4. Social psychology
—Case studies.   5. Erikson, Erik H. (Erik Homburger),
1902–   .   I. Title.   II. Title: Generativity and the
interpretation of lives.
BF724.5.K67   1984   155.6   84-47950
ISBN 0-8018-2507-5

FOR STEPHEN, DAVID, AND MY-LINH,

in anticipation of the time
when they will understand.

CONTENTS

ACKNOWLEDGMENTS

I wish to thank the following people for the role each played in helping this book along. Their contributions ranged from encouragement and sponsorship to critical reading, careful word-processing, and expeditious publishing. In the order of their appearance in the life of the project, they are David Riesman, George Rosenwald, John Brownfain, Tom Cottle, Paul Moceri, Rick Ochberg, Jeff Evans, Hank Greenspan, Greg Kasza, Larry Gruppen, Wendy Harris, Jack Goellner, and Trudie Calvert. Special thanks go to Violet Dalla Vecchia, who was indispensable as a transcriber, reader, and indexer, and to the Dearborn and Ann Arbor campuses of the University of Michigan, which provided small but important doses of financial support. I am grateful above all to the individuals who spent many hours recounting to me the story of their lives. Some of them appear in this book and some do not, but all have left their mark on it.

OUTLIVING · THE · SELF

Introduction

I n the late 1970s professional observers of American society began to worry about a growing incapacity or unwillingness on the part of its citizens to identify with the future—to be interested in offspring and willing to sacrifice for them, to leave the site of one's life in better shape than it was found, to feel one has something of value for succeeding generations. Usually their concern was expressed in footnotes to critiques of "meism" or "individualism" or "self-absorption" or any of a dozen names given to a new flaunting of egocentrism.[1] "We are fast losing the sense of historical continuity, the sense of belonging to a succession of generations originating in the past and stretching into the future," wrote Christopher Lasch when he first discussed the "narcissist society."[2] In *The Age of Sensation* Herbert Hendin reported on a feeling among young college women that equated motherhood with "male assault, the lethal shot that ends your life." Caring was felt by his male and female subjects to be a self-destructive trap, synonymous with losing, and raising a child "an unrelieved chore with no objective rewards."[3]

These observations suggested the presence of a growing ambiguity surrounding a quality that Erik Erikson has called *generativity*. When he defined generativity as "an interest in establishing and guiding the next generation," Erikson was speaking of physical procreation, but he meant more, much more: productivity, creativity, caring for one's sector of the world. "Parenthood," he wrote, "is, for most, the first, and for many, the prime generative encounter, yet the perpetuation of mankind challenges the generative ingenuity of workers and thinkers of many kinds." Indeed, parents may have many children but remain nongenerative: self-indulgent, uncaring, "stagnant." A monk, on the other hand, may strive to settle his "relationship to the Care for the creatures of this world and to the Charity which is felt to transcend it"; he may concern himself with "what in Hinduism is called the maintenance of the world"; he may view spiritual progeny as a welcome trust and have much to pass on to them. Childless, he is nonetheless generative.[4]

Lasch contended that the narcissism of the 1970s—the precise inverse of generativity—was a response to the anxieties created by the growth of monopoly capitalism and large-scale bureaucracy. Others related the egocentrism of that decade to the loosening of familial bonds, to secularization, to rapidly propagating strains of psychotherapy,[5] to a crisis of legitimacy characteristic of late capitalism,[6] even to a culture deprived of belief in public man.[7] Most interpreters sensed a collective mood of despair brought on by economic stagnation, rising inflation, the dwindling of natural resources, disillusionment with leaders, and the growing threat of nuclear annihilation.

Whatever the causes of cultural egocentrism, and however widespread it actually was and is,[8] its portrayal by social critics is the photographic negative of work I have been doing for a number of years on generativity. When Lasch lamented the loss of a sense of generational continuity, I was beginning to interview individuals strengthened and burdened by that sense. My work originated with personal concerns, most of them tied to approaching the age of forty, but it also stemmed from the recognition that the circumstances of our fertility—the setting in which we extend ourselves into the future through physical and cultural reproduction— have been dramatically altered. Not only has the contraceptive revolution of the 1960s and 1970s had a direct impact on sexuality and childbearing, it has also amplified shifts in the life cycle under way since the turn of the century. We are living longer; we are devoting less of our lives to children; fewer generations are living together under the same roof. In this new context, how are we to be fertile?

For a motive so critical to our collective well-being, for one embarking on so radically altered a future, generativity has received only incidental glances from psychology. Recently I made computerized searches of four social science bibliographies for the occurrence of the term. The most productive of the searches took place in *Psychological Abstracts*, which each year indexes more than nine hundred periodicals and fifteen hundred books, monographs, and dissertations. In the seventeen years that *Psychological Abstracts* has been computerized, close to three hundred and fifty thousand citations have been filed. The word *generativity* appears either in the title or in the paragraph-long abstract of only nineteen of those citations, an average of about once a year.

This book is an attempt to redress that oversight by initiating a conversation about generativity against the backdrop of the contraceptive and demographic revolutions. The method is life-historical. Over the past six years I have recorded and studied in depth the biographies of fifteen individuals whose lives address particular facets of generativity. This work combined with the previous writing of two major biographies and some thirty other life-historical interviews to shape a theory of generativity that departs substantially from Erikson's. In this book I present that theory as well as eight life histories that illuminate it, develop it, and, paradoxically, show how the particularities of individual lives elude even the most ambitious of theories.

A word about explanation. The theory I have developed explains generativity, but not in the way that quantitative researchers understand explanation. Though the theory is full of hypotheses that quantitative researchers can pursue, it does not make predictions that are then tested with samples of sufficient size. Rather, the theory aims at a different order of knowledge. It seeks to explain by providing a coherent framework to which individual cases can be linked. Explanation in life-historical research comes down to interpretation, or the discovery of connections. Connections must be found between what is past and what is present, between what is latent and what is manifest in an individual's history. Connections must also be found between histories, and (in the case of the present research) between a group of histories and the larger context of fertility.

In the first chapter of this book I present the overarching theory to which individual life histories will be linked through interpretation. In the second I document how the setting of generativity has been altered by the contraceptive and demographic revolutions. Then I discuss my method: the process of "life-storytelling," which has a minor but long-standing tradition in the history of the social sciences. Beginning in Chapter 4 I retell the stories of eight individuals who have been affected, some more, some less, by generativity's new setting. The subjects of the stories are women and men who range in age from thirty-four to seventy-six. They are people I have known for anywhere from two to six years, and they have read and reacted to their stories. Following each profile is an interpretation that connects it to theory and builds a bridge to the next chapter.

Lives compressed into single stories are like time-lapse films of growing plants. They enable development to be seen whole and enable one whole to be compared with another. My hope in the first instance is that readers will read the stories and form their own perspectives on how particular manifestations of fertility are linked to the entire pattern of a life. Then I hope readers will see how interpretation, which I have kept separate from the biographies themselves, can make lives mutually informative and open a window to broader questions of theory. All in all, I trust that the combination of story and interpretation will take the concept of generativity out of hiding and shape it into the cornerstone of a psychology responsive to the current demographic and reproductive facts of our lives.

PART · I

The Setting

1 · *A Theory of Generativity*

*G*enerativity is a concept that invites us to see the entire range of ways human beings leave their stamp on the future. For Erikson, words like *productivity* and *creativity* are too narrow to span the distance from biological urge to artistic desire, to point simultaneously to the results of our "genitality and genes" as well as of our "works and ideas." *Generativity*, however, denotes a power that is both instinctual and psychosocial, one that engages imagination, reason, conscience, and will. *Generativity* covers both the "low" and "high" in humans, denigrating neither, showing in fact that the two are continuous. The word refers not only to activities as diverse as conceiving progeny and initiating social movements but also to caring for them once they are brought into existence.[1]

In this chapter I wish to summarize and modify Erikson's understanding of generativity, to introduce related theory and research, and to present the model upon which interpretations of the life stories presented in the book will be based.

GENERATIVITY AS A STAGE

Although *generativity* refers to an "urge," an "instinct," a "desire"—that is, to a motive—it is also used by Erikson to denote a specific stage in life, the seventh of his well-known "eight ages of man." In Erikson's view of the life cycle, the crisis of generativity occurs in middle adulthood, when conflicting impulses lead one either to invest in and care for what one is leaving behind, or, out of a sense of stagnation and personal impoverishment, to indulge oneself as if one were one's own child. The outcome of the crisis depends in large measure on the outcome of previous stages—on the trust, autonomy, initiative, and industry that are the legacies of the four stages of childhood and on the senses of identity and intimacy that result from adolescence and young adulthood, the fifth and

sixth stages. Erikson elegantly summarizes the stages leading to generativity: "In youth you find out what you *care to do* and who you *care to
be*—even in changing roles. In young adulthood you learn whom you
care to be with—at work and in private life, not only exchanging intima-
cies, but sharing intimacy. In adulthood, however, you learn to know
what and whom you can *take care of*."[2] The fruit of generativity comes in
the eighth stage. It is ego-integrity, the feeling in old age that life has
been full, worthwhile, rewarding, "the acceptance of one's one and only
life cycle as something that had to be and that, by necessity, permitted of
no substitutions."[3]

The eight qualities that name the stages exist in conjunction with their
opposites, and the achievement of each stage is not that the positive
quality triumph over its negative counterpart but that a favorable ratio
exist between the two. To begin life well, the infant should have more
trust than mistrust, and to close life well, the old person should have
more integrity than despair; but mistrust and despair are never absent
from the personality. Nor do the concerns of a particular stage exist only
within the age limits that define the stage. All eight qualities exist with
their opposites throughout life, each stage representing no more than the
period when a particular struggle is dominant. The analogy is with
embryonic development, in which all parts grow simultaneously, each
part having its time of ascendance. In the human life cycle, generative
strivings peak during middle adulthood and struggle at that time against
tendencies to self-absorption, but instances of generativity have occurred
many times before, even in childhood. These early manifestations are
precursors of the maturational crisis to come.[4]

As researchers since Erikson have become more aware of the effects of
living longer and with fewer children, they have become impressed with
the flexibility of the life cycle and hence critical of Erikson's outline and,
for that matter, of any fixed-stage theory of development. As Matilda
White Riley writes, many such theories suffer from fallacies. One is the
"fallacy of age reification," which occurs in intimations that a certain
psychological stage is entered *because* one has reached a certain age.
Another is the "cohort-centric fallacy," in which theorists searching for
universals overgeneralize the experience of a single historical cohort,
usually their own. Despite overwhelming evidence of flexibility and
variety in the way people age, Riley laments, "misleading stereotypes
and fixed-stage theories still abound."[5]

Though Erikson has always claimed that his theory is a tool for
thought and not a prescription, his scheme does suffer from connotations
of fixedness. As regards generativity, Erikson fails to sort out different
types, and so his schedule for their appearance is misleading. Biological

generativity—conceiving and bearing children—has had a far earlier onset and conclusion, particularly in the case of women, than cultural generativity—the passing on of values. The midpoint of its life (accompanied, perhaps, by the fear of permanent sterility) occurs around thirty, but the midlife of cultural generativity may come decades later. If we look at the full range of generative expression—as I shall soon do explicitly—we will see a number of schedules at work. We can only be impressed by the vicissitudes of this motive in adult life.

GENERATIVITY AS A VIRTUE

To date, generativity has been spoken of by Erikson and others as a desirable achievement, an ideal.[6] From the interplay of generativity and its opposite, self-absorption, comes a virtue: care. According to this usage, adults either impress the next generation for good or ignore it. They are either caring or uncaring. This choice of words overlooks the possibility of leaving a heritage of active destruction, of propagating not good or even neglect—but evil. It overlooks the dark side of generativity, its multifold capacity for perversion.

In his mildly Jungian interpretation of forty middle-aged men, Daniel Levinson shows an appreciation of the damage done in creation. A man at midlife wishes to be creative, but that wish "is accompanied by a greater awareness of the destructive forces in nature, in human life generally, and in himself. . . . In working toward a higher Good, we also produce its antithesis—the conception and the actuality of Evil."[7] The men Levinson studied were at midlife coming to terms with the recognition that they had inevitably harmed others and with the remorse they felt for having done so. And though Erikson does not link destructiveness with the term *generativity*, his treatment of Luther and Gandhi reveals a complex understanding of the dark ways in which one can relate to offspring and followers: how one can turn a deaf ear to them, be horrified by them, vilify them, disown or abandon them.[8]

It would be sensible, then, to avoid speaking of generativity solely as a virtue. Whether fruit is nourishing or poisonous, it still issues from a mechanism of reproduction. Curses leave marks as lasting as do blessings; tales that frighten are as potent as tales that uplift. In the words of Shakespeare's Mark Antony, "The evil that men do lives after them." Failing to classify monuments of destruction as the products of fertility closes our eyes to the full reach of this pervasive human motive. Though doing so calls for changing a semantic habit (one that I myself have practiced), it would be better to view generativity as an impulse that can be channeled into vice as well as into virtue.

FOUR TYPES OF GENERATIVITY

In this modified view, generativity may be defined as *a desire to invest one's substance in forms of life and work that will outlive the self*. The investments are ways of achieving material and symbolic unity with an extensive and enduring future. As a motive, generativity is both instinctual and psychosocial, seeking biological as well as cultural outlets. It is limited neither to virtuous expression nor to a single stage of development. In the life cycle, generativity has precursors in the caring play of children and in the way they teach those younger than themselves. Its first clear manifestation is in the adolescent's capacity to reproduce. Yet it ordinarily does not become a dominant concern until the end is in sight—the end of one's fertility, the end of one's career, the end of one's life. For many, the inevitability of the end is realized at midlife, the point to which Erikson assigns the "crisis" of generativity and to which Levinson assigns the task of "creating a legacy."[9]

The wish to be generative is in many ways like the wish to live forever. Robert Lifton describes immortality as "a compelling universal urge to maintain an inner sense of continuous symbolic relationship, over time and space, with the various elements of life." It is expressed biologically in a sense of "living on *through* and *in* one's sons and daughters and their sons and daughters," a mode of expression central to East Asian culture, especially in traditional China. It is also expressed through works in the sense that "one's writing, one's teaching, one's human influences, great or humble, will live on; that one's contribution will not die."[10] In Levinson's Jungian interpretation, the desire for immortality is an aspect of the archetype of being Young. To feel Young (no matter what one's age) is to feel lively, growing, full of potential, but also fragile, impulsive, inexperienced. To feel Old (and an infant is already growing old) is to feel as though one is in a rut, rotting, coming to the end; but it is also to feel wise, powerful, and accomplished. At midlife, Young and Old are rebalanced, and the cry for immortality is heard from the Young archetype. At this point in their lives the men in Levinson's study began to take pride in the development of offspring, to care about communities, religious organizations, colleges, unions, professional societies—institutions of enduring value. They began to invest the best of their Old in the next generation and to take vicarious pleasure in another's Young. They began, in short, to create a legacy as a claim on immortality.[11]

Despite similarities in meaning, however, generativity and immortality are not coterminous; and not all symbols of immortality (living on in an afterlife, for example) entail creating something in one's own image.

No one has captured the difference in meaning better than Woody Allen, who said on one occasion, "I don't want to achieve immortality through my works. I want to achieve immortality by not dying."

To be generative is likewise to be creative, but there are important differences between what this pair of words implies. *Creativity* connotes, first, that something new is made, while *generativity* connotes that something old is passed on. In practice, this distinction may be lost, for even though creative products appear to emerge *ex nihilo*, they often contain much of the work of previous generations. Connected with this difference in implication is a second: the absence in psychological discussions of creativity of any idea of infusing the self into what is made (*creativity* is typically defined as the ability to discover novel yet appropriate solutions to problems or to make original syntheses). Finally, creativity ends once the product is made, but generativity implies caring for the product as it grows and develops. All three points of distinction add up to greater duration in the generative act—more time antecedent to the moment of birth, more time following it.

The full expanse of generativity may be comprehended by delineating four major types (see Table 1). The first is *biological*, which encompasses fertility as demographers and birth planners speak of it: the begetting, bearing, and nursing of children. The target of biological generativity is the newborn baby, but there may be preliminary focal points: a family's "bloodline," the sex organs insofar as they lead to reproduction (that is, the genitals in the true sense of the word), the growing fetus. Only in biological transmission is material substance passed from the body of the progenitor to that of the creation.

The potential life span of biological fertility is nearly four decades in women and even longer in men. But in practice, most childbearing in the United States takes place over a much shorter period, on the average during the decade bounded by a woman's early twenties and her early thirties. The curtailment of biological expressions of fertility brought on by the contraceptive revolution of the 1960s and 1970s makes imperative an understanding of other outlets.

Distinct from biological generativity is the *parental* type, which is expressed in feeding, clothing, sheltering, loving, and disciplining offspring and initiating them into the family's traditions. In Erikson's framework, these are the activities that produce trust, autonomy, and initiative in children. They also serve to preserve the continuity of the family. Ordinarily, biological progenitors assume the role of parents, but some children's primary needs are in the hands of other caretakers: foster or adoptive parents, relatives, attendants in institutions. Extraordinary reproductive arrangements such as artificial insemination (and other more

TABLE 1. Types of Generativity

Type	Description
1. Biological	Begetting, bearing, and nursing offspring Generative object: the infant
2. Parental	Nurturing and disciplining offspring, initiating them into a family's traditions Generative object: the child
3. Technical	Teaching skills—the "body" of a culture —to successors, implicitly passing on the symbol system in which the skills are embedded Generative objects: the apprentice, the skill
4. Cultural	Creating, renovating, and conserving a symbol system—the "mind" of a culture—explicitly passing it on to successors Generative objects: the disciple, the culture

sophisticated techniques on the horizon) also separate parents from biological precursors. Parental generativity is foreshadowed by the child's experience of playing at motherhood and fatherhood and of caring for younger children.

In a given life the second type of generativity may be "out of synch" with the first. When a teenager becomes pregnant before she is prepared for motherhood, her biological fertility has raced ahead of her parental. On the other hand, when an older woman is emotionally ready for motherhood but has difficulty conceiving, her biological fertility lags behind her parental. When movement along the generative tracks in a life becomes unsynchronized, the stage is set for critical change.[12]

Because of the decline in childbearing and the lengthening of life, the fraction of a life given to parenting, like that given to biological generativity, has diminished. In some cases, as much as half a life remains once these activities are completed, though extensions of both lines of continuity are possible through grandparenthood.

Technical generativity, the third type, is accomplished by teachers at all stations of the journey through life, who pass on skills to those less advanced than themselves. The skills they teach are myriad: how to read, how to fish, how to fight, how to play the violin, how to steal, how to program a computer, how to perform a healing ritual, how to write a legal brief, and so on. Here the object of legacy-making is the apprentice, with whom the instructor identifies as a way of reliving past experiences of mastery and extending those experiences into the future. The successor's sense of "industry" (by which Erikson means competence at *how to*) rekindles and validates the precursor's own. But the object of generativity is not merely the apprentice, it is also the skill itself, whose life is vicariously the possessor's: this craft shall be kept alive and its potential developed. Often there is conflict between the welfare of the apprentice and that of the skill. One instructor declares that the skill has priority: if the pupil cannot fully master the art in question, cannot perform the right way, he will have to be dismissed. Another instructor favors the pupil: recognizing the limit of students, he compromises technique and teaches only what is in their capacity to learn. The tension between the two receptacles of technical generativity disappears only when a follower comes who can fully command technique and carry it to new heights.

Unlike the biological and parental types, technical generativity is normally not restricted to a single period in the life cycle. It finds expression on numerous occasions between young adulthood and old age. Even children teach each other how to do things, and these experiences, like those of playing at parenthood, become components of later manifestations of fertility. They are not, however, generative in themselves. The teaching of skills becomes generative only when it is imbued with the sense of extending oneself into the apprentice or attaching oneself to a lasting art.

Skills are not transmitted in isolation. They bring in their wake symbol systems offering initiates something more than a sense of competence: a map of existence, a view of a place to settle on that map. These symbol systems, along with the techniques they animate, are commonly called cultures. During skill transmission, culture remains in the background and merely sets the scene. When an old man shows his grandson how to preserve seeds from the best produce in his crop, he is ostensibly passing on a craft. But he is also, by implication, passing on a culture—a belief, in the case of one man I spoke with, in the "miracle of life." In teaching *how to do it*, the technically generative individual also teaches *what it means*—but only indirectly. To the extent that body and mind can be separated, the teaching of technique deals with the body of a culture but not yet its mind.

The fourth type of generativity is directly concerned with mind. When a teacher turns from how to do it to what it means, when she speaks of the *idea* of music or healing or law, when she brings to the fore the symbol system that stood in the background and offers her student the outlines of an identity, she becomes *culturally* generative. She is no longer a teacher of skills but a mentor, and her apprentice has become a disciple.

By culture I mean no more than an integrated set of symbols interpreting existence and giving a sense of meaning and place to members of a perduring collectivity. In the metaphor of anthropologist Clifford Geertz, culture is a web of significance spun by humans to give themselves common footing as they live out their lives.[13] Cultures may be religious, artistic, ideological, scientific, commonsensical, social, ethnic—as diverse as the communities that build them. Individuals may belong in varying degrees to numerous collectivities and so partake of many cultures. Or they may belong (consciously, at least) to none and lack an orienting center giving location and direction to their lives.

In the realm of culture, fertility is expressed in the creation of new symbols that augment a community's storehouse, in the renovation of existing symbols to ensure their relevance for future generations, and in the conservation of symbols in precisely the form in which they already exist. The targets of reproduction are both the culture and the disciple, and the mentor must hold the two in balance. If he is content merely to develop the potential of any and all disciples, he neglects or dilutes the culture's central symbols. But if the preservation of culture is paramount, he makes anonymous receptacles of disciples. What the mentor must do is offer an engaging vision of who the disciple might become, a vision that is true to both the disciple's and the culture's potentials. Under ideal circumstances, one and the same act prepares the ground for identity formation in the follower and serves the mentor's stewardship of his culture.

Like technical generativity, the cultural variant is not restricted to a particular phase of adult life, but its most significant forms occur in the years following biological reproduction. From an evolutionary point of view, this postreproductive period is an anomaly. What function could it possibly serve for the survival of the species? Is it as useless as the flight of a rocket after it has delivered its payload in space? One answer offered by Margaret Mead is that it promotes the survival of children and grandchildren through social instead of biological mechanisms. Old people, for example, might be the only ones who know where to find food and water during a drought because they were the only ones alive during the last one.[14] A related answer is that the postreproductive period of life ensures the transmission of culture, which is vital to human survival.

Generative acts that create new symbols, I suspect, occur earlier in life than those that conserve old ones. Studies have found that creative output peaks early in the second half of life (in the thirties or forties[15]); no comparable data exist, however, for efforts at conserving. In their brief discussion of generativity George Vaillant and Eva Milofsky outline two phases: an early one, marked by change, instability, and creativity, and a later one in which "individuals are more likely to be concerned with . . . promulgating the traditions of their culture rather than with reworking those traditions." In the later phase one becomes a conserver, a "keeper of the meaning."[16]

Another timing feature of generativity involves the coordination of technical and cultural movements in a life. If a creator's idea outstrips her technique, her idea will be deformed; it may even abort. If, on the other hand, the technique is sure but the concept mindless, the work will appear hollow. The same is true of teachers, who need both experience and enthusiasm to engage the hands and minds of students. When one's technical and cultural progressions are "in synch," she is in a position to create a rich heritage.

From the standpoint of classical psychoanalysis, which positions itself at the beginning of life and sees everything as an outgrowth of biological urges then present, the cultural acts of adulthood are mere sublimations of instinctual drives. The content of the acts is lost in the distance and is at any rate unimportant; what matters is that an instinct has been convoluted by a repressive culture to allow for its safe discharge. A psychology of generativity, however, stations itself at the end of life and looks backward to the beginning. From this vantage point, culture is not an adversary but a collaborator. It offers a ride to the future in exchange for a human face to concretize its symbols. The individual weaves an aspect of himself into a tapestry of meaning that has extension and continuity. He becomes the voice of a tradition larger than himself, and the tradition flows through him to the young. In this way culture carries on.[17]

As one moves from biological to cultural life, the distance between the subject and object of generation becomes greater. In biological creation, the two are so close that matter—genes and blood and milk—passes from one to the other. The transmission of matter disappears in parenting, but touching and close physical contact remain the rule. In the passing on of skills, touching is greatly reduced and may not occur at all.

The teacher is present to the learner through a medium—the material that is touched by both. Finally, in the transmission of culture, even the physical presence of subject to object is not essential. The concrete medium has become abstract. Predecessors may speak to successors across oceans and over centuries of time. Offsetting the progressive loss in directness, then, is a gain in range. Targets of fertility become less explicitly personal and more social, encompassing ever broader collectivities. Of the four types of generativity, the cultural is the most diffuse, the most variable, the most abstract, the most uncertain in result, the most capable of producing numbers of successors. Seeds that were once physical are now symbolic.

All four expressions of fruitfulness may be present in the life of a relationship between an elder and a young person. People normally care for their own offspring, teach them skills, and pass on a community's understanding of life. What is of interest to a psychology of generativity are variations on this theme, when an array of "fathers" and "mothers" and "sons" and "daughters" enter and leave a life at diverse times and places.

AGENTIC AND COMMUNAL MODES OF GENERATIVITY

In expressing any of these four types of generativity, one's life-interest may fall more heavily on oneself or on the generative object. If the life of the progenitor assumes greater weight, if the creation is simply a clone or a monument to the self, we may speak of an *agentic* mode of generativity. On the other hand, if life-interest is transferred to the generative object with the result that its life becomes more important than the progenitor's, we may speak of a *communal* mode.

Agency and *communion* are terms coined by psychologist David Bakan to describe opposing poles of human endeavor. Agency represents the self-asserting, self-protecting, self-expanding existence of the individual, while communion represents the participation of the individual in a mutual, interpersonal reality or in some larger organism.[18] As Erikson depicts the polarity, agency corresponds to the felt necessity to "survive and kill," whereas communion corresponds to the precept to "die and become."[19] When fertility, of whatever type, is agentic, the progenitor's life-interest is retained in the self, in *me*; the worst thing imaginable is *my* death. When fertility is communal, life-interest is transferred to its object, so that the worst thing imaginable is the death of that object— more precisely, that the object die before its creator.

Examples of agentic generativity are seeking pregnancies to demonstrate *my* womanhood or virility, insisting that children become replicas

TABLE 2. Agentic and Communal Modes of Generativity

	Agency	Communion
	Agency represents the self-asserting, self-protecting, self-expanding existence of the individual. It is represented by the precept "survive and kill."	Communion represents the participation of the individual in a mutual, interpersonal reality or in some larger organism. It is represented by the precept "die and become."
	Agentic Generativity	Communal Generativity
	Life-interest is retained in *me*. Generative objects may be narcissistically possessed, cannibalized, or erected as monuments to the self. The worst thing imaginable is one's own death.	Life-interest is transferred to the generative object. The object is loved for itself, and the worst thing imaginable is its death.
	Examples	
1. Biological Generativity	A pregnancy is desired because one wants to demonstrate virility or womanhood.	A pregnancy is desired because one wants to care for a child.
2. Parental Generativity	A parent molds a child in his or her own image.	A parent allows a child to develop in his or her own way.
3. Technical Generativity	"Do it *my* way!"	"Do it the right way, and as well as you can."
4. Cultural Generativity	A cult leader draws the veneration of followers to himself.	A leader sacrifices a career for a cause.

of *me*, training students to perform exactly as *I* do, drawing the veneration of a community away from its guiding symbols and toward *myself* (see Table 2). In each of these examples, which run the gamut from biological to cultural transmission, the progenitor loves himself in the generative objects. He desperately seeks his own survival even though important parts of those objects may be killed. The agentic progenitor is willing to devour progeny, to possess them narcissistically and feed himself on their talents and admiration.

On the communal side, the biological type of generativity is exemplified in the desire for a pregnancy because one has sustenance to give an infant, the parental type in allowing a child to develop in his or her own way, the technical type in encouraging students to develop skills that surpass the teacher's, and the cultural variant in the willingness to sacrifice a career for a cause. Here, life-interest falls more heavily on the other than on the self. The progenitor loves the other for itself.

Like the outline of four types of generativity, this depiction of two modes is meant to be a lens through which a complex human motive can be seen. These lenses were ground in the process of studying the life histories that follow, and I have found them useful in bringing into focus what is transpiring in the actual and often unclear lives of people. Their magnifying power has opened to view the reproductive situation for which Erikson coined the term *generativity*.

2 · *The Changing Context of Generativity*

*W*hen the context of our lives is altered, the changes occur so slowly that we fail to notice them. Since the turn of the century, two changes have taken place in the setting of generativity. The more obvious and faster-paced of these changes is the contraceptive revolution of the 1960s and 1970s. But meshed with it, and turning at a slower rate, is the demographic revolution affecting the structure of the life cycle. Both revolutions have been well documented, but their impact on the human capacity for physical and cultural reproduction has been largely ignored.

THE CONTRACEPTIVE REVOLUTION

During the 1960s and 1970s changes in contraceptive practice took place in the United States that population expert Charles Westoff rightly called a revolution.[1] As the 1960s dawned, the annual number of births in the United States was still increasing and family planning had not yet gained widespread acceptance. What contraception existed was coitus-related and only moderately effective. A mere fifteen years later, in 1975, nearly 80 percent of America's married couples of reproductive age were either sterilized or using some form of contraception, a figure close to the theoretical maximum.[2] As Westoff said, "We are rapidly approaching universal, highly effective contraceptive practice."[3]

The revolution that, almost overnight, made birth control a feature of everyday life was accomplished through a succession of methods that induced increasingly longer states of sterility: first the pill, which by the end of the 1960s was the dominant contraceptive technique; then the IUD, which never attained the status of the pill but rose in popularity as pill use leveled off; and finally sterilization, which was responsible for the contraceptive surge of the 1970s. If one added to the number of contraceptive sterilizations those undertaken for purely medical reasons, one could state that by the mid-1970s sterilization had achieved first rank as a barrier to conception. At that point, 30 percent of America's married couples of reproductive age were biologically sterile. Couples were becoming interested in sterilization at earlier ages than ever before.[4]

Though few Americans expect to be childless for life, the proportion stating this preference in response to surveys increased during the 1970s. In 1980, Mary Jo Bane and George Masnick projected that a quarter of the women born in the 1950s will never have children—the highest percentage ever recorded. Another quarter of the same cohort is expected to have only one child.[5]

Psychology's first reaction to the contraceptive revolution was to mute the desire to reproduce. Fertility became a "problem," and parenthood ceased to be an "instinct." For example, in 1969 a thorough and competent volume by Edward Pohlman on the psychology of birth-planning devoted only one chapter to motivations for wanting children and viewed these as derivatives of other, often egocentric needs.[6] The bulk of the volume was devoted to research on the costs of having children, the damage done to unwanted children, and the techniques of birth prevention. Feminist social scientists began to insist that motherhood was not instinctual.[7] For a time it was rare to find the desire to have offspring spoken of positively, as a need as "healthy" as those for food, drink, sex, or self-actualization.

Now the pendulum seems to have reversed toward a more nuanced position. We realize that it is possible to welcome the freedom brought by contraception while asking questions that pursue its impact beyond an initial sigh of relief. What, for example, is the impact of lifetime childlessness in old age? Its meaning at that time may be very different from what it was in young adulthood. What function do offspring serve in reducing "life-cycle shock,"[8] in tempering the sting of death, in confirming the life of the progenitor? And who will serve these functions for individuals whose biological lines of transmission were severed decades before? Old age is presently far off for the new wave of individuals who will be biologically heirless, but dilemmas related to their fertility ought to be anticipated.

While abetting the cause of limiting population, in other words, it is possible to seek an understanding of nonbiological, "higher" channels of fertility. Reproduction can be seen as a healthy and even indispensable human constant, one that suddenly finds itself in radically altered circumstances. In such an approach, fertility is not a problem but a resource; it has the power of an instinct and, as such, is not to be denied but sublimated. As we come out of the contraceptive revolution, as more of us become biologically sterile, we must ask the question: how are we to be fertile if not through children?

THE QUIET DEMOGRAPHIC REVOLUTION

A quieter revolution than the contraceptive, turning like the hour hand of a clock in relation to the minute hand, was—and still is—the demographic. It concerns the structure of lives in our population: their expected length, the proportion of them allotted to childrearing, the intimate households in which they are lived, the numbers of young and old people in our country at large. So slowly do demographic changes occur that they are perceived only dimly in a single lifetime. Yet they too shape a new context for the meaning and expression of generativity.

The Postponement of Death

From 1900 to 1980 the average life expectancy of individuals in our population was extended by more than a quarter of a century. Much of the increase resulted from a lowering of childhood mortality rates, but even adults in 1980 could look forward to more remaining years than their counterparts in 1900.[9] Increased longevity did not mean that the biological schedule for maximum life span—something over one hundred years[10]— had changed. It meant, rather, that a growing number of people could reasonably hope to see that schedule closer to completion.

The influence of death on generativity is complex, and not all the intricacies are clearly understood. On the one hand, anticipation of death seems to trigger thoughts of "creating a legacy."[11] If people expect to die in their forties, it is rational for them to make early investments in progeny and successors, to affix themselves to more durable continuities than the self. But if eighty years of life are within reach, those investments can be delayed: it becomes rational to diet, to exercise, to breathe only the purest air, to avoid suspected carcinogens and psychosomatic stressors—to invest in the prolongation of the individual self in ways Lasch called narcissistic. One can only imagine the effects on the human impulse to beget should biologists acquire the ability to rewrite the aging blueprint, should the maximum (not merely the average) length of human life be extended. If we were offered the promise of 150, 200, or 300 years, what need would we feel to generate offspring—in whatever sense of the term?

But although the promise of longevity may diminish generative concern, one effect of longevity is to stimulate it: the number of four- and five-generation families is increasing. Never have so many generations in families been alive at the same time.[12] More children are able to know parents, grandparents, great-grandparents and great-great grandparents; and more of the elderly are able to see up to four generations of their descendants. The potential for feeling a part of the past and future through concrete identification with living individuals has never been greater.

Further, because the lives of parents and children now overlap for an average of more than forty years, there are new opportunities for reworking and repairing relations between parents and children. Parents are alive not only in the first two or three decades of their children's lives but also in the fourth and even fifth. Children, correspondingly, see their parents through more of life's seasons. It is not the mere passage of time that creates new opportunities for refashioning relationships between the generations; it is the fact that old and young have been alive together through more stages of life.

Childfree Years

Not only can we expect more years of life than ever before, we can expect more years without children. This fact is reflected in the emergence in this century of the postparental period—of the "empty nest" and "young old age" stages. Husbands and wives a century ago lived an average of a year and a half with no children in the home; today's couple with two children will have twenty-two years, almost half their married lives. According to demographer Mary Jo Bane, "People, married or not, will spend over a decade in what might be called 'young old age,' between retirement from the labor force and the onset of physical disability."[13] All in all, the proportion of a typical life allotted to child-rearing has shrunk and will continue to do so. Briefer segments of a life will be lived with children present, and even when children are present, they will absorb fewer of their parents' energies.[14] Most of the childfree time has opened up in the second half of life, a point at which concerns for creating a legacy begin to arise.

Women in particular are feeling the effects of this alteration in the life cycle. What they do with their time, in the opinion of Masnick and Bane, may create another demographic revolution: "In 1980, most working women had part-time, part-year jobs or worked intermittently over a period of years. . . . The revolution to come is in women's attachment: more women working full time more continuously."[15] If this revolution takes place—and the picture is still unclear—women's work outside the home will become increasingly important to themselves and to society. How will women's sense of fertility fare during this revolution? There is enormous opportunity for them to become creators and stewards of cultural symbols as well as of children. And there is a complementary opportunity for men, who have traditionally sought to leave their mark through nondomestic work, to take more active roles as parents.

Numerous elderly adults, both men and women, will also be undergoing transitions from full-time work to retirement, a period that is beginning earlier and lasting longer than in the past.[16] (Sixty-five is far above the average age of retirement today.) The passage to different circumstances of living and the sudden surfeit of time for reflection may stimulate thoughts about unfinished legacies, about contributions foreclosed by the nature of one's work. And additional years of leisure before serious failures in health—the so-called "young old age" period—will provide time for those contributions to be made. As Bane writes, "For women, who can now expect to live twenty years after they reach age 60, 'young old age' will last longer than childbearing, longer indeed than youth."[17]

Generational Segregation

When today's sixty- and seventy-year-olds were young, they lived in households populated and visited by a wide variety of people, including boarders, servants, friends, grandparents, much older and younger brothers and sisters, and even other families. A steady stream of individuals from all stages of the life cycle entered and left their homes. According to Masnick and Bane, "The age structure of the household was much more heterogeneous than today's—infants, adolescents, single adults, middle-aged parents and older relatives were much more likely to be present on any given day."[18]

Since that time, however, household size in the United States has shrunk and age segregation has increased. More people now live alone, and fewer households have children present. Those living by themselves are disproportionately old adults (especially widows) and young adults (the single, divorced, or separated). Many who choose solitary living do so in age-segregated environments such as retirement communities or "singles" apartment complexes. Both the elderly and the young adults contribute to an increase in solo living that Masnick and Bane describe as "a dramatic departure from most of our historical experience."[19] It is predicted that by 1990 almost 60 million households, nearly two-thirds of the expected total, will be without children.

As the trend toward generational segregation in day-to-day living heightens, one wonders how individuals will identify with past and future, how they will in this sense be generative, if they do not have the experience of living intimately with forebears and progeny, with representatives of diverse points along the cycle of generations.

But the data on isolation between the generations are not entirely one-sided. The trend toward segregation within households has not been matched by a similar trend between households. Ethel Shanas reports that although the proportion of the elderly living in the same home as one of their children declined from 1957 to 1975, the proportion living at home or within ten minutes of a child remained nearly the same.[20] Improving economic conditions between 1957 and 1975 allowed for discretionary interaction between the generations. The generative possibilities opened up by the introduction of selective contact have yet to be explored.

The Baby Boom Cohort

Outweighing in importance all the demographic movements discussed so far is the fate of the baby boom generation. Individuals born in 1946 turned twenty-one in 1967, and during the 1970s they passed from their late twenties to their early thirties.[21] It is reasonable to assume that the ideals of finding and actualizing the self, of achieving independence from the past—ideals having little to do with progeny—spoke to the major developmental task of their young adult lives. Because the largest age group in a society often colors the way the entire society thinks about itself, it was not surprising to find these ideals generalized to the United States at large, with the result that the 1970s became known as the Me Decade.

In the 1980s, however, members of the leading edge of the baby boom will cross the midpoint of their lives. Overall, our population will continue to grow older, moving from a median age of twenty-eight in 1970 toward an eventual one of around thirty-eight, the upper end of the range for populations like our own.[22] Because of the size of the baby boom (now a middle-aged boom), its struggles with the issues of midlife will command wide attention. Among these issues is that of generativity, the taking of the critical step from Me to Beyond Me.

The demographic hour hand, in other words, did not stop in the 1970s. It continues to move, and as it does, the psychological concerns of an aging population are shifting. This fact above all demands a response from psychology regarding the human capacity for reproduction, a response that takes seriously the desire of humans to extend themselves into the future, a response that is mindful of the contextual changes wrought by the contraceptive and demographic revolutions.

3 · *Life-Storytelling*

*T*hough first-person narratives have rarely dominated the methodological repertoire of the social sciences, they have always had a place therein. Dream episodes of his patients and a number of his own formed the basis of Freud's *Interpretation of Dreams*, the book which in 1899 launched the new "science" of psychoanalysis. The written autobiography of an immigrant occupied a prominent place in the monumental *Polish Peasant in Europe and America* by sociologists W. I. Thomas and Florian Znaniecki; in 1927 they declared that such personal life records "constitute the *perfect* type of sociological material." The development of the tape recorder provided the opportunity to preserve spoken narrative, and at Columbia University in 1948 historian Allan Nevins created the country's first oral history program. In 1961 anthropologist Oscar Lewis used multiple tape-recorded autobiographies to portray the life of a poor Mexican family in his landmark *Children of Sanchez*. At the same time psychiatrist Robert Coles began interviewing black children who were initiating school desegregation in the South and collecting material for the first of his *Children of Crisis* series.[1]

Such first-person accounts have been identified as case histories, life studies, oral biographies—almost any combination of the words *case, life, oral,* or *psycho* on the one hand and *record, biography, history, story,* and *study* on the other. With Oscar Lewis I prefer the simplest of the combinations—life story—and I have used this term to set my posture while seeking to understand contemporary dilemmas of human generativity.

This approach was chosen because it seemed imperative in developing a psychology of generativity to create a language not just of psychological concepts but of the images and incidents of everyday life. I wanted an anthology of experience articulated in people's own words, showing the meaning they attached to struggles with sterility and fertility. First-person renditions of experience would not constitute social science exactly, but they would lay the groundwork for science, raising the questions, creating the hypotheses, and suggesting the perspectives that quantitative researchers could later pursue.

The story form shapes first-person accounts into a particular pattern: a narrative with beginning, middle, end, and dramatic tension. I decided on this form to capture experience for several reasons. One was its accessibility. *Story* is a trigger that nearly everyone can put a finger on. Residing in the common idiom, the term provides a stimulus for a diverse lot of people, most of whom have never heard of a "psychobiography" and do not want to be "cases," to communicate the salient features of their lives. Though *life story* means many things to many people, it never fails to start words flowing. (Despite scholarly arguments about what constitutes a story, no one has ever asked me what to do when beginning to relate his or her own.) I believe a surprising number of persons would remain mute were it not for the story form, however understood, to elicit, contain, and even mold their experience.

If *story* is a trigger, it is also a key. Its appearance in casual utterance has the potential value of other apparently incidental expressions: the trivial slips Freud wrote of in *The Psychopathology of Everyday Life*.[2] A woman acts bizarrely in public, and we wonder what her story is. A middle-aged man tosses a wad of paper at a wastebasket; it falls short, and he mutters something about the "story" of his life. We share a drink with a stranger on the plane and in no time she is telling us her life story. We stand in a line for hours and complain that this predicament is the story of our own life, as if a decade or more of living could be compressed into and understood by an image of waiting in a quiet, helpless rage. Even spoken in jest, the word *story* reaches below the surface and touches semiconscious perceptions of the pattern and meaning of a life. Alan Watts once observed that ordinary language reflects the most profound questions of human existence: "Who do you think you are? Who started this? . . . Where the hell do you think you're going?"[3] Something analogous may be true of *life story*.

BECOMING A GENERATIVE TARGET

To shed light on generativity, then, I defined myself as a collector of life stories. My goal was to identify as many different motifs as possible, to track down varieties of generative experience, and to record a story about each new variety I found.

Three criteria governed my selection of life-storytellers: (1) I approached subjects if signs existed that their story explored unique nuances of the generative problem (a criterion necessarily imprecise). (2) I tried to include in the collection a range of religious/secular, racial/ethnic, occupational, and social class backgrounds, as well as maintaining a rough balance of males and females, middle-aged and elderly (no one below the mid-thirties was included). The point was not to create a representative sample but to ensure variety. (3) I attempted to find exemplars of new demographic trends and of different kinds of generativity.

In practice this meant that colleagues, students, friends, and contacts in many walks of life would suggest individuals to me whose lives seemed, at least from the outside, to address dilemmas of generativity. Usually my contacts made an initial approach to a potential subject, and I would follow with a phone call or letter and then a personal visit. I explained what I could about my project and expressed an interest in the subject's life story. Not everyone understood what I said about generativity, but no one missed the meaning of *life story*, and few declined to let me record theirs, a fact that astounds me upon reflection. People said yes because they were curious, because they wanted to help, because they accepted the recommendation of an intermediary, because they were flattered, because they sensed the telling might be good for them. Not everyone said yes immediately; those who did often went on to tell their story with ease, the major incidents of their lives already encoded in formulas. Others thought about my proposal for months before agreeing; usually their accounts began haltingly, but then a dam was broken and I heard a story in the making. Once anonymity and confidentiality were guaranteed, once people knew they would see the results of my writing, they seemed anxious to participate.

True narrative did not always come forth when someone decided to tell his or her story. I have been struck by an almost elemental difference in the way individuals speak of their lives. At one extreme are those who leap to the concrete, the tangible, the episodic, who relish fables heard and events lived. These are the narrators, and they have usually been among the older of my subjects and those with the least formal schooling. Marveling at their anecdotal ability, I wonder if I am sitting in the presence of a vanishing skill. Older narrators are often befuddled by psychological questions like "How have you changed in the past ten years?" Either they do not answer or they embark on a long and often twisted story that seems entirely irrelevant until its denouement. Like most people, narrators play out their lives on a web of meaning, but the web they spin consists of stories.

At the other extreme are those who interpret their lives with analysis. Usually they have had much formal education and are fluent in psychological terminology. Analyzers fall at the lower end of the age spectrum, which in my research is midlife. They do not need me to ask questions about stages of development or this crisis or that; they have saturated themselves with such introspection. With analyzers I find myself pressing for sights and sounds and smells and feels. I would rather hear from them about an incident in which they looked into a mirror and were repelled than listen to their ruminations about a poor self-image. Analyzers have an advantage over narrators, however: they are able to get the swing of storytelling—to rediscover it—whereas narrators have a difficult time putting on the thinking cap of analysis.[4] Thinking of their lives as stories encourages analyzers to see beginning, middle, and end, to dwell on turning points and moments of climax and resolution. As storytellers, they do not have to appear psychologically healthy or morally upright. They simply have to relate, as one woman said, "what I've been through."

My method has evolved to the point that most recordings are accomplished in four to five meetings of several hours each, not counting an introductory conversation and subsequent visits. I take written notes after each period detailing what the recorder misses: comments made while sitting down to work or walking to the door; the sight, sound, and feel of the speaker and the physical setting. Usually conversations take place a week apart. The interlude allows storytellers to rummage through memorabilia, talk to relatives and friends, and evoke deeper memories. It allows me to check previous tapes against a broad set of questions each story should address; if the questions have not been covered spontaneously by the speaker, I ask them at an appropriate moment. The break also allows the implicit contract binding the subject and me to be renegotiated. I realize the story I hoped to record is not the one I will finally leave with; I decide to pursue the new one. The storyteller, who may have begun because of the recommendation of a friend, now finds her inner life fascinating, or she starts to see coherence and even value in what might have been disorderly and painful; she continues for these new reasons. In other words, what each of us draws from the interview changes, and intervals are useful for readjusting expectations of benefit. After my final visit, I keep in touch with subjects, taking notes on or taping descriptions of further developments in their lives, verifying or discarding interpretations I have made, allowing our contract to be altered even further. On one occasion, I reminded a man whose story I had recorded the year before that he might not live to see what I would fashion from his materials. (Following a heart attack, he had already outlived one physician's prediction of longevity.) We agreed, nevertheless, that we should continue to meet and record his experiences. After this quiet renegotiation, his reflections took on even more the quality of creating a legacy.

Like mental life itself, the stories to which I listen come in layers. There is the manifest story, a public version of the life that includes the basic biographical facts, the outer journey. Beneath this is the latent story, the private version that depicts the inner course of the life. The latent story has many levels, some of which are slowly revealed to the speaker and me, some of which remain hidden. Feeding the latent story are unconscious images that Freud called the primary process and that comprise mental life "at bottom." Even at this chaotic basement level we find material organized into the primitive narrative of fantasies and dreams. Which layer of a story is transmitted, that is, how "deep" the story is, depends on the teller, the listener, and the climate the two of them create. At whatever level a story is told, it is an interpersonal construction of these two individuals, a compromise between the needs of each. Because life-storytelling is an interpersonal event, it is distinguished from solitary narratives such as journals, diaries, memoirs, and formal autobiographies.

To highlight the difference between the manifest and latent story, I sometimes open my interviewing with a request for a five-minute overview of the subject's life. Then I ask, "If your life story came in chapters, what would they be?" Not only do these requests guide subjects into thinking of their lives as wholes and provide me with an outline of what is to come; they also produce a manifest version of the life that can be contrasted with the latent one that will appear in the weeks ahead. (Like many ordinary practices, these often have to be abandoned. Once, I was about to explain my research to an old man in the hopes of enlisting his cooperation. Before I got the first words out of my mouth he sat down and started recounting his life. He was a narrator with a hair trigger. Needless to say, my ordinary openers were discarded.)

In these interviews I either stimulate or observe a naturally occurring process that Robert Butler has called the *life review*. Butler was speaking of a process in which past experiences and conflicts return to consciousness to be surveyed and reintegrated. Butler claimed that the life review was a universal phenomenon set in motion by the anticipation of death. Though characteristic of the elderly, it was not restricted to them; it might occur at any turning point in life. Subsequent researchers have refined his concept. Peter Coleman distinguished the life review from informative reminiscing, which was akin to storytelling; the latter's purpose was to entertain and to use the past to teach others, whereas the life review analyzed the past to achieve an acceptance of one's own life. John Meacham argued that reminiscing in later adulthood provided integrity for the individual in the present context of his or her life.[5] When the storytelling I record is successful, it seems to do both—it creates the sense of generativity of which Coleman wrote and the sense of ego-integrity to which Butler and Meacham referred.

Recent studies by sociologist Daniel Bertaux have illustrated that extent to which a life story is shaped by a life's present condition.[6] Bertaux and his collaborator, Isabelle Bertaux-Wiame, collected the life stories of elderly French bakers and found that present outcomes were justified by renditions of early career experiences. For example, bakers who never became masters omitted from their stories youthful attempts to do so; others did not. I have found it equally true in my work that life stories are as much revelations of character *now*, and justifications of conditions *now*, as they are renditions of what happened *back then*.

It took time and the comments of several subjects to make me realize that as I let the concept of *story* shape my interviewing, I began to be seen by my subjects in a particular way. Doctor to some, friend to others, professor, sympathetic ear, therapist, imagined lover, son, recruit, person in need of assistance to still others, I became something constant to all: a mirror in front of which to puzzle over a life, the record that had to be set straight, a conduit to carry a life to permanence, a receptacle for the hope that something in the life has been of value, a catalyst for the unusual experience of creating something in one's own image and likeness. As a writer making use of the material of subjects' lives, I became a focal point for their life review and a symbol of posterity—a generative target.

In subtle ways, conversations with storytellers are designed to achieve this effect. Before we begin, subjects are told that they will receive copies of the tapes we make and that their words, with names and places disguised, will appear in print either as full stories or as brief illustrations of certain motifs. Those whose lives become full stories know they will see the finished product and be able to react to it. The microphone and tape recorder, intruders in some forms of interviewing, are allies in life-storytelling—visible reminders that a record is being made. As a further reminder, after several sessions I present subjects with copies of tapes made to that point, and at the end I give them the rest.

The generative cast of this life-review activity sets it apart from psychotherapy and in particular from psychoanalysis.[7] In psychoanalysis, the analyst comes to stand in the patient's mind for a significant person in the past; Freud called the phenomenon transference. In life-storytelling, the listener and the recorder signify not the past but the future; in a kind of generative transference they become a target for whatever fertility exists in the teller. In psychoanalysis, the goal of enlightenment is to extract a poison, to cure the self. In life-storytelling, the goal is to extract that part of a person's experience which others can incorporate. The ground rules of psychoanalysis are that all should be spoken and nothing remain buried; those of life-storytelling state that, although depth is pursued, some secrets should die with the teller.

Although forms of a generative transference no doubt occur in much oral-historical research, its presence in my work offers a bonus: it brings together content and method. *What* I study falls in step with *how* I study it. Instead of photographing generativity in some pure (and inaccessible) natural state, I create a situation that exaggerates and compresses it. As I listen to accounts of lives, I watch people create legacies. Thus when I write a story and reflect on it, I attend not only to the content of the life but also to the process of the interview, to what happened in the course of the storytelling.

In comparison with other models of recording first-person narratives that are available on the shelves of social science, the one I have selected is both less and more formal—less in its use of only a few set questions, more in its attention to the design of the interpersonal situation. From my point of view, the definition of that situation is critical. Because flexibility is essential, because I am more than one thing to the people I speak with, control over the situation is never complete. But to the extent that our conversations are true life-storytellings, to the extent that they are generative events, to that precise extent does material emerge that illuminates the meaning of fertility and sterility.

WRITING AND VERIFYING THE STORIES

All the accounts I record are analyzed, but only about half—the most enlightening—are written up in full. In this process, *story* still guides the work. I hope that the result has something of art, something of life, and a great deal of communicable truth.

In writing, the process of compression continues. A lifetime of experience, which has become several hundred pages of typewritten transcript, now becomes a single story of twenty-five or thirty pages. I take a wedge to a life and attempt to break it open at just those places from which long vistas are visible. Concentrating on those critical points, I select and arrange material to highlight the dramatic tension in what I have heard. I try to bring out the succession of conflict and resolution, the changes in character, the inner pilgrimage that led to each story-teller's type of generative engagement. Doing so, I keep in mind the criteria for a life history developed by psychologist John Dollard in 1935: while not neglecting the contribution of bodily changes to the life story, Dollard recognized the impact of culture; he recommended that the individual be seen as "a link in a chain of social transmission," as "one of the strands of a complicated collective life which has historical continuity."[8] Except for disguising identities, I fictionalize nothing. I constantly check to see whether a particular stroke of editing—putting together words spoken on different occasions, for example—is justified in terms of the overall truthfulness of a person's life. The tape recordings, the transcriptions thereof, and notes written at the time of the recording constitute a primary record that is accurate in the literal sense: they set down what has been said and what has been seen. The finished stories are accurate in a secondary sense, not as facsimiles of the transcripts, but as literary depictions of the ebbs and flows in the lives that created the transcripts. Admittedly, the story in each life is a construction of mine (more precisely, of the speaker and me), but the construction, like good scientific theory, can be verified in the primary record.

The story can also be verified in the interpersonal dyad from which it emerged. To verify a story in this living reality one takes as an analogate not the method of the historian, who uses stories of the past to establish what happened *then*, but that of the psychologist, who views stories of the past as disclosures of character *now*. (This is not to say that in the pursuit of character I bypass historical truth; using memory and memorabilia, the life-storyteller and I try to build as accurate an account as possible.) Verification of character is an ambiguous task at best, but a critical moment in the process comes when the subject reads the written story—a moment parallel to when the patient hears an interpretation of the analyst. The keys to verification at this time are three: (1) whether the subject makes allusions, direct or indirect, to being seen and understood; (2) whether the subject's reactions, favorable or not, are consistent with story motifs; and (3) whether the subject is impelled to reveal fresh and deeper material.

Allusions to Being Seen and Understood

After reading her story one woman told me she felt as if her "bare ass were hanging over a fence" for all to see. Another expressed surprise that I "left so much the way it really is. . . . It was like looking into a mirror." Both were amazed and stunned to see so much of themselves on paper, and both had a reaction shared by others: to cover up what was exposed—more precisely, to cover up their association with what was exposed. Taking their responses as confirmations of the truth of the story, I went through the text with each and disguised their identities even further.

The shock of recognition comes not so much from seeing one's own words but from seeing the pattern into which those words fall, to seeing the plot of one's life. The coherence of the written stories intrigued their tellers and gave them a sense not simply of being seen but of being understood. "You pulled it all together" or "You really got the essence" are reactions showing an appreciation of coherence. As the next example will show, a person need not like the story to feel that he or she has been seen inwardly. Being flattered is not the same as being understood.

Reactions Consistent with Story Motifs

Another check on the psychological truth of a story is whether the teller's reaction to the written version enacts story themes. An overriding emotion in one story to which I listened was a feeling of personal failure despite extraordinary public accomplishments. When the story was published as a full-length biography,[9] the subject reacted in print:

> *Am I the man portrayed in the book? Probably, and I wish I weren't. . . .*
> *The book terrified me because I did not find the life described therein attractive, which I suppose means that I don't find the leading character all that attractive. I found myself saying, "What a wasted life, what a tragic misuse of time and energy and ability.". . . I've worked very hard over the last quarter-century, frequently to the point of exhaustion, in the production of an inordinate amount of printed pages. I see it all neatly arranged in the Kotre monograph and realize how much the effort was a waste, how worthless the product. Better never to have started.[10]*

The sense of waste was central to the story and to the teller's reactions. The parallel constitutes a verification of character.

In a book called *Simple Gifts* I wrote of a couple who were generative in many senses.[11] They had four children, adopted a fifth, took numerous foster children and foreign students into their home, and began an international religious movement—activity that on occasion forced their own children into the shadows. In the book I gave more attention to a foster child than to the couple's own children. Seeing the manuscript, the mother objected: the picture activated a motif that had caused regret in the past. The onetime foster child, however, was overjoyed: the manuscript gave him a place in the family for which he longed. The reactions of the storytellers, negative and positive, were consistent with what appeared in their stories.

In addition to comparing subjects' reactions to story themes, of course, one can also see whether events in the life since the initial recording have followed trajectories forecast in the story. The year or two that elapse between the recording and completion of a manuscript give ample time to track how the life has been lived, not merely spoken of.

The Emergence of Fresh and Deeper Material

Robert Langs has written of the psychoanalytic interview that a particular interpretation made by the therapist may be confirmed or disconfirmed by seeing whether it unlocks heretofore repressed memories, dreams, or fantasies. Even if the patient objects on the surface to the interpretation, the emergence of fresh material shows that he or she has felt understood at a deeper level and that the interpretation was essentially correct.[12]

In life-storytelling an analogous situation prevails. If, after reading his or her own story, a teller suddenly remembers more, or has a new insight, or feels the pressure of "all the things I didn't say," we can be confident of the basic truthfulness of the plot. In the story of one woman, I dwelled on her relationship with her grandfather. When she read the story, this emphasis served as a net that collected far more memories of intimacy between them. When the protagonist of *Simple Gifts* read the manuscript of that book, she not only objected to the coverage given a foster child, but she also, somewhat paradoxically, produced two documents I had not seen before. In fact, no one outside her immediate family had ever seen them. One was a letter written by a psychiatrist friend to the family after her husband died of cancer; the husband had sought counsel from the psychiatrist in his dying months, and the psychiatrist had conveyed some of the husband's last concerns to the family. The other document was a meditative note the husband had scrawled on a yellow pad the evening before his second surgery for cancer. These two privileged documents revealed the substance of her husband as no others had done. I took her bringing them forth at that moment as a sign of verification of interpretations made to that point.

In general, new revelations that emerge in a feedback meeting do not alter the main line of the story. Rather, they deepen and enrich the plot with color, affect, and texture.

Simple Gifts was a mixture of life-story recording and biography, two activities that should be distinguished conceptually, though they often merge in practice. In formal biography one need not speak directly with the subject of the work (in many cases he or she is deceased). If one does make direct contact with the subject, the subject's version of events must be checked against other sources. In life-storytelling, on the other hand, the listener does not go outside the relationship to check the account. The life story is an interpersonal construction, and the boundary surrounding it must be kept intact to preserve trust and to facilitate the revelation of personal mythology imbuing a life. Maintaining a boundary does not preclude a researcher from recording other stories that intersect

with and even contradict aspects of the first, but each story is left intact.[13]
Thus there is no story of a life that is "true" to the exclusion of others.
There are, rather, as many "true" stories as there are teller-listener dyads
in which they are spoken and verified.

I want to be very precise about the nature of the truth that is verified
in life-storytelling, and to do that I have to be very clear about the nature
of life stories. With Bertaux, I regard the life story (*le récit de vie*) as but
one part of life history, the part that is told to another.[14] To become life
history the oral account must be supplemented with personal documents,
official records, letters, conversations with others, and the like. In verifying a life story, then, all we can hope for is what psychoanalyst Donald
Spence calls narrative truth: coherence that takes on "aesthetic finality"
and fits the present character of the storyteller.[15] The three criteria for
verification speak to narrative truth. A story is returned to the dyad from
which it originated, and the storyteller begins to remember events and
even act in ways that fit the pattern she now perceives in her life. If the
written story reinforces our mutual understanding of that pattern, it has
been verified.

In actual practice conceptual precision is often lost, as it must be if we
are to be responsive to the phenomena before us. In my own writing I
often use *life story* and *life history* interchangeably. But while we are being
clear, let me state that because my emphasis is on the telling of a life, the
profiles that follow are first and foremost life stories possessing narrative
truth. Because I also make use of personal documents as checks, the
stories have elements of histories, and the narrative truth in them has
been nudged in the direction of historical truth.

INTERPRETING THE STORIES

Though life stories have their own intrinsic interest, to be useful to
psychology they must be interpreted. By examining a number of stories,
a researcher can formulate generalizations that will, on the one hand,
serve as conclusions to discrete projects and, on the other, set the stage
for further investigations. Interpretation is a matter of making connections within and between stories and using them to build and refine
theory.

The passage from story to interpretation is like that from the *idiographic* approach in psychology to the *nomothetic*, a distinction first made
by Gordon Allport.[16] In recording a life story, I take the idiographic
view, trying to set down in an artistic way the uniqueness of a particular
individual. But once the story is constructed, I cross over to the nomothetic side, searching the story and others like it for themes common to

the experience of generativity. The contrast between story and interpretation is great. The element of surprise, for example, is the essence of a good story but the bane of a good theory, which seeks to rub out chance and make lives predictable. If psychologists overstress the idiographic, they miss the universal for the particular and simply make a string of unrelated lives. But if they are wedded to the nomothetic, they overlook vast differences between individuals, differences that can bring sound theory to its knees.

In interpretation, I try to extract the generative thread from each of the life stories I have recorded. In contrast with psychoanalysis and depth psychology, I attempt to view a life from where the thread ends, not from where it begins—looking backward, that is, from the nature of its fertility rather than forward from the nature of its infantile attachments. Once extracted from each life, the threads are woven with others into coherent statements of a general nature. The statements do not represent universal psychological laws (as the term *nomothetic* implies), nor do they depict age-bound stages of growth. They are nothing more nor less than summaries of recurring motifs, of varieties of generative experience. Once motifs are stated, each transcript is inspected for illustrations of it. The inspections are not quantitative but qualitative, their purpose to uncover variations on a theme. All in all, this method of interpretation is akin to what Geertz, following Gilbert Ryle, calls "thick description," the aim of which is to draw conclusions from cases that are few in number but rich in significance.[17] And the theory that emerges fits the description of what sociologists have called "grounded theory."[18]

Among the first-person methods used in social science, then, the one employed here is distinctive in its attempts to collapse entire lives into single narratives, to verify the psychological truth of those narratives, and to draw from them general observations that contribute to the development of theory. We need collections of stories to complement psychology's collections of studies, but we also need to state what may be learned from the stories.

PART II

The Stories
of Four Women

4 · *Mirror, Mirror*

*H*er small apartment is nearly empty. A folded cot and a few cardboard boxes stand in line against a bare wall. Plants sit on the floor, their foliage spread carefully on the carpet. Odds and ends huddle neatly in a corner. On a stereo is a bust of a young black woman, and on the wall by the dining table, just behind me, is a painting of a black ballerina dressed in white, her slender arms extended in a graceful arabesque.

She has been packing for a move. As she rests at the table, her dark eyes seem to scan an inner horizon, straining to see the future. Occasionally her eyes rest on the painting. She is a wisp of a woman with skin the color of coffee, a face that is instantly reactive, and a natural elegance in her bearing. She appears to be in her late twenties, but her hands are those of someone older. When she speaks, her words are barely audible, but they come in clear, precise rhythms. She is wearing blue jeans and a T-shirt. Where the pocket of the T-shirt would be are the words *Sweet Honesty.*

She struggled with the decision to tell her story, one day saying yes, the next, no. She is a "private person," she says. "No one knows what's inside of me." In the end, I believe, the sheer power of the events that shook her life compelled her to speak. She overcame her apprehension and agreed simply to tell me "what I've been through."

I

Dorothy Woodson's life began on a Connecticut farm in 1942. She was born Dorothy Brown, the last of seven children and the only one born in the North. Because her mother started to hemorrhage while carrying her, she was also the only Brown born in a hospital. Dorothy's mother was an orphan who suffered a devastating childhood at the hands of a cruel aunt; her father was a farmer. The two met somewhere in the Carolinas, started a family, and eventually migrated to Connecticut, where a shack with a dirt floor became Dorothy's first home. Memories of it jump at her like ghosts, memories of breaking out in hives after eating a tomato, memories of hearing her brothers and sisters scream at a snake she does not see, memories of running lost and terrified through grass over her head. When she was three, the family moved to a crowded apartment in the city, and there a new fear stalked her: "Fires. There were fires every weekend. Someone would be drinking or they'd fall asleep with a cigarette or knock over a wood-burning stove. One night a friend of the family died in one of the fires. I used to stay awake at night and wait for somebody to yell *fire* because I knew there was going to be one." Throughout her childhood, however, one feeling dominated: "I thought I was a horribly ugly child. Sometimes my mom will show me the only picture she has of me as a baby, and I cringe. Hide it please!

"My mother was very beautiful, and I think she reacted to my ugliness. She was fair-complexioned, with long hair, and very slim. She loved me in her own way, but because she did not have a parent, she did not know how to show love. She'll tell me very, very often, 'I had to go to the hospital to have you. Because of you I lost a couple of years' work.' Her favorite daughter is very pretty, and her skin is very light. I remember my mom buying nice things for her but not for some of the other girls. She rarely bought me anything new. I thought I was the darkest in the family. I was not, but I thought I was.

"My dad was not a handsome man, but he had such a pleasant, accepting face that you just liked him. I'll always remember him balding. Everyone in the neighborhood loved him. He was the kind of guy that, if you were in need, he would give you his last dime when he should be paying a bill. If he saw you depressed, he would cheer you up. He'd come around and tell jokes or a story from back on the farm or something ridiculous. There were times he gave us money he didn't have, but we would ask him, 'Dad, can I have a quarter?' And he would give us one. I don't remember my dad ever talking harshly to me.

"My dad used to drink, and that would upset my mom. When he got depressed, he would go out and gamble to try to earn money for the family and to buy nicer things for us. My mom used to be furious. As I became older, I was able to see that my dad had a lot going on inside of him, but he made that secondary to his dealing with other people, especially his family. He felt so inadequate in everything. When I think of the socioeconomic factors that impacted his life and the sensitive, feeling person that he is and his sense of dedication to his family, I can understand the reasons that he drank and gambled. I think that was his way not only of coping, but, in a desperate hope, of trying to do better, to get more for his family, because he was totally a family person.

"My sister Carolyn was the family militant. She was so aware of what was going on. She was the most intelligent in the family, and she would always be speaking about social injustices. My mom would voice a certain sentiment or feeling, and Carolyn would attack it, 'No, it's not that way.' My mom used to say, 'You're being disrespectful.' But she wasn't. She was just using her mind. I remember how it used to frustrate my mom. She did not have the words to combat Carolyn. Carolyn was just the type of child that read voraciously. Her head was constantly in a book. I remember when she was in school and she was asked to report on *Uncle Tom's Cabin*. She refused. The teacher told her she'd better do it, and she said, 'I don't talk that way and I won't report on this,' and she left school. I remember my mom crying and saying, 'I never had any trouble with any of my children. What is this child that I've borne? What's wrong with her?'

"Carolyn was in the business course. We blacks were all told don't take college courses because I guess they felt our brains were too small. So Carolyn took shorthand, and she was so good at it. Her outlines were so perfect and so beautiful and I admired her so much that after she would finish with her books I would get them and make the outlines too.

"There were times when Carolyn felt so strongly about a thing that in her expression of it she would not consider another person's feelings. That would upset me because I was just the opposite. I was very sensitive. If I saw a person who was crippled or even ugly, I would cry. I would think, 'Oh, that poor person! How is he getting through life?' But she didn't allow those things to enter her thinking. Not that they didn't bother her, but she cut them off. We were different in that sense.

"In high school I remember starting to look at guys, and I thought, 'Boy, why aren't I popular like the other girls?' I just seemed so homely, and because of it I didn't do anything to make boys like me. In school I felt very inferior, even though when I look back now, my skills were great. Once, one of my teachers, a science teacher, kept me after school and tested me for the final exam. He gave me a hundred questions and I got ninety-nine of them right without studying. So he had *me* give the exam to the class! I've not thought about that until maybe a month ago. In high school I was taking 135 words a minute in my shorthand class, and my teacher never said to me, 'Why don't you try for a scholarship?' She would encourage the other girls to do so. I wonder about things like that. I've not been able to see my ability as other people do. I don't even begin to say I know all of the reasons why.

"I was so self-conscious. I thought, Oh, don't look my way! Inside I was very fearful and very uncertain, but I would give the impression of knowing what I wanted and going after it. My mom says to me, 'Oh, Dorothy, I've never had any trouble out of you. You were such a good child! When you were sick, you would go to the hospital all by yourself. And you would tell me, Mom, I don't want *you* to do it, *I'll* do it.' And when I sit down and hear her tell these things, I marvel because I've always wanted somebody just to hold my hand through something. I didn't want to do anything by myself. It's like she's talking about a different person.

"I don't recognize that person at all. Not at all. And I hear people tell me things today about how they perceive me, and I sit there and I marvel. But within the last few years I'm beginning to listen and to try to see myself as other people see me, and not as the fearful backward person I've perceived myself as. About a month ago I was asking myself, 'Why can't I see myself the way others see me? Why is it that I'm so negative? Why is it that I'm always saying I'm not good at something?' I went to the mirror and looked at myself really carefully. I examined every part of me, and I thought, Well, I'm not so bad. I'm *not* ugly. I'm not *beautiful*, but I'm not as ugly as I've seen myself."

II

"When my first son was born, he was very dark, and he was oh, so homely. He was just so little, you know, so withered. He was just three pounds, and he wasn't fully developed. I used to go up to the hospital every day to see him, and I'd think, 'Why couldn't my first baby be more beautiful? He's ugly just like me. Why couldn't he have taken after his dad?' And sometimes I wonder, well, is that the reason he died? Did he sense that I didn't really accept him because he wasn't a beautiful baby? Didn't he have the will to live because he sensed that? I used to think that way. I try not to entertain those thoughts anymore."

Dorothy had met her husband when she was sixteen. Alan was counterpoint to her: outgoing, optimistic, personable, at ease with people. He quit high school before graduation, entered the service, went overseas, and proposed to Dorothy when he came back. Not until later did she discover that he had been jilted by another girl and made his proposal almost out of vengeance. Alan Woodson and Dorothy Brown were married in 1961. She was eighteen.

"I depended on him totally after our marriage. He was my everything. He used to tell me I was possessive and clinging. He felt like he was in chains, like I was smothering him with my love, and I probably was. I thought we were to dedicate our lives to our men, and I didn't know how to deal with the fact that he wasn't reciprocating. We had difficulty in the marriage the day after I said I do.

"It was very difficult for Alan to keep a job. Something always went wrong, and he would wind up quitting. What was really in his heart and mind was to sing. He had a beautiful voice. I tried so hard to encourage him to go to school and learn music and perhaps teach it, as long as he could be involved in what he loved to do. But he couldn't see it. After we were married he had an opportunity to sing with a well-known group, and he did, in spite of the fact that it took him away most of the time. There was no stopping him.

"I didn't plan on getting pregnant so quick, but I did not try to prevent pregnancy. After I found out I was pregnant, I was very happy about it. At first, Alan was disturbed because it was so soon, and then he seemed to like the idea, but then he would go off and wouldn't come home for a day or two.

"I had placenta previa and started hemorrhaging when I was three months pregnant. I was admitted to the hospital for several days of bed rest. As I was going into my seventh month, the hemorrhaging became quite profuse and I was admitted into the hospital for the second time. The hemorrhaging was so bad they decided to perform a C-section."

Her voice became fragile. "My baby was like a prune, so tiny and helpless. It was all from me. It was as if Alan had not contributed at all to the appearance of this child. I felt responsible for the child's ugliness, but I grew to accept that, and I really tried my best to be a mother—whatever that was.

"The baby stayed in the hospital, I don't know how long, because he was so tiny. They wouldn't allow him to come home until he gained five pounds. I remember when I was finally able to bring him home from the hospital. I dressed him up in this cute little yellow outfit to make him look so pretty! I brushed his hair down—it would want to go this way and I'd brush it that way. I remember taking him to my mom—my mom had not seen him—and I'll never forget the look. It, she, just crushed me. She looked at him as if to say, 'Is that him?' He was just so ugly, and she was so cold. She didn't want to touch him. She didn't want to hold him. I took him and I thought, I won't even bring him around anymore.

"I don't remember how long the baby was home. All of that seems so vague. He was with us at least a couple of months and was beginning to gain weight. His appearance was even changing. He started to look an awful lot like Alan, and he seemed to be a happy, happy child. He used to spit up constantly, I mean not just a little, and I was very concerned about that. But the doctors told me it was nothing wrong.

"So he just died one night. I got up one morning and found him that way, and they just said it's something they didn't know anything about. They don't know why it happened, but it seemed to happen with premature babies that they would just give up life.

"It was a great loss. It was very, very difficult to accept his death. I guess it taught me the uncertainty of life. I mean, you have your own feelings about things, and then it doesn't work out because of circumstances you have no control over. It made me feel very insecure about existing. Alan was very much affected by it also. I could tell he cared, he grew to really care for the child, and I wondered if that was one of the reasons he was incapable of drawing close to his other two children."

III

"When Diana was born the following year, I felt as if I had been rewarded because of the tragedy of my last child. It was a complete reversal. I thought that here was a gift to make up for all of it. During the pregnancy I experienced some of the same problems, but they were not as severe. At the eighth month they decided to take her even though I wasn't hemorrhaging as badly. She was healthier, she was stronger, and she weighed more, just under five pounds. She gained quickly. She was extremely beautiful and precocious.

"As she grew, she was bright and alert. It was frightening. I remember her trying to form words at an incredibly early age. Even at five months the lights would fascinate her. I would tell her that's the light: 'Light.' Then at night I would take her for a walk in the stroller, and she would look up at the stars and the moon, and she would point to them. It was incredible. She was just too little to be doing many of the things she was doing. By the age of two she had a vast vocabulary. She was talking fluently and clearly, and she was very, very beautiful.

"At the time, Alan was away more than he was at home. Marriage to me was 100 percent giving and 100 percent hurting. I don't think he did the things or said the things intentionally, but he was so frustrated and so confused. He was supposed to get a job and send for me and the child, but he never did. I heard from him occasionally. He went from little groups to singing in night clubs. He was involved with many things and many women and many people, and that was a nightmare.

"Then he got a job at the Apollo Theater in Harlem. I so desperately wanted to be there, to be with him. So I left my daughter with a thirteen-year-old girl. I couldn't find anyone else to take care of her, and I just felt the need to get away and be with the man I loved. It was the strangest thing when I left that night. I looked at Diana and had a premonition that I would never see her again in that form. It was more than a feeling, it was almost a warning. I started not to go, but then I thought, oh, that's ridiculous. I mean, it was not logical. The need to be needed by this man and to show him I cared, hoping that he in return would show the same kind of love for me . . . I left.

"Shortly after I got to New York I received a call stating that Diana had been very badly burned and that I should return right away. When I got the call I wasn't surprised. I was terrified but not surprised. I just felt I knew something was going to happen.

"Alan would not leave before his show, and I felt trapped. I felt I had to get to Connecticut, yet I didn't want to leave him either. He convinced me to stay. The next thing I remember was being at the hospital in Connecticut and there was a female doctor and she came over to me and she was very hostile. She questioned me very curtly. I mean, there was no understanding on her part for what I was going through. All she could see was this beautiful child burned, and I was nowhere around. She finally told us that Diana was resting comfortably, and we saw her. It was terrifying. Her little body was swollen and blistered and black from the burns, but Diana, as was her nature, was just there. When she saw me, she smiled. She was talking, and she was very alert. I don't know to this day if she was in a lot of pain. That's the kind of child she was. The doctors were dumbfounded that she didn't cry, or that she didn't show that she was experiencing pain. I don't think I could have borne it if she had exhibited that.

"I don't understand this today, but the babysitter said she was going to bathe her, and she ran a tub of hot water, scalding hot water. She said Diana fell into the tub, but that could not have happened because she was just burned from the waist down. She had to have been sat in the tub. She experienced third-degree burns from the waist down.

"I wanted to stay at the hospital, but Alan wouldn't let me, so we went home. There was nothing we could do there. I went back the next morning. Alan wouldn't come. He went back to New York and stayed there.

"Diana lived for two days after that. The miraculous part of it was that she did not cry. I am very thankful for that. I was with her those two days, and she . . . just died.

"Alan drifted further and further apart from me. My son James was born by then, and he was just beginning to crawl. Alan wanted us to move, but I was petrified of New York. I was terrorized by the pace and the indifference of the people. I felt that if I went to New York, I'd die, I'd just die, and the people wouldn't even know it. So I expressed that to him, and he left. But he knew he could always come home.

"And James, I couldn't get attached to him. I couldn't go through that again. I remember thinking, you're just going to die anyway, I'm not going to love you. For the longest time he was crawling and I was performing my duties as a detached nurse."

IV

Religion had always contributed to the atmosphere in which Dorothy Woodson was raised. God was rarely talked about at home, but the children learned nevertheless that He existed, that He had a higher moral law, and that it was to be obeyed. On Sunday they were dressed in special clothes and sent off to church to hear what the minister had to say.

But the churches to which Dorothy was exposed were "too emotional." Sometime during the confused year after Diana's death—the twenty-fourth year of Dorothy's life—a friend told her about another church. "She told me about how different it was and how people's lives were being transformed because of their submission to Jesus Christ. She told me about a radio program, and she asked me to start listening. At first I thought, oh, I can't be bothered, and then she called me up one morning—it was about seven o'clock and I was asleep—and she said, 'Turn your radio on. I want you to hear the program. It's on.' So I said, 'Okay, okay.' And she said, 'That's all right, I'll put the phone to the radio and then you can hear it.' I remember dozing back and forth, but there were certain things that stuck in my mind. This guy was saying that he needed milk, and he didn't have any money, and he prayed so fervently, and he knew God was going to answer him. And as soon as he got off his knees, it was brought to him. I thought, boy, that's having contact, I'd like that kind of contact! I didn't do anything about it right away, but it stuck in my mind.

"I started reading the Bible. I didn't understand a lot that I was reading, yet I felt as if I were being instructed by certain statements. One night I was reading, and it was as if I was being spoken to personally. I read a passage that said, 'Come out of her.' I knew that was speaking about society, and I thought I've got to make a decision on how I'm going to lead my life. I put my cigarette out, and I called my friend. I said, 'I'd like to go to your church.'

"I remember my first visit there. It was as if the entire church came over to welcome me. I had never experienced anything like that before in my life. The people were so warm and friendly and helpful, and there was a spirit of such unity that I felt I'd like to be a part of this. That started my commitment. After attending the church services and counsel-

ing with the ministers about my marital situation, I was told, very
thankfully, that I was my husband's dishrag and didn't I realize I could
catch all sorts of diseases by having him come back and forth?

"I think I wanted a God that satisfied my intellect as well as my heart.
I thought these are people that really believe in the Bible for what it
states. I guess that's called literalism or something, but at any rate I was
impressed that they really tried to live a moral, 'righteous' life. My friend
told me I should start studying, but I didn't know where to begin. So she
said, 'Why don't you come live with me? I could take care of James
while you work and then we could study together.' I lived with her and
devoured all of her literature. I'd jump up at five o'clock in the morning
and shower and go into a little corner with a desk and a little lamp, and I
would sit there for an hour and a half and study. I was very faithful. I
was amazed at the content of that book. I became aware of my human
nature and God's nature. I would pray. I didn't feel God was hearing me,
but because the book said He heard me I thought, well, He does. I had to
accept that on faith even though I didn't feel it. You're not supposed to
go with feeling, you're supposed to go with faith, with what the book
states. I embraced it 100 percent. That's my nature."

Dorothy's next five years alternated between her home in Connecticut
and the church in New York. For a while she commuted from one to the
other; then she spent several years in New York living with a church
family. She returned to Connecticut but then got a job in New York and
moved once again to the city she hated. Finally, she saw an opportunity
for something different. "One Saturday we had a lecturer from the
church's college in California. He had done some research on the brain,
and it was just fascinating. After the lecture I went over to him and asked
him what were my chances of being employed by the college. And he
said, 'Why don't you send in an application and, when you do, let me
know.' So I wrote and got an application and then let him know I had
forwarded it. And very shortly after, they called me and asked me to
come out. They needed a secretary.

"I flew out Thanksgiving Day 1972, and it was so cold that day. I
remember stepping out of the airport in California. It was like going to
heaven! I couldn't believe the warmth of the sun and the palm trees. I
thought this is home! I loved it from that very moment."

V

Dorothy was thirty when she moved to California. She was welcomed as
warmly there as she had been in the local church in New York. But with
time came questions and then serious disillusionment. The church she

attended back East was all black, but the college in California was predominantly white. Subtle prejudices began to bother her. Rumors circulated about excessive spending, and she found them to be true in the case of some leaders. In New York there was doctrinal unity, but here there were confusing arguments. "It was traumatic because I expected everyone to be perfect. In the local churches I was a part of, people's lives were being transformed. They were dedicated people, and they really believed in a higher moral law. They tried to keep it, and they realized they needed spiritual guidance and help. They leaned on God in order to get that help. So when I went to the college and saw people who were being unkind to one another and insensitive, it was disillusioning. And then I discovered there were people who were there just for the money. It caused me an enormous amount of problems, even to the point of questioning God.

"After a couple of years I was going to quit because of the mentality of the people there. Then I got a promotion and began to work for a very likable person. He used to travel quite a bit. One day he returned from Europe, and I said, 'You're the first boss I ever had that I hate to see go away. I can't understand that!' And I couldn't! I just enjoyed having him in the office.

"I began to discuss my thoughts with him. It was incredible to me that he would even sit and talk to me, yet he would spend hours out of the day. I learned an awful lot. He made me aware of studying critically. He's an extremely intelligent, sensitive person, and he had a lot of doubts about so many things. He started me wondering about a lot of things. He planted a lot of seeds in my mind, things I never even considered or aspired to. He would question me about everything and make me think about how I really felt, my gut reaction to things rather than parroting what I thought somebody wanted to hear. That opened up a whole new world for me. I received only support and well-being from him, and it was a new relationship for me. No one ever took that amount of time, nobody was ever that interested to say, 'Hey, what's going on inside of you? I know there's a lot going on in there, I see it, why are you so closemouthed about it?' He helped build me and my mental image of myself. He helped me see that I'm made in the image of God, and that gives no one the right to make me feel inferior.

"I felt, I saw, a person accepting me, for *me*. I was just able to say things. I would start taking risks, and I would get angry. He didn't say naughty girl. He would allow me to be me. And I started thinking about that: I had never been *me* with anybody! If I was angry, well, I didn't say anything about it. If something upset me, I would just suppress it. He said that was okay, and we'd talk about my anger. Then I would feel better, and he would tell me that he learned just from talking to me. It was always give and take. At times his aspirations and his ideals about me were so high they were frightening even to think about. It was almost blasphemous.

"He started inviting me to his home to be with his family. Wherever his family would go he'd invite Dorothy and James. I began to feel a part of the family. After about a year and a half I realized I was falling in love with him. I remember we were at an amusement park. We were having the best time, and the park was about to close, and we just made the last tram over. He was sitting next to me, and all of a sudden I felt this chemistry! I couldn't believe it! I sat there, and I thought, What on earth is happening? It was then that I realized I was in danger, because I had just enjoyed him as a person and had never thought of him in a sexual way.

"But I continued to talk with him, knowing better, and he continued to talk with me. I told him once, 'You know, you're like a doctor. A patient falls in love with a doctor because he helps. He removes something from her, and she's whole again.' And he said to me, 'Well, it's more like you're the doctor and I'm the patient.' I thought about that for a while. I couldn't really understand it.

"Then he started confiding in me about some problems he was having in his marital relationship. And that didn't help matters either. It was really sad, because they're such a fine family. He wanted to marry me. He asked me once, and I just said that is out of the question. It would have meant him divorcing his wife and his children. I could not bear that, because I just love her and I just love his kids. I could not allow it.

"I told him I had to leave. I tried to leave several times, and he would talk me out of it, but then I found that I just could not go on that way. It was sheer torture. I couldn't *stand* to be in this guy's presence. And I'm sure it was that way for him. I had to make the decision to leave. I just closed my eyes and my ears to him. I handed him my resignation and started packing."

VI

In November 1977, after five years in California, Dorothy and James flew to Buffalo, New York, to join the church family she had once lived with. Her "sister," as she refers to the mother of the family, knew why she had come. In fact, she and her husband had all but ordered her to do so.

It was a chilling return East. "For five years I had been far removed from winter, and I couldn't remember the extremely cold temperatures and the mountains of snow. Oh, it was just frigid! I think I must have cried the first month I was here. Every morning, I hated to see morning come. Every night, I hated to see the night come. I could have willed myself to die, that's how miserable I was because this man had become such a part of my life and such a part of my mind. The thing that was so bad was he was married and he was white and the church would have put us both out. We were adult enough to realize the direction our lives were taking was wrong, but we did not realize the extent of the pain we would both go through because of the separation. It was like coming off drugs. I decided I had to communicate with him. I called him a couple of times and I bawled. He said he was unable to pray. He almost cursed God for allowing me to go. We determined we would communicate and ease the pain—come down slower, so to speak.

"I had to go out and look for a job, and every step of the way was agony. Yet I knew I had to do it. I couldn't just lie there and die. I had to deal with the elements as well as the condemnation of my 'sister' and her husband: 'Just don't communicate with this man.' They were moralizing because I was receiving letters from him. I couldn't get across to them that I couldn't *not* get them. I needed something. I felt for the first time in my life as if I could not see the future. I tried so desperately to tell my 'sister' that, but she just couldn't see it. So it was terrifying to me. It was as if there was no more hope, no more alternatives. It was as if my very soul was speaking out and nobody was hearing it but me.

"I accepted a couple of jobs. I quit. After I did that two or three times, people were beginning to say, 'Dorothy, you're unstable, and you're going to establish a very poor reputation.' I kept trying to say, 'Well, the job has got to fulfill something in me. I can't work under adverse conditions right now. The rest of my life is so upset.' I guess I was looking for something comparable to what I left in California.

"To drive in the snow was another story! I was totally unfamiliar with the area. I remember one day it started snowing in the morning, and by one o'clock it was blizzarding. Visibility was maybe ten feet. I didn't know where I was going. I felt so lost. I almost panicked. I thought, Where on earth am I? Momentarily, I reflected on that being the condition of my life, and then I really panicked! I remember stopping at a stop sign, and a guy stopped near me. I rolled down the window and *yelled* to him, "Where's the freeway?" He said, 'It's right there, miss.' You know, it was right there, but I couldn't see it. *That* spoke to me in a very specific way about my life."

Finally, Dorothy landed a job with a utility company. The first day at work marked the beginning of another episode in her life. She was thirty-five.

"On the date of hire I had an eight o'clock appointment with the company doctor for a physical. It was the most thorough physical I ever had in my life, and that's when I discovered I had a tumor, a uterine tumor. He said it was a tiny little thing and it was nothing to be concerned about. How did he put it? 'They're not uncommon in women. It's probably just a fibroid. And as long as it's not bothering you, I think we should not bother with it.' I accepted that. It didn't bother me so much although it stuck in the back of my mind. A tumor—why? Why that? I'd read enough about the mind and the body, and I wondered if the stress that I had been under contributed to the growth of the tumor, because there were many days I'd wake up or go to bed, one or the other, and I just didn't want to see the sun.

"The following November, or maybe October, I started having difficulty during my menstrual period. I was in severe pain. I couldn't get up. I couldn't do anything. This happened several times, and I decided to go back to the doctor to find out what was happening. He examined me and said that the tumor had grown and perhaps I should have it removed because of the rate at which it was growing. He said I should seek another opinion. I was upset, naturally. I counseled with a friend of mine, and she gave me the name of Dr. David Henry, and I contacted him. After the examination he felt I should have it removed surgically as soon as possible. I consented. I felt, well, that was the less of two evils: if I don't do something, I won't know if it's malignant. I was admitted to the hospital on December nineteenth, 1978, and surgery was to be performed on the twentieth.

"The doctor assured me it was perfect surgery. I found out two days later it was benign. That gave me relief. But during the examination by one of the student doctors, I noted that he spent an awful lot of time on my right breast. It got my attention, but he didn't say anything and I didn't say anything. After I was released from the hospital, I was home for about six weeks, and I really couldn't do very much. I was utterly alone. Then I felt a very tiny lump in the breast. It was startling because it was, oh, very, very tiny, about the size of a B-B, and I thought that's not anything to get upset about. It's not that large, and it will go away. Weeks later, I don't remember the time span, I examined my breast again, and it had gotten larger. That's when I really got scared.

"During this time I was having conflict in my mind about God. People from the church would call and send cards and they'd bring food, which was very much appreciated, but I felt that there was something missing. I thought, I just don't understand where God is in all of this. Where is He? Why did I have to go through this surgery? I thought, how can I pray to a God if I don't even know if He's concerned about me? I'm just angry with Him. If He is there, I'm just angry. I don't like this treatment. Here I tried to serve Him and live according to how I felt we should live, and all of a sudden He's not there.

"The lump didn't go away. I felt, why is this happening to me? Did I will myself to die? I guess many times I've wanted to. So often I wanted to die. Is this the result of the nights that I would lie in bed, and my soul would just groan? I don't know. I thought about James. What would he do? Where would he go? I talked to him about it. Not about the lump in my breast, but if I died where would he like to go? Would he like to stay with his father? Would he like to remain with my 'sister's' family? What would he like to do? At first he said, 'Well, I would like to go with my dad because he is my other parent,' but days later he told me, 'Well, I really don't know him at all. I don't know if he's the person I want to be with.' So I still don't know what he'd like to do.

"I decided to go back to the company physician. He examined my breast and said there's definitely something there and I should go to a doctor. I didn't right away. I thought, oh, it's nothing. I'm not going to bother about it, it's not malignant, it's just that I'm getting older and I'm changing. Perhaps even the surgery had something to do with it. Maybe it caused chemicals in my body to form this thing. So I still refused to believe that it was a lump, I guess. Weeks later again, I decided I better go because it had gotten a little larger, and so I made an appointment with Dr. Henry. He examined it and said it didn't feel like cancer. What did he say? Oh, it was still movable, and based on his experience, he felt it was not cancer at all. He also did not want to give me a mammography because I was still young. He said, 'If we can get you through forty, then I would feel more comfortable in giving it to you.' He also said that he would like me to make *daily* self-examinations and report to him any change. I felt better. I was appeased after that but still not at peace."

VII

All through our conversations Dorothy had mentioned her son James, an affable young man of thirteen, who usually busied himself in a back bedroom while I talked with his mother in the front of the apartment. For the first seven years of his life James had been a fearful child who cried constantly and clung to his mother. His full name was James Thomas and everyone called him Tommy. But in California, as his mother became happier and more confident, he too became happier and more confident. One day he announced that he wanted to be called James because "that's my name."

"One of my thoughts is that I've got to make every day count with my son. I mean every day. Not a day should pass that he's not loved and that his ideas and he as a person are not acknowledged and guided in some way. I guess all along I've tried to instill in him principles that can help him through life. I feel he's an old philosophizer at thirteen! Sometimes he feeds back to me some of the things I've taught him, and I think, boy, he *did* listen!

"We've had occasion to talk about death and do things I would never have thought to do. Weeks ago I asked him, 'James, do you pray?' Because there was a time when James and I would pray daily and we would have formal Bible studies. We'd sit down and we'd either have a question-and-answer session or I would select something out of the Bible and read it and then we'd discuss what it meant to us. We've gotten away from that, especially since we've been here in Buffalo. I used to say, 'James, don't forget to pray when you go to bed.' And I've not been doing that for the last year and a half. So I asked him several weeks ago, and he said to me, 'Of course I do, every night! I'm almost afraid not to!' " She laughed. "I don't want him to have *that* approach, and I will discuss it with him!

"I look at him now, and I marvel. I think how balanced he is. He's such a beautiful child, I can't believe it. He finds his happiness in creating happiness. When I'm down, he senses that and does things to make me feel good—crack a joke or tell me good news or just talk. He has a great deal of his father's personality. I feel it's genetic to a degree. But exposure has contributed to it also. We've been all over, we've met all kinds of people, and that has given James the confidence to relate to anyone. The fact that he's gone from sitter to sitter, not had any kind of structured family life, and not gone to the same school more than two sessions has had its drawbacks, but James has developed an awareness and an overview about different types of people. He can relate to his ghetto buddies as well as to his other friends. I tease him. I tell him he's bilingual. All his teachers mention that he loves people. He feels very responsible for his friendships and puts a lot into them. Sometimes I'm fearful for him because I feel he's going to be hurt a lot.

"He instructs me often, believe it or not, just in his approach and his outlook. He is very optimistic. Maybe he will arrive at where I am now by the time he's twenty because he's not afraid to take necessary risks, he's not afraid to ask questions, and yet he does it with respect. He does have feelings of inferiority. He doesn't do that well academically, and he's bored very easily. He's not been motivated. I've had to fight bad guilt trips about coming home and being too tired to sit down and give him the necessary instruction where homework is concerned.

"I see family traits that I have, that I've seen in my sisters and my mother and my son. It's like ancestral influences I'm trying to overcome and replace with stronger, more transcendental values. I guess that's what I'm trying to do with him, to let him see that I've passed things on to him—and his dad has too. He's got some pretty good stuff from both of us, but he's got some weaknesses too. If he doesn't focus on them and just concentrates on those strong areas and replaces the weak areas with the creative things he likes to do, then he's going to be that much more valuable to society.

"James will be gone in five years. He wants to go to college, and he's discovered there are girls in the world, so it won't be long. I feel I've got to teach him more. There are still some areas in his life that I feel I've got to impact—at least get some things in his head. He's turning out to be such a fine, fine individual that I want to be a part of that and his posterity." Her voice was a whisper. "I guess what I'm saying is that there is a reason to fight for life."

VIII

In narrating her life Dorothy Woodson had an exquisite touch, a grace so natural she was unaware of it. Despite the suffering she had undergone, she laughed often. She had an infectious giggle that rose like a bubble, took over her entire body, and broke in a single burst. The laugh was set off by the images she saw in her mind's mirror, by the sight of her childhood fears, of her naiveté in expecting a perfect church, even of her anger toward God. She never pitied or derided those images, nor was she ever cynical about them. Her laugh, rather, was one of compassion and insight. It released tension and pain. Followed by a sigh, it accepted the events life dealt her. Often it trembled and held back tears, and sometimes it collapsed in formation. It disappeared when she spoke softly but not numbly of the deaths of her children. Then it returned to lighten her movements and speed up her pace. The laugh eased her into the tragic and accompanied her out of it, giving her the capacity to continue.

One of our conversations took place on a summer evening, one of the longest days of the year. The setting sun seemed to stay in the sky forever, sending soft rays through drifting dust to illuminate the wall behind her. On that occasion Dorothy was even more reflective than usual, her thoughts turning to the life that seemed to be ebbing from her.

"After discovering the lump, I just felt, oh, I wasted my life! Now I may not have it tomorrow. What have I done? I've not done anything worthwhile. I've not done anything I've wanted to do. I've just been forced into things. I thought, what am I going to do? Worry and contribute to the bad chemicals that are induced by stress, or live each day to its fullest and make purpose for my life? Because in the final sense it's up to me. I tried to evaluate my last few years and my condition, and I determined that I wanted to *live*." She seemed surprised at the simplicity of her answer.

"I thought, well, if it's just for a month, I want it to be to its fullest. And I thought, well, I can't live my life like it's going to be my last day, because then there's no motivation, at least not for me because I have this extreme mentality. And I thought, well, I'm going to live each day like it's my first because then I'll be able to plan. Then I can go about planning and setting to bring those goals about. And that can give me hope.

"I feel stronger as an individual. I feel stronger in my relationship to God. In a greater sense, I feel as if conversion has taken place in my life for the first time. All the other stuff was preparation for this, because now my relationship with God does not depend on anything that's visible, anything that's tangible. It doesn't depend on the minister getting up and preaching exactly what he should preach. I mean, he can deviate, but it does not change God. So I feel that I can go through almost anything now, and I know it's okay. I can be very, very happy as long as I have my son to instruct and my plants.

"I had gotten to the point where I was very angry with God, and then I even questioned His existence. Then I thought, well, I believe in Einstein's God: He's just the cosmos, He's not involved with man at all, He set things in order and they're still in order, but He's just too big to be concerned about man. Then I reflected on my life and the changes that have come about, and I thought, no, no, I need a personal God. I remember when the crabapple trees here just blossomed over night. One day everything was barren, and the next day everything was beautiful. I remember reflecting on how everything was dead and the fact that something died doesn't mean that it won't ever live again. It's evident by nature. I remember marveling and just drinking in the beauty of the area at the time. It was beautiful to see things grow again where there was nothing but barrenness two or three weeks before. I thought, there is a God, there is. There's just too much design, too much harmony. I need God in my life. I just do.

"I don't believe I go to heaven when I die. I believe in a resurrection at an appointed time. I draw the analogy of spring.

"I feel life is a process and that your experiences bad or good, specifically bad experiences, can either build character or destroy character. And if individuals are seeking a higher good or a higher reason for life, then the experiences will add to their character and add to their life. I don't know, I do believe that God is building people. I know last night I sat watching the news, and I almost couldn't bear it. I sat there and bawled like a baby because there's violence and no natural affection for another human being. I looked at the truckers and the policemen beating on the truckers and a sniper killing one and it was almost too much. I thought, what has happened to this country, what has happened to the world, what has happened to humanity? Then I thought that there is something basically evil about capitalism. After I thought about it, I said, well, no, it's just the extreme of it, because you get to the point where you just want to accumulate and accumulate and you're not willing to sacrifice. We're used to a standard of living that we're not willing to give up. So what if the country goes to pot, so what if twenty years from now the air isn't worth breathing and our kids have to walk around with gas masks. I know that's extreme, but we've just become so selfish as a people. We're so spoiled. It's very sad. We're not willing to lower our standard of living. We continuously buy, buy, buy, buy. And to hell with the country as long as I'm comfortable, as long as I can get my gas, as long as I can watch my color TV. There's nothing wrong with those things, but when it affects another person and it affects your neighbor and it affects your country, then there's a need for reassessment, there's a need for sacrifice, there's a need for cutting back. Because we can be very happy with the minimum. We really can, as long as we have the ingredients of love and giving to one another. I mean, that's what really makes happiness. People think that acquisition of goods will satisfy, and it will, but it's only temporary. Then they've got to go out and get more. They're missing the point. It's human relationships, your relationship with your brother, with your wife, with your children, that make life worthwhile. Preparing for them. Thinking about them, that *they* can have a better life. Well, it's just sad, very sad.

"I am very dissatisfied with my job. I detest it, and I know that it's no good for me. I perceive the job as a group of people perpetrating their own existence. They're just making work. The whole department could be cut out —ten people like that! I'm typing the same things I typed a year ago. It's just nonproductive work, and that kills me. I feel as if I'm wasting my life there and my time. I'd rather be doing something else at a tremendous reduction in salary, as long as I can feel I'm making some kind of contribution.

"At any rate, that's where I am right now. I'd like to get out of the rat race. I reject it totally. I really do. I'm in it because it's a means to an end, and I have no choice. If it were not for the benefits, I would have an astronomical hospital bill. What I would really like to do is study to become an interpreter for the deaf. I've sent away for some of the brochures. The classes seem to be exciting, and I think I can really become involved in that. It would be doing something that would be a service, and I would get to relate to the souls of other beings that are handicapped. In a sense their handicap is no different than mine because I feel that what I have is a handicap. It's a handicap emotionally, and I'm sure their deafness is a handicap for them in many ways. I'd like to learn the psychology of being deaf.

"I've thought a lot about it. I believe you can tune into somebody's soul by putting yourself in their place because I've done it with my son. It's scary. It's scary to do that. I don't like it when I do that because I become them in a sense. I remember often I would walk down a corridor at work and I would be aching inside, I mean really aching, and sometimes there would be a smile on my face. And I would wonder, how many people am I passing daily that are going through what I am emotionally? They just need someone to say, hey, how are you? To have someone care enough to hear them, I mean really hear them. Not necessarily do anything about what they're going through, not to give great edicts about what to do, but say, look, I understand. Just be a soulmate, going through it with them, not so much even going through it, but just being right there to say, 'Hey, I'm here and I *hear* you.' "

IX

Dorothy was moving from her apartment when I first visited her, and when I saw her fifteen months later, she was making yet another move. She had quit her job with the utility company, spent some time with her ailing parents, and was on her way to California. She wanted to get away from frigid northern winters, and she wanted to pursue her goal of becoming an interpreter for the deaf. She had already taken a class in signing but was still a long way from fluency. Leaving a secure, well-paying job for the unknown was frightening, but at thirty-eight she felt it was now or never.

Her friend in California knew she was coming and wanted to see her, but she had broken off communication with him months before. In the past year he had left his wife, the ministry, and the church, and his beliefs were somewhere between agnosticism and atheism. Another man in California, a church member, wanted desperately to marry her, but the "mental chemistry" wasn't there, and so she had to face the difficult task of refusing him. Her son James had suddenly grown taller than she. "He'll pick up my ankle and put his whole hand around it and laugh. He says it's so strange to outgrow me. He is, I think, becoming more serious about his future."

The lump in her breast had not changed, she had not gone back to the doctor, and she still did not know how much life was left for her. The stress of the move was more than she had anticipated, and she was often sick to her stomach and "neurotic." Dorothy laughed and sighed as she said that, implying she knew she would always be that way. She was explicit, though, about her need for the strength and the clear guidelines that God and His moral law gave her, about her commitment to the church and the "spiritual realm." "My move to California is very scary for me, and I've got to have the faith that wherever I am and whatever I'm doing, as long as it's pleasing to God, then it's going to work out. It may not work out in the eyes of other people, but as long as the spiritual growth is there, then I feel as if I'm serving the purpose for which I draw breath." Dorothy still relied on an inner tautness to bring her from one fearful situation to the next, pulling the passages off and speaking of them with an unconscious grace. As I left her the second time, I thought of an incident that had occurred when I said good-bye the previous summer.

Just before I had left her apartment I happened to ask about the painting of the ballerina on the wall behind me. During our conversations, it had often engaged her eyes. I was surprised to discover that it was a portrait of her, a mirror reflecting still another self-picture, one more hidden and fragile than that of the ugly child, but with a history almost as long.

"That was done by my friend in California. He painted that for me, and it means an awful lot. He told me what he was doing and let me see it a couple of times before he had it completed. I love ballet. I didn't mention that, did I? As a child I wanted to become a ballet dancer. My family couldn't afford to send me so my mom sacrificed one year and gave me lessons when I was twelve years old. And I remember I used to cut out my sister's old gowns to make my own tutus. They could never afford to get me the hard-toe, but I was able to get ballet slippers. Black ballet dancers were not in vogue then, and there are very few now. It was what I wanted to do. Ballet is beautiful.

"I remember during that year the instructor would take me aside, and she would say, 'Well, I didn't show it to you that way, Dorothy, but what you're doing is absolutely beautiful.' You know, I would feel it, and I would do what I felt rather than what she would instruct. I just feel it's something I've been given—a natural gift of grace."

INTERPRETATION: DAMAGE
AND NOURISHMENT

In Dorothy Woodson's elegant story of death and life there are allusions to all four types of generativity. She speaks of meanings associated with the biological transmission of life, in particular of her lack of readiness for it and of her sense of passing on bodily ugliness. She wonders if a sense of inadequacy is "passed on in the genes." She tells of tragic failures and then success at parenting, a capacity that matured in her long after she bore children. Few of her comments deal with technical generativity, though she mentions teaching her son to read the Bible and touches on failures in instructing him in how to be a student. Much of what she passes on to him (and to me as she tells her story) falls into the realm of culture. As death seems to approach, she feels a great urgency to nurture in her son the religious understanding on which she bases her existence.

What is intriguing about Dorothy's generative life is its dramatic change. Two of her children die. She is numbed and fails to respond to her third. For seven years that child clings fearfully to her, and then, rather suddenly as lives are measured, he becomes confident and outgoing, seeing himself so differently that he insists on a new name. What changes in his mother permitted this to happen? Though Dorothy's narrative illustrates a number of motifs, two in particular address this question. In tandem, they speak to the link between what enters a life and what comes forth from it.

PRODUCING WHAT IS DAMAGED;
DAMAGING WHAT IS PRODUCED

It is almost inevitable that in the course of a life one will bring into being something crippled, flawed, or evil, that one will harm or even kill the good things under one's care. Abortion, mistakes and abuse in rearing a child, failures as a teacher, fatal errors on the part of a doctor, miscalculations by a leader, incompetence in an artist: in some way what emanates from *me* will be deformed; in some way I will injure the target of my generativity or damage the object of my stewardship. The destruction may be passed on willfully, accidentally, or even as the inseparable counterpart of creation. Generative damage may be no more than a blemish in an otherwise masterly work. Or it may be so great that the progenitor will say, as did a creator of the atom bomb, "I am become death, the destroyer of worlds."[1]

Dorothy Woodson feels responsible for the deaths of her children. In her thinking, the first died of rejection, and the second, for whom she holds herself less accountable, died because she failed to act on a premonition. For most of her adult life Dorothy has also had an elemental sense of growing weak, shriveled, and deadly things within herself. Because she believes that mind controls matter, she feels responsible for these too—for the ugliness of her first baby, for the tumors she now fears. As she puts it, "The seeds of cancer are sown in the turmoils of the mind." The somatic knowledge that her insides produce bad things is expressed even on the surface of her narrative, in what I call the manifest story.

But the knowledge appears with greater force in the latent story. It is significant that whenever Dorothy's life turns toward the positive, she experiences the removal of an evil growth within her. The biblical words that speak to her are "Come out of her!"—a command to God's people in the Book of Revelations to come out of evil Babylon. Dorothy takes this as a command to extricate herself from her unhealthy surroundings, but the words also recall the many times Jesus extracted unclean spirits from deep within possessed bodies by demanding that they "Come out!" In California, Dorothy perceives her loved one as a doctor who cures a patient. "He removes something from her, and she's whole again." In New York she has an actual and potentially dangerous lump removed surgically from her body. When I later ask her what she wishes could now be removed from her, she says, "That six-letter word: cancer. I'd like that element removed, whatever it is, wherever it is. I believe it's dormant there waiting for my mind to command it to grow." Though other narrators surely experienced it, none expressed as directly and poignantly this bodily sense of producing ugliness and poison. As Dorothy said of her first child, "It was all from me"—words that illuminate the dilemma of anyone who looks at his creation, biological or cultural, and sees that it is bad.

Recognizing that creations are flawed, knowing that one has in some way "slaughtered the innocents" under one's care can be devastating. Mirrorlike, progeny and works reflect on their creator, misshapen ones saying that the creator's essence is deformed, for it grew and gave birth to this. From the subtle accusation lying in the product flows the urge to shatter or disown it, or, more commonly, to dim the recognition of damage. In the narratives I recorded, reactions to the recognition of damage varied from mild regret to extreme guilt, one of the most powerful emotions I encountered. Some realized that destruction was a part of life, that one had both received it and dealt it out, and in neither case could it be undone. Some were silent about the harm they had done, while others alleviated their guilt by denying that harm existed, by blaming their victims, or by attributing their behavior to an uncontrollable disease that had afflicted them. A few rightly saw that their hand had been forced by external circumstances, and they were embittered; while they grieved, they retained their anger. The responsibility that Dorothy Woodson feels is almost beyond guilt, grief, or anger. No twisted defense mechanisms hide from her the fact of what happened. Her knowledge is tempered only by a belief in a resurrected life in which Diana will be "just as I last saw her, but whole, not blistered." In this intuition of the future, the damage is emotionally undone.

BEING NOURISHED

During the years Dorothy felt little good emanating from her, she also felt little good entering her. As a child she took in fears rather than confidence, a feeling of ugliness rather than beauty. When she married, she was ignored by her husband, and she clung to him as one starved. Lying in bed after the death of her second child, Dorothy was moved by a voice on the radio saying that he desperately needed milk and that, after turning to God, it was brought to him. That voice crying for milk— the most elemental nourishment—struck a responsive chord in Dorothy.

She started reading the Bible and was deeply affected by the words, "Come out of her!" Instantly she stopped putting bad things into her body. As she later explained, "I used to smoke very heavily. Every time I got hungry I reached for a cigarette." When she read that passage and decided to do something about her life, "I felt I shouldn't be smoking." She went on to devour her friend's religious literature, embracing it as totally as she had her husband. In the church she found warmth and unity, and "I had never experienced anything like that before in my life." Here was a fundamental experience of being nourished, of receiving a kind of milk.

More sustenance came from her loved one in California. Not only did he remove a sickness from her, "He planted a lot of seeds in my mind, things I never even considered or aspired to." Literally and symbolically he gave her a beautiful picture of herself. "It was a new relationship for me," says Dorothy, describing another primary experience of taking good things in. The immediate effect of this new food was on Dorothy's generativity. For the first time in his life her son became relaxed, confident, and outgoing.

The link between nourishment and generativity—between what enters a life and what comes from it—is inevitable. Though I have studied far too few lives to be conclusive in this matter, I suspect that each type of generativity requires its own kind of nutriment, both in the critical moment of its birth and throughout the course of its life.

Dorothy's life story illustrates the connection between nourishment and generativity in the parental and cultural areas. Parental generativity draws on founding experiences in the first years of life, in the convictions of trust, autonomy, and initiative that one received in the beginning, as well as on the support one receives while rearing a child now. At neither time did Dorothy receive enough nourishment. Because of her own upbringing, Dorothy's mother "did not know how to show love." Dorothy remembers the beginning of life as a frightening time in which she just wanted someone "to hold my hand." She had not the slightest idea of what motherhood entailed, nor did she receive any encouragement from her husband or mother while she learned. In a familiar pattern, she parented as she was parented, with little sustenance flowing through her.

Cultural generativity in a life may be traced to origins in the discovery and confirmation of identity, an event that Erikson assigned to adolescence, but one that can take place more than once and long after the teenage years. Just as parents need to provide nourishment that is "good enough," so too, in ways that are symbolic but nonetheless real, do cultures. While parents' nourishment consists of affection and control, that of cultures consists of templates of existence that offer adherents meaning and belonging. It consists of prescriptions for action, the support of co-believers, and access to a storehouse of mythical lives and heroic deeds. Through the medium of their personal identity, partakers of a "good enough" culture draw on the symbolic order sustaining the social life of a community.

Dorothy's life changed when she began to receive cultural nourishment. It was given to her by the mediators of a mythic and moral order, in this case, her church. To the warmth and unity that first greeted her she responded by forming an emotional bond as strong and total as that between an infant and its mother. She accepted counseling from church ministers. She incorporated wholeheartedly a religious understanding of life, began to live in accord with its principles, and moved in with church families. In California she fell in love with another representative of the same culture. In this relationship the involvement of identity is clearly seen. "I felt, I saw, a person accepting *me*, for me. . . . And I started thinking about that: I had never been *me* with anybody!" The benefit of Dorothy's new-found intimacy was its fostering of a beautiful and graceful sense of self, a "me" that existed only when supported by the culture. So strong was her attachment to the culture that when a conflict developed between it and her love for this man, she chose the culture, though he was ready to abandon it.

Entries into cultures were memorable experiences in half the stories in this volume, and I shall explicate a psychology of them in subsequent interpretations. My premise is straightforward: cultural entrées are marked internally by experiences of identity. As one steps into a culture, one discovers "me" and finds that "me" energized. Particular dimensions of the personality are linked to the collectivity's symbolic life, there to draw on its sustenance. Normally, the first such experience comes in adolescence, when one consciously recognizes the atmosphere of meaning one has been breathing all along. The recognition may be aided by rites of initiation, which specify the role the young person is to play in the next stage of life and confirm his or her suitability for that role. Supported by the group, the initiate says: here is where I belong, here am I. In this founding experience of identity the individual is set on a path leading to a particular kind of generative engagement.

Because of increased longevity and the ever-changing array of cultures and subcultures in contemporary society, lives today are more likely than in the past to be characterized by a number of cultural entries (and exits)— by experiences of identity not just in adolescence but in young and middle adulthood as well. These later entries often contain the sense that the newly discovered *I* has been present all along, lying in a dormant state and waiting to be activated.[2] "I had it all along, but I didn't know I had it" is a typical expression of the sense of dormancy. Or the following words from a recovered alcoholic: "As I got sicker and sicker something in me was saying you can do better." For certain reasons, which the life-historical researcher can never fully determine, the mythic substratum of *this* culture speaks suddenly to the subconscious of *this* person, and that self is awakened, like Snow White or Sleeping Beauty. Dorothy Woodson longs for recognition, acceptance, and love; she wishes she could recapture the clear sense of right and wrong she had as a child. Mediators of a religious culture offer her these values, and she finds a "new" self. As she enters the culture, something else happens, nearly unnoticed: she reviews her life with representatives of the church. Events from her past are recounted, stripped of whatever interpretation they carried, and seen in a new light. In the process Dorothy feels as though she is peeling away an ugly self and uncovering a beautiful one. The larger reality is that she is stepping from a diffuse and almost nonexistent culture into a highly focused one. To secure her footing in her new environment, she attaches her life story to its symbolic framework.

The refashioning of personal history at the entrances to cultures is illustrated by the process of thought reform.[3] In the late 1940s and 1950s the Chinese Communists used terror, the manipulation of guilt, and a direct assault upon identity to strip their prisoners of their familiar interpretations of life. Captives were forced to relate every detail of their past life to interrogators and to cellmates already advanced in their personal reform. These details were then reinterpreted. Innocent comments about horsedrawn artillery were reconstrued as acts of "military espionage." A discussion of the price of shoes became an act of "economic espionage." As prisoners' life stories were ripped from their accustomed symbolic context, their identities were blurred. A doctor questioned whether he had ever really been a doctor, a priest whether he was not in fact a spy. Only when prisoners began to accept the rewritten history of their lives did a sense of identity return. Their captors understood that to get from one culture to the next prisoners had to tell their story and that the story had to change in transition.

Initiation into psychoanalysis offers another example of cultural entry. At the gate of the culture, in place of Dorothy's minister and thought reform's interrogator, stands the analyst. The patient is asked to delve into every aspect of her past life, and the analyst interprets: one memory covers a "wish for a penis," another a "fear of seduction," a third a "desire for impregnation." If the psychoanalytic culture fits the patient, the concepts speak to her unconscious, unlocking memories, providing insight, and connecting the previously hidden past to the present. A bond, the transference, develops between analyst and patient. In a conversion that is both intellectual and emotional, the patient removes her history from whatever symbolic framework she brought to the analyst's door and attaches it to the framework she finds inside. Images that arise from her unconscious are blended with the myths of her new culture. An old identity has been "unmasked," a new one "found," and the analysis has been "successful." The initiate leaves with a new life story keeping her identity affixed to a sustaining culture.

In several lives I have studied, experiences at cultural entry sensitized the individual to a particular kind of nutriment, so that he or she could incorporate that kind later on, so that later experiences could have the quality of recapturing the energizing beginnings. The way of life prescribed by Dorothy's church, more than anything else, feeds her now. Her attachment is not as total and unquestioning as when she first entered, but she maintains her belief in God, remains involved with church members, and follows the moral law outlined in the Bible. These commitments strengthen her. I believe analogous relationships can be found between nourishment in the beginning and nourishment now for each of the four types of generativity.

More than anything else, the presence of a sustaining culture led to the change in the quality of Dorothy's generativity. She now felt good things growing inside her that she could pass on to her son. As he received them, he saw a picture of himself so novel that he called for a change in name. Though Dorothy had produced a beautiful child before, this was the first time she was able to sustain her care for one.

Dorothy not only wishes to pass on a religious understanding of life to her son, she also wishes to become an interpreter for the deaf. Somehow this would make up for the times when the world was deaf to her, when she would be "aching inside" and no one, God included, heard her pain. Although her desire appears to flow from a sense of deprivation, of *not being heard*, the wherewithal to accomplish the desire derives from one critical episode of *being heard* by her loved one. Thus it is mixture of deprivation and nourishment—of sustenance suddenly given and suddenly withdrawn—that appears to motivate her choice of how to make a contribution. Her choice, incidentally, is slowly becoming a reality. A year after our last visit Dorothy phoned to say that she was well, that her lump had gotten smaller (she was convinced it was affected by diet), that James had adapted well to California, and that she had progressed sufficiently in sign language to have a community of deaf friends.

There are other motifs touched by Dorothy's life, and I shall refer to it again while discussing other lives. But no one felt as strongly as she both the sense of producing ugliness when malnourished and producing beauty when sufficiently fed. Hers is a life that illustrates a basic dilemma of generativity.

5 · Journey into the Lie

My mother always said that when you get married you put a big apron in front of you, and if there is any problem you put everything behind that apron." She circled like a hawk above those words as if they were the prey, as if they were the belief that, having deceived her, had to be exorcised.

"My mother was a liar. Part of me says it's not nice to be angry at a woman who loved you so much and who went through so much hell of her own. But her whole life was a lie, even, from what I can piece together, down to the last minute. Never once, as far as I can see, did she face life as it really was. It was hidden behind her religion, behind the stories she told herself, behind that apron. After her death I started researching. I wrote friends and relatives trying to get as much information as I could, trying to answer questions that bothered me. Why was my mother the way she was? Why am I the way I am? I would like to be understanding. I would like to say this is what she had to do to survive in her own eyes. But there are all these blocks in front of me, and they all have so many sides! If only I knew which side of each was supposed to face me, if only I could right the pieces, then the puzzle would have meaning. It would be whole. Maybe then I could cure my anger."

She was a thirty-eight-year-old woman, well dressed, with auburn hair and a broad, handsome face. She was obviously attentive to her appearance. When I first asked to record her life story, her face became passive and impenetrable. She avoided a response for several months. Then, suddenly, she said she was ready. But she warned, "I can be very devious."

I

We are sitting in a shaded room on a warm summer afternoon, and her voice is full of expression as she begins. I am amazed and confused at what is coming forth from one who wavered so long before this telling, who spoke of unsolved puzzles and uncured anger, and who referred to herself as a deceptive maze of "levels" and "parts." She speaks in a low, clear voice, never hesitating, never fishing for words, her English fluent but lightly accented.

She was born Erzsébet Rácz in 1940 and spent the first years of her life with her grandmother in Nagykanizsa, Hungary. When she speaks of her beginnings, she recalls terror: a grotesque statue of a dwarf in the back yard of her grandmother's house, a spanking after "going potty" in some dishes, her head being shaved and bathed in petroleum to protect against lice rampant in a bomb shelter. Her mind jumps to nightmares in which she still runs from the horror that rained on Budapest in 1944— from hunger and cold, from bullets and falling walls, from Dobermans and men in green shirts. She speaks with awe and fear of a nun who took her and her mother into a convent, fed them, and gave them blankets, and she shudders to dwell on the few days her mother left her alone with that courageous but stern sister.

Then she retreats even further and remembers the loving voice and smell of an old man who smoked a pipe. She called him Pöpö—the puffer. Pöpö came by her grandmother's house in Nagykanizsa every day, took his little Erzsike on his lap, and let her grab his pipe. She did not know or care why he was there. "He was gentle and warm and giving and patient, and he always came to my defense. He died when I was four. I remember my mother coming down on the train for the funeral. It was a rainy day in spring, and I sat in the pretty room—they called it the pretty room because it was used only on special occasions— and all these people came by and felt very sorry for my grandmother because Pöpö died. My mother refused to take me to the funeral parlor. My nurse Wilma took me to the cemetery, but we never entered it."

When her grandmother died a few months later, Erzsi's mother came to take her to Budapest, four hours by train to the northeast. From her mother Erzsi learned that her grandmother was a saint, that no one was as beautiful or holy as she. "My mother always quoted me the saying that if you honor your parents, they will live a long life."

Erzsi and her mother survived the Allied bombing and siege of Budapest, but her father, she was told, was killed. Just before the war he had gone to Rome and obtained some medals blessed by the pope. Erzsi's mother told her that those medals had guided the two of them safely through the destruction.

After the war, Erzsi's mother remarried. Her new husband was affectionate; he kept his family fed; but he was crude, just the opposite of another stranger, an exciting man whose meeting with Erzsi must have been arranged. "All I know is that an Uncle László talked to me for quite a while in a beautiful office at the company where my mother worked. I was six at the time. He told me beautiful things, some of which I still remember. 'Whatever you learn, whatever you take inside as knowledge, nobody can take away from you.' After the conversation was over, I went downstairs feeling forlorn. Then something shook me out of my thoughts."

Though she never saw him again, the mysterious stranger planted a seed in Erzsi's mind. In a few years she began to long for a true father, for someone wealthy and handsome and sophisticated, for someone like Pöpö or Uncle László. She had seen so many fathers: who was real and who was not? Reality and illusion began a dance in her fantasy, and at times they spun so fast she could not tell them apart.

In a catechism class she was shown a picture of God's Eye peeking out from behind a cloud. She learned that He was always watching and that "He doesn't beat you with a stick." When you get what is coming to you—and you surely will—it will not be as obvious as a clubbing. By the age of eight Erzsi had figured out where heaven and hell were, but she was confused about purgatory. "I knew God was up there because His Eye was there, and I knew hell was down there. I knew the locations, who belonged where, how you got up there, how you got down there. But then the nuns talked about purgatory. I asked, 'Where is purgatory?' I was very serious, and they got upset with me. They called in my mother and said I asked impertinent and stupid questions that did not belong there."

When the Communists came to power in 1948, reality and illusion began another bewildering dance. "They started making bad jokes of priests. They said the church had taken all the land. They said look at all the church members who were in cahoots with Hitler and the Nazis. They said everything that was ever discovered was discovered by the Russians. No matter where we went, there was Uncle Joe smiling at us, mustache and all. We were taught that he was the upholder of world peace. When he died I cried for a day. I thought world peace was going to end."

Then she discovered a source she could believe: books. You did not have to agree with them, and you could let your imagination run free in their pages. "I would read and I would read and I would voraciously read. There weren't enough books I could get. We always had books around, and there was a family across the hall that had a fantastic collection. The boy had a crush on me, and he brought me books by the tens and twenties: English books, American books, French books, Hungarian books, classics and trash, books on the black list. If I read a book and said it was hogwash, that was the end of it. I didn't have to nod. I didn't have to take what was in there if my own eyes saw something else.

"When I was nine I got scarlet fever and spent six weeks alone with my books. My sister had just been born, and I had loathed her from the moment my mother was pregnant with her. My mother wouldn't let me go to the hospital because, she said, you go to hospitals to die. So I stayed at home in my room in total isolation. The doctor came twice a day. My stepfather came before he went to work and after he came home. He took my bedpan, washed me, brought me food, and then went out and washed himself. He lived in the middle of the apartment. My mother and sister were locked up together in the front.

"I was alone with 120 books. Alone and miserable, alone and scratchy, alone and lonely. I tried to tell myself this was the best my mother could do under the circumstances. But somehow I felt she was more interested in protecting that baby. When I got better, they came and fumigated my room. They burned my mattress. They burned my books. That was the most painful thing I had to witness. When I came out of that room I rejected them. I rejected my mother. I rejected my sister. I rejected my stepfather. All of a sudden my mother's touching repelled me. It caused me pain when she would want to kiss me. I became painfully aware of being ashamed of my stepfather. From then on I spent most of my time in my room with my books, acquiring more and more books, borrowing more and more books. I don't know how much of it was an escape from reality. I put a rope around me, and I didn't want anybody.

"My whole world was changing. At eleven I started menstruating and didn't know what was happening. My mother hadn't told me about it. I was on the beach when it started. I panicked. Somebody drew me aside and said, 'It's all right. Don't cry. You're going to survive. It's woman's fate and isn't it awful?'

"All I wanted was for my real father to be alive. I began to feel he *was* alive. He was in Rome where he got the medals. He didn't know I was all right. He didn't get in touch with me because he thought I was dead. But soon he would find out I was alive and then he would take me out of this misery and take me to Rome. He would hold my hand, just like Pöpö did, and he would take me where I wanted to go, and he would give me everything I wanted, and we would live happily ever after."

Alone with these thoughts, Erzsi was rummaging one day through a box of family pictures when she came upon her parents' marriage license. Róbert Rácz and Kati Kiss, it said, were married in Budapest on August 18, 1939. The date startled her, for she had been born only five months later. She checked her birth certificate: She was indeed Erzsébet Rácz, and her birthdate, as she had thought, was January 13, 1940. Then she discovered some letters written in the interval between marriage and birth. They were addressed to her mother but signed by a man named Laci. On that point she dared confront her mother: "I thought my father's name was Róbert, and I thought he died during the war."

"Yes," her mother replied, "he did die during the war, and his name was Róbert, but he liked to be called Laci."

Says Erzsi today: "It was a very simple lie."

II

Now she stares vacantly to the side and speaks of a man she does not name. When they met on a blind date she was fifteen and still in love with an imaginary father who would carry her off to Rome. Her date was twenty-six and a conservatory student who played the piano in a bar. "He wasn't like anybody I ever knew before. I didn't like the way he looked. I didn't like the way he talked. I didn't like the way he any-thinged. I just couldn't stand him. I thought, as soon as I can get this over with, I'm going to exit. Then we started walking down by the Danube and sat on some blown-up pieces of bridge. He told me of his childhood and of the nuns who raised him in the orphanage and how much he was beaten by them. He had never had anything good in his life. All of a sudden I felt very sorry for him. I wanted to do something for him that would lift him up and show him that life could be better. I slept with him."

In the streets of Budapest a revolution was brewing, and he drew her into it. "It was the last thing in my life that I blindly believed in. When the Russian troops came in 1956, it was logical that I want this revolution, that I want the Russians out, that I want freedom for Hungary. When the revolutionaries knocked a Red Star and Stalin off a pedestal, I was in the center of tens of thousands of people, and we sang the Hungarian anthem. I remember goose bumps going down me, and I remember this absolute oneness with the people around me. Twenty seconds later they started dragging out the AVH agents, stringing them up with their heads down, and cutting them open. That was the end of my belief. That was the last time I was completely taken in by anything.

"At five o'clock one morning the Russians came back. I remember the radio: the government leader was talking in three or four languages, begging people to come in and help because the Russians were coming from the East with tanks and troops. Fear started in me at that point that things would go back to what they were during the war. There was lots of noise and destruction. Tanks were firing on each other and on houses.

On the surface I was fearless. I would stand in bread lines with bullets flying over my head, fearless. I would go out in the middle of the boulevard with the revolution shooting on one side and the Russians on the other, fearless. I don't know if I did it because I was sixteen or because I was an idiot. Maybe I was suicidal and asking for it. I don't know."

At the height of the revolution, Erzsi's mother took her aside and handed her a slip of paper. On it was a name and address Erzsi had never seen before: László Lamos, Mecsek Utca 2, Pécs. Her mother said, "If anything happens to your stepfather and me, your real father is alive. Go to him at this address."

Erzsi was stunned. "Why didn't you tell me before?"

"You didn't need to know."

A short time later the phone rang. It was Erzsi's boy friend. "I just wanted to say good-bye because I'm leaving tomorrow morning."

"Where are you going, East or West?" East meant the Russians were taking him to Siberia, West that he was going to escape to Austria.

"West."

"I'm going with you."

"No, you're not."

"Yes, I am."

"My mother overheard the conversation and locked me in. The next morning I broke out. All I had was a winter coat. I went to meet him and told him I was going to go with him. He said it was dangerous and besides, 'What the hell do I do with you anyway?' It took us three days to make a trip that ordinarily took forty-five minutes. We spent the night in a peasant's house, and we paid him to take us to the border in a hay cart. When we arrived we got out of the hay, and he said, 'That's the border, but you have to cross that bridge first.' It was a hundred yards away. We got out and started running through a cleared area. There were others trying to escape. Tanks and jeeps appeared behind us and started shooting. The bridge came—it was a split log over a skinny frozen river. There was nothing to hang on to. I said, 'I'm not going,' and he said, 'Yes, you are.' I said, 'No, I'm not,' and he turned around and gave me two gigantic slaps. He grabbed my hand and pulled me across the bridge crying. Three men close behind us were shot.

"We ran, and we got to Austria, and they welcomed us. We gave our names to the International Red Cross so my mother and father would know we had made it. We slept in hay and schoolhouses. We went by train from Vienna to Salzburg, and then we went to Camp Roeder.

"I was pregnant, and he knew it. 'Well,' he said, 'it's easier for married people to get into the United States, and since you are pregnant anyway, don't you think we might as well get married?' Don't ask me why, but I was very happy. This is what I wanted for a year and a half: for this man to marry me. We had to have bus fare to go to Salzburg, so a Protestant minister gave us twenty-four shillings for the witnesses and us. He married us. It could have been in any church. It didn't matter to my husband. It didn't matter to me. It lasted about five minutes. No pomp, no ceremony, no passage of time, nobody there I knew. It was five in the evening on December 31, 1956. From everything I read about marriage it was a letdown.

"My husband put some conditions on our marriage. He was going to have twenty-four hours free time every week, once a week, and I would have no right to ask him where he went or why he went there. He was going to be free. Just because he was getting married, he was not going to be tied down, because he was not really the marrying kind. He expected me to be faithful. I was not allowed to be jealous. He could hit me but I could not hit back. I could not defend myself. That was the rule, and I agreed to it.

"He started hitting me even before we got married. If I said something he didn't like, he slapped me. I did not kick back. He told me I had a very pretty face but that I was disformed bodily. My shoulders were too narrow. My fanny was too big. If I were normal, I wouldn't be built like this. When you say that to a sixteen-year-old kid, it's no good. I was pursuing him, and he was running from me. He put me down, and I kept trying to prove something to him. Or to me.

"We stayed in Camp Roeder until the fourteenth of January. Then the U.S. Army flew us to Camp Kilmer, New Jersey. Three days later I miscarried. My husband came to me and said, 'Well, since you lost this child we might as well get a divorce because we're in the United States and there's no sense for us to stay married.' I cried and said, 'I don't want to divorce you. I love you.' I told him about three million times that I loved him. I have no idea if I did or not, but I clung. I wanted him to need me and want me and love me.

"Imagine me at that point. I think I was very pretty. I was absolutely dying for my husband. I was trying to prove something. I don't know. I was working for his affection. I was doing this very openly, nonashamedly, and I got very little in return. When people would come and say, 'Your husband last night in the john with such a woman ...,' I would pretend that's part of us, that's all right, or I would sigh and try to elicit their sympathy. It was a very sick situation. I'm not sure I could ask you to understand it. I'm not sure I want you to understand it. It was very, very sick.

"It started on the night we got married. He ran into a girl he knew in Budapest. I had a toothache. The girl was there. . . . I was hurt, but I knew if I said something, first, we would fight, second, he would be right because I agreed to that on the train from Vienna to Salzburg. I wouldn't have a foot to stand on. And I was deathly afraid. I was afraid of nothing worse than losing him.

"In Camp Kilmer he was diagnosed to have tuberculosis, so they sent us to a hospital in Arizona. I got a job washing dishes for room and board and $114 a month. I gave him everything I earned and never missed a day visiting him in the hospital.

"He was there for five months. By August he was fine, fine enough to have a nurse for his mistress, fine enough to rent a room for the two of them, fine enough to go out and buy a car without consulting me. But I accepted it. In my dreams I said that someday he will be all right, he will be well. When I give him a child, then I will assume my rightful place."

III

Giving him a child was no easy matter. By the time Erzsi was eighteen, she had lost her third; in addition, she had had an abortion while in Hungary. "With each miscarriage I got the same thing: 'Listen, we're having a lousy marriage. I want to divorce you. I don't want to live with you. This isn't working out. I don't like married life. What I want out of a woman I can get outside marriage.' There were absolutely no bones about it: he wanted out. I cried and I carried on. I hung on and I clung. After I lost the last child he said, 'If you don't give me a kid in a year who is going to be alive and normal, I'm getting out.'

"I got pregnant again and went to a group of Roman Catholic gynecologists. I was told they would do everything in their power to keep a child in you, and by damn they did. I was working in a lab, and when I was eight and a half months pregnant, I fell. Our janitor had dropped a gallon of formaldehyde solution, and the gases came out of the formaldehyde and I slipped. I fell stomach down. I cut my hand and arm open and passed out.

"They took me to the operating room and started working on me. I had cut tendons and nerves in my right hand. Four and a half hours later they had my hand back together, saying I would never feel certain parts of it. My husband came to the hospital. He did not want to talk to the doctor who did my hand operation. He wanted to talk to Dr. Thomas, the gynecologist. He said to Dr. Thomas that unless that kid comes out healthy and normal, he doesn't give a damn about my right hand. That really shook the daylights out of me. That was the first time it was spelled out to me that I was nothing but a vessel for him.

"I left the hospital and stayed home for about ten days. Then I went to the hospital, and I had Marie. She was very small, but she was healthy. I had the biggest disappointment of my life when I first looked at her. My mother had told me that when they first brought me to her, she looked at my eyes and they were big and blue and she looked into my face and she said, 'Finally, there is a person in this life I can love.' She said it was the most beautiful moment of her life, and I believed her.

"I wanted to believe that when my first child was brought to me I would look into her eyes and it would be the most beautiful moment of my life. I wanted to believe that all this crap could be shoved behind me. They brought in Marie, and I started crying. I wanted to see the big blue eyes, and there was nothing. There was this red, wrinkled, ugly, horrible thing, moving with absolutely no coordination. I told my friend her nose was broken, and she said, 'No, it isn't. Everything is fine.' My husband was crying with joy. He was absolutely ecstatic. Here was a living being, ten fingers and ten toes, and it was his. It even looked like him. He said she was the most beautiful child in the world because she looked like him. There she was making these noises and everybody was saying how cute she was. But I was either crazy or blind, because I was the only one who didn't feel how cute or beautiful she was.

"I lost my name when Marie was born. He never called me Erzsi again. He called me 'the dear little mother of his child.' That was my name—that whole long phrase. I didn't like that. I didn't care to be the dear little mother of anybody's child."

IV

By the time she was twenty-two, however, Erzsi was the mother of two more children—a boy, Paul, and a girl, Anne. She had no maternal feelings. "It was an avalanche. I was unhappy as a woman. I was unhappy as a mother. I was unhappy as a wife. I would look at Marie, and there was a frustration in her that was so evident, even at five. I would look at her face, which would immediately make me feel guilty as hell. Then I would get upset and yell."

She began to tyrannize her children. They had to be clean and they had to be dressed alike and they had to wear good shoes. The apron around *her* marriage had to be spotless. She was jealous of the attention her husband denied her and gave to the children, and she felt guilty about her jealousy. She envied his ability to be a parent, to be tolerant, patient, playful, loving, and proud—all the qualities she lacked. She shoved them onto him. With pain Erzsi admits that "the only salvation my kids had was that he was there and that he was a parent. It perplexed me: how come he had it and I didn't when I was so much more intelligent than he?" And then, not without bitterness, she salvages what she can: "It cost me more—the little I gave them—it cost me more than what he gave."

She began to seek an escape. In *The Sandpiper*, a movie with a title reminiscent of Pöpö, she found another imaginary savior to lift her out of her misery: Richard Burton. His love and caring were so powerful and the beach on which he lay so inviting that she began to search for them actively and intensely and promiscuously. The affair she wanted could not have been casual. "It could have ended tragically, but it had to be lasting, and it had to be warm and meaningful and beautiful. I went through sleazy and dangerous things without ever finding it. You wouldn't believe the people I went with. I don't believe it. The risks I took were idiotic.

"One summer morning in 1967 my husband wanted to sleep late. He had had a job the night before. I was yelling at the kids, trying to keep them quiet, and he got up and beat the hell out of me. Kicked me and beat me. The kids still remember this incident, and I am very sorry about it, but what can you do? Then he packed them up and took them to the beach. I was awfully angry, and I wanted to show him. I took something, I don't remember what, and I wrote a note: see how you do without me. I was definitely going to show the bastard. He came home and took me to the hospital. They washed my stomach out and kept me for a week."

A short while later she started to have headaches, and whenever she picked up a book, her vision blurred. "Somebody told me to see an eye doctor, and I did, and I was told I was going blind in my right eye. They said the muscles were weak, and I was not able to focus, and it was possibly an inherited condition. So I had an eye operation and during the course of the operation the anaesthesiologist asked if I had myasthenia gravis in my family. I said I didn't know what myasthenia gravis was. When I woke up he asked me again. I said I still don't know. I started questioning myself: Do I really want to live with this? I thought again of suicide as a way of handling things, as a wonderful possibility: if things don't work out, you have the control of getting out. How was no problem. There were all kinds of poison and ether in the lab. It was no problem to go quickly and painlessly.

"I thought of nothing at that point except one of my children, and that was Anne, and I cannot tell you why it was her. How could she live with the thought that her mother had committed suicide? Right now, if something would happen and I would decide, well, I don't want to live with it, I'm going to exit, I would very strongly think of Marie and would sort of think of Paul and I would very much think of Anne. But at that time I remember the only person I thought of: how will Anne live with this? 'Suicide-mother': that's a label you have to live a lifetime with."

She had surgery that enabled her to read again, and she went on as before. In the course of her affairs she met a man twenty-two years older than she. Like the man she had married, he terrified her: "I had known Don and feared him for many years. I had absolutely no rapport with him. To talk with him was impossible. I respected him, but I didn't know what I was respecting. I had admiration for his brains and all his diplomas. No liking as a human being. I never loved him or had the desire to have anything to do with him. One New Year's Eve he asked me if I would like to have a drink with him, and I said no. That was about six months before it started. It started like any other affair. It had absolutely no promise, and I was very mixed up because I had more negative feelings toward him than positive feelings. I feared very few people in my life, but he was one of them.

"But from the beginning I got an awful lot out of the relationship, more than I can verbalize. It wasn't love. It wasn't *The Sandpiper*. He was a fumbling, clumsy, soulless person, but from the first moment on he needed me, *me*, my complexity, my warmth. Something was broken in him. We didn't do anything well together except have good sex. There was an awful lot of friction, but there was something on the bottom of everything that was very solid and very secure, something I could depend on, something I never ever remember having before."

For several years Erzsi agonized over a divorce and then, in January 1972, fifteen years after she fled Hungary clinging to a man who abused her, she decided to obtain one. On the day after a dinner honoring her thirty-second birthday, fighting enormous guilt at the thought of what she was about to do, she assembled her family. "I sat the kids down on the couch and said, 'I would like to talk to you. I am going to leave.' My husband was silent. Paul said, 'I understand.' Anne started crying. And Marie looked at me with dark, deep brown eyes—I still remember her eyes piercing through me—and said, 'I'm very angry at you.' It was probably the first honest response I got from her from the time she was little and I was nursing Paul. I tried to bring it up a year later, but she didn't even remember sitting on the couch. All she remembered was her father telling her later that I was going to leave."

V

Throughout the years in which Erzsi was bearing and attempting to raise children, having affairs, thinking of suicide, fearing blindness, and finally divorcing, she was also pursuing a secret—the secret behind the slip of paper her mother had handed her during the revolution. Shortly after arriving in America as a seventeen-year-old, she had written the man at Mecsek Utca 2, Pécs, and she had been brutal: Why did you knock up my mother and then go off to greener pastures? Why were you not a father to me as you were supposed to be? Why did you never let me know you were alive or reach out a hand when I needed you so much?

"He replied. He wrote intelligent, beautiful, witty letters that gave me everything but an answer to what I asked. He was civilized. He was cynical. He was skeptical. He was complex. I admired him instantly, but at the same time he infuriated me. He said he would have been a monkey father had he stayed around. He could not have given me what a father is supposed to give a child. He would have tickled me and nothing more.

"I was proud of everything in the letters but the contents. He never lied to me. He rationalized. He wrote everything so convincingly that I'm sure he told himself these things so long that he thoroughly believed them. And he liked himself. If he had done anything that he didn't like in his life, he had justified it a long time ago so he could keep liking what he was."

Though Erzsi was far from satisfied with her father's answers, she did learn some facts from him. Her father was the Uncle László who had charmed her in his office when she was six. He had never received medals in Rome, but he was, as she had guessed, the author of the telltale letters she had discovered at the age of twelve. Erzsi's mother was visiting in Arizona when her father died in 1964, and on that occasion a few of the blocks covering her past were overturned. But the picture was far from complete. When her mother returned to Hungary, Erzsi was still angry and confused, still torn between guilt over her anger and a sense of betrayal. Besides, her own marriage had come out a lie. Erzsi had been led to believe that childbirth was exhilarating, but the arrival of Marie was a chaotic disappointment. She had hoped children would turn her husband into the caring, sophisticated man of her fantasy, but they only increased his tyranny. She had thought that her problems could be kept behind the apron of family life, but they burst forth in an attempted suicide. What seemed responsible for the lie in Erzsi's life, and what drew her fury, was the deception surrounding her own birth. After her mother's death in 1973, she began tracking down lifelong friends and relatives of the family. Slowly the deception was unraveled.

"My mother grew up under a continual stigma. When she was a girl, she had to go to her aunt's house every afternoon because her own mother, a widow, was seeing Pöpö. The house had only three rooms, so my mother had to get out when Pöpö came. She admired her mother but was terribly stigmatized by the situation. She was pushed and pulled at the same time. I pictured her as a teenager going through an awful time, not being able to talk to anybody about what was going on in her. When she was eighteen she chose to leave Nagykanizsa and move to Budapest.

"She was there a long time and was very proud of her virginity. She won several beauty contests. When she was twenty-nine she met my real father at the English company where she worked. He was forty and living with an older woman named Klára, who had given up a lot to pay for an operation of his.

"My mother fell very much in love with him. She was warned not to get involved, yet she went ahead and had an affair and got pregnant. Then she went to him and said, 'Now you are going to marry me!' My father said no, he was not the marrying kind, and he was proud of it. My mother told me that Klára offered her my weight in gold if she would give me to her. My mother said no. So my father asked Klára to buy a name-marriage for my mother. In a name-marriage you purchase a man, and he goes to the church and gives his name to the woman. The marriage is legal. My mother met Róbert Rácz when she married him in August of 1939 and never saw him again. He was paid off and he exited, but he left his name. Five months later I was born.

"In front of her mother and Pöpö, my mother kept up the pretense that the name-marriage was a real marriage and that I was really a legitimate person. The distance between Budapest and Nagykanizsa was sufficient that this could be done. In 1940, when men were being drafted into the army, it was easy to say, 'I have to raise this child alone, would you take her?' So I was shipped down to Nagykanizsa.

"My father and Klára bought my mother an apartment. Klára died in 1945, three months after my father married her. Then my father got in touch with my mother and said to her, 'Why don't you and Erzsi come down and live with me in Pécs? I won't marry you but I'll support you. I have all of Klára's money now.' My mother said no. I asked her why, and she was very, very bitter. She said, 'When you were born, your father sent me a white lilac tree, the expense of which was astronomical. Yet when we were starving to death and absolutely insecure during the war, he refused to give me money, and when he first saw us together after the war, he looked at me and said, Are you still alive?'

"My mother was visiting us in Arizona when the letter came announcing his death. It was addressed from Pécs. She didn't open it. In this respect she was very honorable: she would never read a letter that belonged to someone else. She lived with that letter for six hours until I got home from the lab, and then I opened it and she looked at me and said, 'He died, didn't he?' And I said, 'Yes, he did.' She was touched by his death. There was no gloating in her reaction. I'm firmly convinced that until the time she died she had very strong feelings for my father.

"But I was very, very angry that he died. I cried with anger and pain. I said, 'How dare the bastard die before I had the chance to meet him and get everything I want out of him?'

"A year after my divorce, in 1973, I received a telegram in Arizona. It said: your mother is dead as of the first of September. For the last year and a half of her life, she had not walked, and I very actively and very openly wished that she would die. I wished she wouldn't be suffering and helpless. To me this was common sense; to her it wasn't.

"When the telegram came, I went to bed. I cried and whined and held myself. I talked to myself. One of me said, You idiot, why are you crying now, when for a year and a half you wished that she would die? The other one of me said, because this is final. My mother is no more, and there is no way I can do anything. I felt guilty for what I didn't do for her. When she was out here I should have done more for her. I remember her horrible joy when something would be happening between the two of us, but I would refuse to communicate with her.

"When I was in Hungary in 1976, I asked my sister and stepfather, 'Did she ever consider suicide? Did she ever wish that she were dead?' To me it would have been normal. But they both said very emphatically, 'No, not even at the most painful moment when there wasn't anything to be done.' I think she felt she deserved her suffering. 'God doesn't beat you with a stick.' If you do something bad, you're going to get it eventually. No matter what you do, you're going to pay for it. If she did something at twenty-nine that she wasn't supposed to do. . . . Maybe I shouldn't be so sure, but I think she felt a tremendous amount of guilt for the affair with my father. She had tremendous guilt for giving me birth. It was the wrong time to give birth—the wrong time privately for her, the wrong time in the world—and it was not a nice thing to fool her mother with the name-marriage. My mother kept saying to me in 1964 that my grandmother died without ever finding out the shame and the horrible thing that my mother did. But I'm not so sure.

"History repeated itself with me. I went through a farce for over a year before she died, pretending I was still living in my first marriage so she would never find out. But the last time I was in Hungary, a neighbor woman told me something that cut into me like a knife. I wish I could forget it, but I can't. This woman had been very good to my mother toward the end, and she said to me, 'Did you know your mother was in absolute agony that you got a divorce?' I said to myself, No, no, it isn't so! My mother *didn't* know. I never wrote her about it. But I couldn't say it with much sureness. One of these days I'm going to face it. One of these days I'm going to say it's 99 percent sure that my mother did know that I was divorced while she was sick and that she was very much pained by it."

VI

"Is it stupid to try to tip the blocks upside down and look at them? Is it senseless? Does it make any difference in the present?" She has learned that the blocks do not fall like dominoes in a chain reaction. When one falls, six more appear, all of her own making. Why did Klára offer her mother an infant's weight in gold? Why did her stepfather never learn the story of the name-marriage or her birth? Why the countless little lies? "My stepfather married my mother in 1946, but he never found out her true age until 1964, when she retired. She lied about her age successfully for eighteen years! I never knew her true age until she came out and I saw the visa. To me, this is a senseless lie. And yet she went to confession. Why?"

So the journey will not end, nor will the puzzle finally be solved. But what is the solution she craves? She says she wants to know, but part of her wishes that time could be reversed, that knowledge could fill her up with secure and happy and blessed origins. She says she wants to see, as if seeing could vent her anger toward a fantasy savior who never came. She says she wants to understand, but she wishes that understanding could absolve her of guilt, guilt for the anger still felt toward her mother, guilt for the abuse heaped on her children, guilt for the pretenses and prevarications and lies repeated in her life. In her middle years she fears that the neuroses and sins of parents are visited upon children. And she faces a question: how can one purge a simple lie from the chain of being?

No, she insists, the journey is not senseless. It matters in the present, and, even more, it affects what is to come. "I reach in there and I try to tip the blocks up, and it means something in my future, in my going on. You see, I pass what I learn on to the kids. I feel that I am giving them something that is not just words, not just a story three generations back. It's part of them: things my mother told me, things my mother had to endure with her mother." She would like to understand and forgive her mother, and, even more, she would like her children to understand and forgive *her*.

Her children. When Erzsi married Donald Domier in the summer of

1972, she won a respite from day-to-day living with them. The following winter she and Don spent three months in Hawaii, where he had a temporary assignment. She was able to indulge herself as though she were a child. "We had a beautiful apartment. I got a library card, and I walked around, and I just loved it. All my life I had dreamed that I would have a nice place around me, and everybody would just leave me alone, and I could have books and music. In Hawaii, all this selfishness came to the surface, and I didn't have to feel bad about it. Every hour of every day I was able to enjoy. Every hour I was aware of things. It was hitting me that life was fantastic. Why would anyone want to step out of it?"

The children visited her in Hawaii, and she saw them frequently when she returned to Arizona. When they became teenagers, she began to see them in a different light. "They'd bring successes to me, and big hurts, but not everyday things. Maybe that's why I started to enjoy them." Then in 1976, when Erzsi was thirty-six, she and Don moved permanently to Minnesota. Her children have never left her mind, and she finds that distance, time, and her own patches of happiness are working balm into their relationship. "I like my kids much more now that they're becoming adults. I enjoy Marie tremendously. I still can't handle Anne and Paul, but I enjoy them when we're alone, one to one. When Anne plays the violin, tears come to my eyes, and it hurts because I try to control it. I say, Oh, my God, I wish my mother were alive and could see this! And I feel an anger that my father never saw the kids. If only he could see them now!

"I'm very proud of them, but I worry an awful lot. There is a big danger. I want them to be strong and do everything well, but it doesn't work that way. It's not realistic. If anything went wrong—and do you know how many things could go wrong?—if anything happened I would blame me. I have no control over this. It's something I have to work on: to prepare myself to survive no matter what happens.

"I wish to God I could get rid of the guilt. If someday—I don't want to start crying—if someday they all make it, I think it will go away. I have terrible fears because of my guilt. A year ago the kids went on the plane back to Arizona, and all of a sudden my life just went out of me. I stayed in bed for a week. I didn't cook or anything. I was aware of what was happening, but I wasn't able to control it. It scared the hell out of me. I cried, and I said I've ruined their lives. I've ruined everybody's life. My poor mother. Don was very worried. It never happened before to this degree, and I hope it's not going to happen now.

"I know they love me very warmly, but I have to keep asking. I have to keep having the reassurance. I have a feeling that the older they get, the more critical they will be of me. That's not for sure, but I feel that way right now. I don't want them to have the same feelings toward me that I had and probably still have toward my mother. I want to pass on the good. I have tried like crazy to pass on anything that's good in me. Anything that I have to offer I want to give them. I don't want to pass on the bad, but it doesn't work that way. So I don't know what you do.

"Half a year ago I discovered that Paul has intelligence. I had a long talk with him, and all of a sudden thoughts came to my mind which I have never been able to put together, and I gave that to him. I talked to him about the worth of family and the fact that I had not realized until recently what it means. I'm very scared that he will not be able to trust a woman because his mother walked out when he was twelve. I asked him, if he chooses somebody for a so-called life-mate to put the possibility of family and children and tomorrow onto it. I told him about my father, who obviously didn't have this feeling. And I said you don't do it for yourself, but you're feeding into something out there. You're just a part of the chain, and if you screw up it will affect. . . ."

VII

After her arrival in Minnesota, Erzsi decided to return to school. Apprehensive at first, she quickly discovered while attending a local community college that she had superior ability. She earned a bachelor's degree at a four-year institution in 1978 and then embarked on a graduate program in East European history.

Our last meeting was over lunch in a city where Erzsi was in her first year of graduate school. Nine months had passed since our first conversation. It was a mild but damp day in March, and the grayness outside contrasted with the springlike green and white of the café. Erzsi was happier that day than I had ever seen her. She was doing well in her courses and had finished high in competition for financial assistance. She had found a mentor who would steer her to field work in Hungary. Marie was due to visit her in a few weeks.

She had to shake herself to believe where she was. Sitting in the library from time to time, she would be pierced with unaccustomed but distinct surges of sheer happiness.

"Once I didn't really think that I was worthy to be alive. Right now I think it would be criminal to kill me because I'm beginning to be worth more and more. All my life there wasn't meaning, there wasn't purpose. But starting in 1973, and more and more since I have been in school, I *don't* want to die. If blindness came, I think I would try to cope with it.

"If all goes well, I would like to live as long as my mind is functional

and sharp, as long as I can put something into it and get something out
of it. This is a very good time in my life because I am finally doing
something that I wanted to do, which is going to school and getting a
direction for this thirst for knowledge. It sounds corny as hell, but it's
not. I have always wanted to *know* things. We have to go back to the
blocks. This is why I read so much.

"I have to tell you about a man I haven't mentioned before. For five
months when I first came to Arizona he was very important in my life.
His name was Zoltán. He was a Hungarian who had just come out after
the revolution to be with his sister, who was my boss when I was
washing dishes. He was about forty or forty-five and I was seventeen.
He had been a secretary to a Catholic bishop, he said, and he had known
Mindszenty, and he had been in Rome, and he knew the pope—the same
pope who gave my father the medals. Ninety-eight percent of his conversation was taken up by the saints, or by the church, or by the holy Jesus.
But he said beautiful things to me, and I loved him very much. He said
things to which I said, 'No, no, that's not so,' but I believed them
underneath. He resented me because I smoked. He called me a diamond
covered by soot, so I was really a piece of coal, he said, but I had a
diamond inside because I was so intelligent."

She wants to use that hard, cool intelligence to write. She wonders
whether writing will transform the guilt she carries with her, whether it
will cure the anger and make use of the pain—and she desperately hopes
that it will. She wants to be fertile in a way she was not with her
children.

All through her life, all through her journey into the lie, she has been
"gathering." "I will never have all the answers, but as long as there is
togetherness in me I can gather the answers. I will never be able to say I
have it all, there's nowhere else to go. I will never be satisfied.

"I had the gathering potential all along, but I didn't know I had it. But
I *did* have it all along. I didn't concentrate on the *right* things, but I had it
all along. For example, my reading. From every book, even a trash book,
I got something. I learned how to spell a word or learned the meaning of
a new word. I enlarged my vocabulary or found out there was a place
called Capri.

"For a long time there were questions like, what is the meaning of
life? Why am I here? If this is so horrible, why can't I croak? Believe it or
not, I was gathering in those years too, and if I can face it now, and if I
don't run away, and if I don't try to put a cover on it (which would be
very easy to do), that's material my kid can use. If you face it the way it
is, with little distortion, it's very valuable, as crappy as it was.

"The gathering is not aimless, it's not senseless, it's not passive, it's not an escape. You integrate what you gather, and that's what's marvelous. And I'm so good at it. I can get this from here and put it with that from there, and something entirely new comes out. Many, many times I have thought that this is the first time in my life that I am doing something totally fanatically. Don is asking me, 'Why are you pushing so hard?' But nobody can slow me down.

"I've always loved books. Can you imagine if I were to write one? Or edit one? I wrote a diary when I was a kid, and I wrote one again when I was in camp, and now I write myself out of my depressions. I would be overjoyed to have something in print! You go to the rare book section of a library, where everything is locked up, and you pick up a book that was published three hundred years ago. It's permanent. Why do you write? Because you want somebody three generations from now to say Erzsébet Domier said that. I wonder who the hell she was. You're going to generate a thought in that person's head three generations from now. Writing is something that's lasting, something that's active, something that integrates all the gathering. And I'm going to leave something like that behind. Many somethings."

She clings to that hope as to a life raft. Nothing, she tells herself, will interfere with her goal. But there's a new danger: cracks have appeared in her life with Don, and strange emotions she had thought forgotten make her crave the approval and caresses of fatherly men who say beautiful things to her—rescuers who walk on water and promise her Rome. Still at thirty-nine? she wonders, condemning herself for lunging after mirages and loosening her grip on the future. Why can't she be totally focused? Why can't she follow her brain—and it alone? She does not want her fertility poisoned by a lie from an archaic part of her being.

She struggles, therefore, and speaks of her conflict. As we left the café she was talking furiously. My mind drifted from her words to occasions in the past when she had paused in the telling of her story. These hesitations, I knew now, were less resistance than invitation, moments when something in her said, turn over this aspect of me, tip over this block, let what is covered be seen. When she rationalized, when she hedged, she would wave a flag, and if I missed the signal, she would say, "You didn't see that." Then she would take a breath, and I would know a block was being tipped. Her next words would be, "There, why was that so hard to say?" Once, when I turned over a piece for her, she could hardly speak for the emotion she felt. She only said, "Keep talking." There were matters she chose not to speak of and questions I chose not to ask, but at the end I realized that when she had spoken, she had spoken the truth.

INTERPRETATION: HIDDEN LEGACIES;
SECOND CHANCES

Erzsébet Domier's story unravels the relationship in one human being between conceptions of the beginning and end of life, between the questions, Where do I come from? and What shall I leave behind?—a relationship near the essence of this book. In doing so it touches on the themes of damaging progeny and obtaining nourishment, which were discussed in the last chapter. It portrays the usurpation of one's generativity by another, as Erzsi became "nothing but a vessel" for her husband's offspring. The specter of death is present in this story as it was in "Mirror, Mirror." But I believe the principal value of "Journey into the Lie" is its illumination of themes other than these, specifically, opening hidden legacies and receiving second chances at generativity.

OPENING HIDDEN LEGACIES

I think of Erzsi Domier's story as a variant of the legend of Oedipus, with the obvious difference that its protagonist is a woman, not a man. In the ancient Greek story, Oedipus is launched on a predetermined course from the moment of birth. He learns of his destiny through an oracle, but because he does not know his true parentage, he steers himself to a fate he believes he is escaping. Unknowingly, he kills his father and marries his mother, becoming king of Thebes as a result. Extraordinary intelligence and curiosity have brought him to this point, but they prevent him from leaving well enough alone. Driven to solve the riddle of his origins, he looks backward, opens his hidden legacy, and discovers the truth of where he came from and what he has done. Only in midlife does he awaken to his life's true course, but by then it cannot be changed. Horrified by what he sees, Oedipus tears his eyes out and becomes a beggar.

Although everyone whose life story I recorded was mildly curious about his or her background, only Erzsi Domier treated the past as a puzzle that had to be solved at all costs. She seemed to believe that a secret planted at the beginning of her life was propelling her as inexorably as the fate steering Oedipus. She was impelled to discover the secret not only because it was buried but also because it was powerful. Until she discovered it, she felt, her life would continue off course.

Erzsi's journey into the past began in her late teens, when she arrived in Arizona. At that point she wanted to make contact with a powerful figure who had lived for years in her imagination—the father of her Roman fantasy. She harbored the dream of being saved by this man, but at the same time she was furious that he had abandoned her and furious that she was deceived about him. Erzsi wished to understand the lies affecting her life by tracing them back to their roots; she wished to scream at whoever was responsible for them; perhaps she felt that doing so would enable her to start over. As her treatment of her children worsened, another motive entered: she wished to find in the story of her own childhood the water that would cleanse her of guilt. In her mind, the secret surrounding her birth was like an inherited disease one learns of too late. Seeing the disease in herself, she felt betrayed. Seeing it in her children, she felt guilty. Above all, she had to discover everything she could about the secret, for it still governed her present and future.

The truth about the past never came to Erzsi in a single blaze of insight, as it did to Oedipus. Like Oedipus, however, she eventually turned her anger on herself, he destroying his eyes, she attempting suicide. Life also threatened her with blindness, and that led to another reason for her search: the urgent need to know whether her condition was hereditary. Could a forebear have died of myasthenia gravis, and were her children already in jeopardy?

Erzsi's was not the only story I recorded about a secret steering a life in an alien direction. A father I spoke with "felt trapped in a life I knew was not my own" until, after the birth of a son, he came out as a homosexual. Suddenly he seemed to be on the right trajectory and in control of his destiny. Just as suddenly his entire past had to be reinterpreted. He pored through old diaries and yearbooks and asked questions of old acquaintances, seeking proof that he (and others he had thought straight) had been gay from the beginning. His search was not motivated by anger or guilt, as was Erzsi's, but by the need to root an identity that had just appeared. He had entered gay culture, and now he had to authenticate his gay self by rewriting his personal history, by uncovering previously hidden indications that he had been gay all along. An academic, he currently devotes a substantial portion of his research to finding evidence that historical figures avowed to be straight were actually gay.

It is possible that Erzsi will have to clear up her grievances with the past—to "cure" her anger as she says—before she can devote more energy to generativity. It is equally possible, however, that the "uncured" anger will itself motivate the creation of a legacy. Whatever the case, the search Erzsi makes of her origins currently affects her generativity in two ways. First, she delivers the material she uncovers to her children. The children are growing older, and Erzsi tells them about her newly discovered past for several reasons: to be a parent in some way before time runs out, to break a concatenation of lies, to assuage her guilt, to receive their understanding and forgiveness. Erzsi also broadens her personal search by embarking on a career of unearthing the cultural past of Hungary—the second way in which her generativity is affected by her journey. The extension of her personal search into a career is like that of the homosexual mentioned above: both she and he envision a life project in which a major component is the reconstruction of a culture stretching from the past into the present—a logical outcome for individuals who pour such energy into opening hidden legacies.

The prototypical story of Oedipus does not end with his blindness nor with his fall from power. In the trilogy of Sophocles Oedipus leaves Thebes for Colonus and dies a hero. Though blind in this life, he becomes a guide to others in the next. His body is left behind to protect Athens. In the end, contact with his terrifying origins and a change of place have led Oedipus to purification and fruitfulness. When he opened his hidden legacy, it was too late to change what had happened, but it was not too late to become generative.

SECOND CHANCES AT GENERATIVITY

There is little emotion in Erzsi Domier's life as powerful as the anguish she feels, and will continue to feel, over her children. On one occasion her guilt was so great that she was bedridden for a week, unable to control her fear and despair. She wants desperately to know that her children are "okay"; when I said as much she wept. I received the same message from her eldest, Marie, whom I interviewed at Erzsi's request. Erzsi wants to hear from the mouths of her children that they are okay, and she wants to hear it from me, as though I were a doctor who could give them a clean bill of health after a conversation over lunch. Actually, her children are far more resilient than her fears suggest, which is not to say that she will ever lose the sense of having damaged them.

But Erzsi's life illustrates not only the tragic experience of damaging progeny, it also reveals several ways in which individuals receive opportunities to rectify or compensate for generative failures. When she "changed places" as Oedipus did near the end of his life, that is, when she divorced, remarried, moved, and began school, she took in nourishment and was able to begin life anew. At that time two things happened in the generative dimension of her life. First, her children grew older and she discovered a new channel on which to communicate with them. Second, she returned to books, which had provided her nourishment as a child. In short, the nature of her parental relationship changed, and she entered the sphere of culture. Both changes presented an opportunity that I name after the words of a woman who had an "accidental" pregnancy late in life. "Since I screwed up on the other three," she said, "I thought here's another chance. My whole feeling through the pregnancy, the delivery, and when she was an infant was different. I felt calm. I felt nurturing. I was getting another shot at being a mother and not messing up." Like Erzsi Domier (and like Dorothy Woodson), she experienced a second chance at generativity.

I believe the theme of second chances was common to many of the stories I collected because of two features of the demographic revolution. One, of course, is the postponement of death. Longer lives give individuals more time to try a variety of generative expressions; they also mean that successive generations will overlap for longer periods of time, creating the conditions for the renovation of relationships. The other is the decline in childbearing, which, coupled with longevity, opens up a span of childfree years in the second half of life. Women in particular are being presented with opportunities to be fertile in technical and cultural ways after they have done so—or failed to do so—biologically and parentally.

Second chances are not experienced simply with the arrival of another infant or project. Rather, second chances are felt to initiate new segments in a life, a new phase of childbearing or teaching or politicking or composition. The segments begin with feelings of nourishment, of taking in sustenance so as to begin again. Second chances are perceived as opportunities to redo or make up for what has been done badly before. *Redoing* is not what psychoanalysts refer to as *undoing*, a defense mechanism in which an individual repeats a painful event in fantasy or even in ritualistic action in order to make it come out right. In redoing, an attempt is made to rectify damage *in reality*. Redoing refers to repairing relationships with children when both child and adult have moved to another stage in life. It refers to making up for damage that cannot be undone by creating something else that is damage-free. Because the knowledge of having damaged generative objects never disappears, because guilt lingers on despite confession or therapy, second chances allow that knowledge and guilt to animate new undertakings in constructive ways.

Second chances can occur with the very children one has harmed. Several of the stories I heard involve a mother who separates from her children and, after a "leave of absence," begins to refashion her relationship with them. The separations are brought on by divorce, by a child growing up and leaving home, by a geographical move, or by some combination of these. The leave enables the mother to receive nourishment and embark on a new path; in the meantime children are reaching a new stage of life.

The more adult Erzsébet Domier's children became, the more she was able to enjoy them and refashion her relationship with them. For the first time she had something to give that they were capable of receiving. On the phone and in letters and on visits, she communicated what she was learning in school, she passed on what she discovered of her personal past, she expressed pride in their cultural accomplishments. Because the plane of her generativity and their receptivity shifted from the parental to the cultural, a line of transmission opened up and she was able to redo what she failed to do before. She hopes it is not too little too late.

Some of my subjects, however, were unable to remake relationships with the children they had harmed. Instead, they attempted to make up for their failures by investing in other children. A woman already alluded to concentrated on a child born late in life. A father who neglected his children worked at becoming an ideal grandparent to his children's children. Another remarried and started a new family. In varying degrees, these individuals viewed a new phase of parenting as a chance to make up for mistakes in previous periods.

Second chances are also experienced when the target of generativity changes, when one moves, say, from biological to cultural objects. These changes are occasioned by career shifts such as those from motherhood to the world of work, from one kind of work to another, and from work to retirement. Each shift requires a transition, great or small, from one culture to another. Such a change was integral to Erzsi Domier's second chance.

That chance came in her early thirties, when she finally extricated herself from the influence of her first husband and married a man who "needed me, *me*, my complexity, my warmth." He was a brilliant man, a representative of the culture of "brains" and "diplomas." With him and with a return to school she entered that culture and found a favorable identity. Her life story was told to me, another representative of higher learning. In a way characteristic of individuals making new beginnings, she began to feel she had had "it"—in her case, a "gathering potential"—even through the bleakest periods.

The cultural legacy she wishes to create is one of knowledge, and her hope of generating a thought in someone "three generations from now" has deep and intricate roots. She has had a passion for knowledge from the time her catechism teachers told her one thing, the Communists another, and her books a third, a fourth, and a fifth. By the time she was sixteen she had rejected religion to turn to communism, rejected communism to believe in the revolution, and then rejected the revolution.

She developed a Dream of knowing a man and painfully separated the real from the illusory in that Dream.[1] All the while she unraveled the deception surrounding her parentage, solving riddles as Oedipus did, and nearly developing the blindness that came upon him. Unlike Oedipus, she discovered that the end of one puzzle was merely the beginning of another. Her curiosity will never be satisfied; at best it will animate from below some valued intellectual quest.

The timing of events in Erzsi's early thirties was far more propitious than in her late teens and early twenties. Then her biological and parental generativity were "out of synch." Biologically, she was conceiving and bearing children, but psychologically she was unprepared for parenthood, "nothing but a vessel." The results were abortion, miscarriages, and abused children. But in her early thirties, she left the scene of her domestic failure, married a man who addressed basic elements in her Dream, reestablished contact with the world of books, and saw her children become adolescents—all in the space of a few years. The synchrony constituted a new beginning in which she was narcissistically nourished. On leave in Hawaii, "all this selfishness came to the surface, and I didn't have to feel bad about it. Every hour of every day I was able to enjoy. Every hour I was aware of things. It was hitting me that life was fantastic. Why would anyone want to step out of it?"

Thus, as I closed my interview with Erzsébet Domier the clocks affecting her generativity seemed coordinated for the first time and the promise of fruitfulness was substantial. Already she has been asked to publish some of her papers. A year after the last interview, however, another timing feature was coming into play. Did enough years remain to her, she wondered, to accomplish what she envisioned? According to her internalized *social clock*—a term introduced by Bernice Neugarten to refer to society's idea of the right moment for life events[2]—she was indeed "off time": forty years old and still a student. Even in our interview she noted, "Don is asking me, 'Why are you pushing so hard?' But nobody can slow me down." Her husband is in his sixties, and the collaboration of her life tasks with his will become increasingly difficult. Further, she will enter the job market at a time when few positions are available. In short, the synchrony she enjoys now may be disrupted in the future.

Despite the uniqueness of her experience, the timing of Erzsébet Domier's renaissance is typical of many whose life structure has been altered by increased longevity and diminished childbearing. In the middle of the nineteenth century a woman could expect to live only twenty-five years after the birth of her last child and less than two years after that child married. In the middle of the twentieth century her counterpart could expect fifty-two years after the birth and nearly thirty years after the marriage of her last child.[3] This quiet demographic revolution is resetting the social clock. Not only is there life after parenthood, there is ample generative opportunity after parenthood. There is time for second and even third chances—chances to repair existing relationships with offspring who become adults, chances to bear fruit in new ways. No matter what lies in one's origins, more and more it is not too late to make a new beginning.

6 · A Chosen Life

I decided. . . ." Although she often used those words in interpreting her life, she never did so carelessly. Always there was the sense that the essence of a decision was its either-or quality, the way it closed off one avenue even as it opened up another. I remember her pointing out the title of a book on her shelves: *Consider the Alternative*. "I haven't read it yet," she said, "but I love to look at the title."

Jo Biondi is a pretty woman in her early fifties, with eyes that bulge slightly and skin that would darken quickly under the sun. Short graying hair is cut in an exact line across her forehead. Although her face shows the effects of age, no single temperament has settled into it. On this cold, drippy April day, she wears a blue sweater and slacks, and as she sits on the couch and looks with determination out the window, her fingers play with a gold cross on a fine chain about her neck. She speaks rapidly, sometimes burying words to produce them faster.

"I'd like to be three people," she says at one point. "I'd like to be one person who is pretty much what I am. I'd also like to be a person who is married and loved and the mother of children. And I would like to be someone who has the freedom and finances to go wherever I want, see for myself what's going on, and then write about it." She has chosen to be one of those persons and, to hear her tell the story, she lives daily with the consequences of her choice.

I

Jo—for Josette—is a name she chose at nineteen. Her given name was Ann, and the Ann that comes back in memory was an adventuresome, even reckless little girl with imagination to spare. When a Sunday school teacher told her that animals do not go to heaven because they were not baptized, she and a friend rounded up the neighborhood cats and baptized them. When she found a pillow by a garage and thought it had been left by a witch, she set a match to it. The garage caught fire. When she learned about parachutes, she demonstrated to the boy next door how to jump off a stoop holding a shot glass and a string. She cut her hand, and the wound had to be stitched. Jo's earliest recollection, though, is a metaphor for something she has felt throughout her life: "I was in a carriage. I don't remember if I was too big for the carriage or what. I just remember feeling restless, uneasy, and unhappy. I was bored being in the carriage, and I wanted to get out."

Both of her parents were immigrants from the region south of Florence. They came to America around the turn of the century and married in New York in 1916. Her father was thirty-four at the time of their marriage and her mother was ten years younger. They lived in a neighborhood of Italians, Irish, and Germans, where the men worked as milkmen or postmen or trolley conductors. The two desperately wanted children but had to wait twelve years for their first, Ann, who was born in 1928.

"My mother had tried to adopt but she was deaf. She must have been an excellent lip reader because I never thought I had a mother who was deaf, except that a black box sat before her on the table when we had company. It was an old-fashioned hearing aid. Her father was a gambler and a show business person. He brought over Italian actors and actresses—operas, vaudeville, whatever. My mother had to work in the box office when she was just a little kid. There were people who said the noise of the overhead el—the train—caused her deafness.

"Her reputation when she was growing up was that she was a daredevil. She'd try anything. I think she even flew a plane not long after the Wrights had done it. She was older when I was born, and she tended to be plump, but in the pictures of her as a young woman she was really stunning. Her features were beautiful. She had dark hair, fairer skin than mine, and dark eyes.

"What I remember most about my mother is an awful lot of humanitarian things. I remember one time when we and the people next door were going on an all-day outing. My father was in the car and my mother wasn't there. Finally, exasperated, he said, 'See what's keeping your mother.' And I went in, and there sitting at our table was this old tramp. He was unshaven and dirty, and she was fixing bacon and eggs for him. And I went out and said, 'Mommy's feeding an old man.' Oh, my father was going to die! But she did that kind of thing. People came to us. The garbage men came to us for water in the summer. She bought paper roses from an old hag, and she'd have to hide them before my father got home.

"She was generous and loving. I guess her desire for more children engaged me, because one of my earliest recollections is of kneeling at the side of the bed and saying my prayers out loud. The prayer I remember saying every night in her presence was that when I woke up in the morning I would have blue eyes, blond hair, and a baby brother.

"When I think of my father, I think of him in vest and tie with spats and cuff links. He was meticulous about his appearance. He did some housework, not a lot, and he did most of the grocery shopping. He was very strict. My knowledge of fathers was that when you woke up in the morning, your father had your orange juice fresh squeezed and waiting on the counter for you. When you went to bed at night, you left your shoes and they were shined in the morning.

"He came to America when he was sixteen. It was a time when there was excitement and adventure in the New World, and I think he had that in him. He didn't come to escape poverty. I think he first went to Pennsylvania and began work in a bottle factory, and then he went to a barbershop, and then somehow he got into real estate and house construction. As a child, I was never totally interested in what he did, but I found out later that he was known in the area as the real estate king. I knew that his associates were lawyers, real estate men, builders, and contractors. At one point he was president of the Republican party in our neighborhood. His opera partner owned the nearby candy store."

When Ann was six her mother had another child, a girl who was named Christina. Shortly thereafter, the family moved to a house in a newer neighborhood. Two years later, on the day after Christmas of 1936, her mother was taken to the hospital.

"All I knew was that she had to have an operation and that she would come home. I guess they thought it was gallstones but, as I was told much later, the doctors opened her up and found her filled with cancer. They said, let her die. I remember the day she came home. I was waiting for her, and as far as I was concerned, once she came home she was well. I was very excited. She came in looking thin, and to me, young and pretty. I remember the way she hugged me and my little sister! Everything was okay now that she was home.

"One day I was terribly bad. I don't know whether she wanted to curl my hair, or what she wanted to do to me, but I was apparently very fresh. I may have learned a little independence while she was away. I was running around the table to get away from her, and then—I had never seen her upset—she went into the bedroom, and there was a big picture of St. Theresa the Little Flower over her bed. It was a religious painting that was very popular at that time. She was crying and praying that I would be a good girl. I was scared to death. I got good so fast!

"Soon after that she was in bed, and then we had around-the-clock nurses. Everything was different. Toward the end my mother was in a great deal of pain and didn't want us to know. I remember going into the bedroom with someone who had stopped to visit her. She didn't know I was there. The lights were on and she said, 'Who is it? I can't see you. I can only see shadows.' I was terrified, absolutely terrified, that she was going to die.

"She died on a Monday. I don't know why my father kept me home from school, but he did. I was out in front of the house bouncing a ball, and the lady next door came out and asked, 'What are you doing home from school?' I said, 'My mother is dying so I'm staying home.' And her eyes just filled with tears, and she said, 'Oh, you shouldn't say that. You don't know what you're saying.' I just . . . continued playing. I was being very cool, I remember that. I knew she was dying, but I didn't know what dying meant. Then the lady next door's reaction disturbed me, so I started to go in every few minutes and say to the nurse, 'How is she?' The nurse would say, 'She's the same. She's the same.' And then one time I went in and she said, 'Your mother just died.' I said, 'Can I see her?' She said, 'All right,' and she brought me into the bedroom. A sheet was over my mother's head. I waited at the bottom of the bed, and I was looking up at that picture of St. Theresa. She pulled the sheet down, and I looked at my mother and I looked up at the picture. There really was a resemblance! The nurse said to me, 'Do you think your mommy looks like the picture?' I said, 'Yes,' and she said, 'She does.'

"Whatever that meant, I don't know, except it was a beautiful picture and she was a beautiful woman. When she died, she didn't look ravaged by illness.

"I was given a choice. I could either go to the funeral mass or I could go to my aunt's house and play with my cousin Donna. I remember having a very hard decision. I was being pressured not to go to the funeral. I decided I'd go and play with Donna, and I resented it the minute the car pulled off. I've never been comfortable with that decision. I should have gone to the funeral."

II

"The night of the funeral, my father came home and sat at the head of the table. Christina was close to me, and my father took our hands and he said, 'Now that mommy's gone . . . ,' and he was going to make a speech, and he stopped and he put his head on the table. It was the first time we ever saw him cry.

"The poor man didn't know what to do with two little girls. He spent hours at night trying to curl our hair. He would take some hair and wet it and roll it and tie a knot at the bottom of it. That was supposed to give us curls. In the morning he would have to undo all that knotting to shrieks and screaming. Then he took to sending us to the beauty parlor once a week. And then I picked up lice in school and brought them home. And my father, who was so careful with us, so meticulous, couldn't get rid of them. He had turpentine, benzene, all the home remedies. We'd wake up screaming in the middle of the night with a pillow full of bugs. He was just destroyed. He didn't know what to do.

"In little more than a year he married my mother's younger sister, who was twenty years younger than he. She became pregnant, and almost from that time she was jealous of my father's affection for Christina and me. I had a room in the attic, fixed very nicely, and if Christina would come to talk to me about anything, my stepmother would sneak upstairs behind her. There would be a terrible scene because I was not supposed to speak to Christina alone.

"Once Maria was born, the slightest problem she had was exaggerated out of all proportion. She was sick with bronchitis one winter, and we had the doctor in two or three times. I was in sixth grade, and it was January and very cold. I came home for lunch and had to go back for a final exam in spelling. When I came in, my stepmother said, 'Your sister's dying. Maria's dying. She can't breathe. Where's your father? I called the office and he's not there.' I had no way of knowing where he was. She said, 'He must be with your Uncle John. Go get him.' Well, Uncle John and Aunt Rose didn't have a phone, and they lived about two to three miles from where we lived, and there was no bus service. I said, 'I can't. I have a spelling test. I don't even know that he's there.' And she went to the window and tore the curtains down, screaming at the top of her lungs, and then she turned to our lace tablecloth, which was my mother's. I knew it was my mother's, and she started to tear it, and I said, 'I'll go, I'll go.' I went to the front closet to get my coat, and she said, 'You've no time to get your coat. Go!' I had to run out in January without a coat on. When I got to my aunt's house, I couldn't even talk. I had no breath and I was frozen and I just sobbed and sobbed and sobbed. Of course my father wasn't there.

"It was an irrational act, and our home became filled with them. There were fights. She would nag and nag and nag and nag and nag. The voice never stopped. I can remember a Thanksgiving when there was a turkey in the oven. My father and stepmother had a fight, and the turkey was thrown in the garbage pail. When they fought, I felt it started with complaints about me. I always thought if I had been a better kid maybe there would have been less trouble at home. But I never hated her, and I don't to this day. I always knew her behavior wasn't normal.

"My father was completely frustrated at his inability to change what was going on. He was a man who was always in charge, and he was not in charge anymore. He had a tiger in the house.

"As a result of the terrible unhappiness, the *incredible* unhappiness at home, I was sent away to boarding school when I was in seventh grade. My godparents were well-to-do people, and one of their daughters had gone to a high-class boarding school—Ladywood Seminary. They were very pleased with their daughter's education and apparently convinced my father that sending me there would be the best move. We went to see the place, and it was a beautiful building in the country. There were all sisters there, and I'd wanted to have sisters because my cousin Donna went to Catholic school and she loved it."

Ann was twelve when she entered Ladywood, and she stayed through high school. Classes were challenging, and the nuns cared about students. Ann's schoolwork, which had deteriorated after her mother's death, improved dramatically. She went on a self-imposed diet and lost thirty pounds. She became literary editor of the yearbook and coordinated the school's first junior prom. She fell in and out of love. "When I think of high school, I think of laughing my way through it. There were eight of us students who had a dormitory together, and we were very close. In my junior year we met a bunch of fellows and had a lot of fun with them. I loved dancing. Two of the girls in my group ended up marrying two of those fellows."

Ann also relished regularly scheduled retreats, periods when she could indulge her appetite for books. "One book that attracted me was *A Woman Wrapped in Silence,* a free verse rendering of the life of Mary. I loved stories about Jesus Christ. I remember feeling very personally the call to come and follow Him because I wanted to do the good things that He did." Actually, Ann wanted many things: to be a nurse, to be a journalist, to have a husband, to be a mother. She cannot pinpoint when the idea of being a sister first entered her mind, but by the end of her senior year she had made a decision to enter the convent.

The most difficult part of her choice was informing her father, a man who had rarely gone to church and whose only expression of religion was caring for the grave of his deceased wife. He was now sixty-four. "One Sunday afternoon in early June he drove me to the train station after I had been home for the weekend. We were sitting in the car waiting for the train, and all of a sudden I knew I had to tell him. I don't remember the words I used, but I told him I was planning to enter the convent in September. I didn't ask him. I told him. I thought that this was the moment when we were going to have an explosion.

"There was an awful silence that seemed to last forever. When he spoke it was in a terribly controlled voice. He said it wasn't what he had planned for me. He had wanted me to marry a rich man and go to Europe. He had provided for me. He was going to give me a car for graduation. He had worked his whole life so I would have a good life of my own. But then he said, 'I don't understand what you are doing, but if that's your devotion, I won't stand in your way.' Those were the terms. 'Devotion' is not a word that he used or that even particularly fit, but I knew exactly what he meant.

"So I proceeded. He gave me money to buy things I needed. My cousin Donna was planning to enter a different community of sisters, and the day we went to buy our black shoes—it was July 22, 1946—I got a phone call to come right home. My father had had a stroke. By the time I got home he was in a coma, paralyzed."

III

"We didn't know if he was going to live or die, if he was ever going to walk again. He was in the hospital, completely disoriented, for five weeks. Then he came home and was in bed for two or three months. The whole world just slowed down.

"I was supposed to enter the convent on September 8, and I let the day go by. I told the community I would have to think over my plans. I started to go out regularly with one fellow. I told him I was considering the convent, but you can't always control the way things go. He was drafted and went off to camp, but he wrote every day, and every time he had leave we went out together. We were serious. He proposed. I said no, but we continued to see one another.

"One evening—it was a Tuesday night in November, around midnight—my father announced, 'Ann, I'm going to Florida on Thursday.' I said, 'Daddy, what are you going to do in Florida?' He said, 'They have good therapy in Miami Beach. I want them to cure me.' I said, 'Daddy, you can't go there by yourself.' He said, 'I'm not going by myself. You're coming with me.'

"He hired a man to be a chauffeur and attendant, and two days later my father and I and this chauffeur went to Miami Beach.

"There we were, a thousand miles from anybody I knew, living in a hotel suite right on the ocean. I was alone much of the time and spent a lot of time thinking and walking along the beach. I was fiercely devoted to my father and very solicitous of him, but I realized he could live for many, many years and never get any better.

"Part of me had been content to let the idea of the convent slip into the background as a high school girl's romantic dream. But in the summer of 1947 I got a letter saying it would be courteous to let Reverend Mother know if I was coming. It was like cold water in my face: wake up, kid, you've got a decision here. I knew because of the direction my life was taking that I was either going to enter the convent or be married within a year. I didn't know what to do. I wanted too many contradictory things. I wanted love and affection. I wanted a husband, I wanted a family, and I wanted it to be special. I wanted everything all those movies said that you had when you had a man, and I wanted to be a nun and have none of those things.

"I was conscious of a passage in the Gospels: what person who is going to conquer a city doesn't estimate the number of forces and whether or not he can meet this many with that many? I calculated it very carefully. Could I do it? Was it worth it? Could I pay what it cost? For some reason I felt called to do this, and I felt it was not easy. I talked it over with a priest: 'Tell me what to do.' 'I can't tell you what to do. It's your life.' Finally, I said to him, 'I think I'm going to have to go. If I don't do it now, I never will, and I'll never know.' I felt that insofar as I could make a judgment about my own integrity, I had to go. I was going to pay very heavily to try. It was going to mean a lot of flak at home, a lot of personal anguish leaving my father, a lot of uncertainty. I never expected to be 100 percent sure that I was doing the right thing, but I felt I had to do it."

IV

Six months after entering the convent, in March 1948, Ann was formally received as a novice. In the ceremony she wore a wedding gown, symbolic of becoming a "bride of Christ." Her father cried when he saw her in it. The next two years were a period of austere discipline: rules governing every detail of life, long stretches of silence, hours of prescribed prayer and meditation each day, nearly total exclusion from the outside world—and absolutely no choice. She was allowed visitors once a month, and her father never failed to appear. Cloister was an endurance test for Ann. "I spent hours in chapel with my mind wandering all over, unable to get any sense of devotion, watching the second hand on the clock. I worked with books or scrubbed floors or sewed and felt there was so much suffering that needed to be relieved, so many people who needed to be talked to. When I wondered if this was the best thing I could be doing, something inside me said maybe it wasn't the best thing, but as long as I remained in community, people would be reminded of faith in God. In the novitiate I had so much energy and vitality, and it seemed to be suppressed. I was saving it for something, but I didn't know what."

In March 1950 Ann concluded the novitiate and made her first vows. Like the other sisters in her order, she was immediately assigned to teach elementary school. Over the next thirteen years she taught in three parishes, averaging seventy children per class, and earned a bachelor's degree by attending college on Saturdays and in the summers.

"My first assignment was in the inner city. The kids were black, I was white. Still am. They were really poor. Often they came from one-parent families, from rat-infested places. I felt they had a terrible, terrible need, and I wanted to meet it any way I could. They didn't learn an awful lot no matter how I tried. Some of them did. There were some great kids! I can see them: Marcia Davis, Don Bradshaw. They're very present to me. But there were a lot of kids who just were never going to learn. They should have been in special schools. I remember one girl . . . it was funny. I told you about the day of my spelling test when I had to go out in the cold and look for my father. There was also a final spelling test at the end of one term, and I had warned the kids not to come back late because there was a time limit. And this girl, LaJewel Henderson, came in late, and I was angry because she disobeyed me. I said, 'Sit down!' and she sat. When the test was over I called her aside and said, 'LaJewel, why were you late?' She burst out crying. When she'd gone home for lunch her father had come—her father was an alcoholic—and was trying to break into their home. The mother called the police to take the father away, and she couldn't come back to school until the police came. Now, that happened to me early on, and it was another learning experience: don't ever jump on kids, listen to the reason first. I had learned that myself as a student who had been jumped on. As a teacher I wanted to be someone who was not a pal, but someone students could come to when they were in trouble and know they would get a fair hearing.

"Teaching became a wonderful outlet for my energies. I always had a priority. It was the children first, *my* children first, community life second, and study third. Every place I have ever been, every school, I have come to love the kids, to care about them, to consider them a part of my life. Whenever I left a school, I thought I'd die. In the old days, we got a letter in the middle of August that said where we were assigned for the next year. We packed our trunk and were gone in a week. We'd never see those people again. That was hard. I would go through a withdrawal, and then I would immediately find myself falling in love with a new group of kids."

In 1957, in her eighth year as a teacher, Ann's father died. He was seventy-five. "Toward the end I went to him any time I could manage it. I bathed his feet and cut his toenails and made sure his clothing was clean—whatever I could do within the limitations I had. One time my stepmother was ranting and raving in another room. My father and I were talking very quietly, and he said, 'You know, I thought when you entered the convent I was going to lose you, but there is no one in my life who is closer to me than you are.'

"I should tell you that on the day we wore the wedding gowns, we were to relinquish our baptismal name and become known by a religious name. Now, this is a tradition which has since gone, but at that time we were allowed to suggest three names with reasons for them. One of my sister's friend's name was Josette, and I liked the sound of it. Josette was a form of Joseph, who was the patron of a happy death. Well, I thought of my father, and I guess I wanted an assurance that he would have the grace of a happy death. I wanted him to die with the support of the church, and I wanted to be sure he went to heaven. So I decided I'd ask for that name. I'm not a pact-maker, and I don't pray to saints, but I made this pact with Joseph. I said, 'Look, if I get your name, Joseph, wherever you are, I promise you that I will honor your name and I will pray to you for the rest of my life. You take care of my father.' I was surprised I got the name. I was one of the very few people who got the name they chose, and I must say that for the next ten years, every day, I did pray to Saint Joseph.

"Well, my father lingered for eleven years after the stroke, and some of those years were terrible. Toward the end he fell and broke his hip and was admitted to the hospital. I helped him through admissions on Sunday and then I got permission to see him after school on Tuesday. I had about forty minutes with him. He was conscious and didn't seem to be in too great pain. I remember bringing him an orange, peeling it, and helping him to eat it. It was a very loving time for us. Before I left, I said, 'Daddy, how would you feel about seeing a priest?' I thought he was going to say, 'Oh, cut it out. Don't start that nonsense.' But he didn't. He said, 'I wouldn't mind.' I said, 'Did you hear what I said?' He said, 'Yeah, I wouldn't mind to see a priest.' When it was time for me to leave, I said to myself, where am I going to find a priest? This is a big city hospital. It's not a Catholic hospital. I don't know any chaplains. And as I was thinking this, I walked out of the room into a priest! I mean *into* him! In thirty seconds I told him that my father was in such and such a bed, would he consent to see him? He said, 'Sure, Sister.' My father died the following Saturday. After the funeral I wrote the chaplain and thanked him for taking care of my father. He wrote back a post card: 'Dear Sister, You can rest assured that your good prayers won for your father the grace of a happy death.' Later I discovered that he was the kindest chaplain in the whole metropolitan area. He had a reputation for it.

"Well, I am not much about coincidences, but I really felt that that was an answer to prayer. So when we sisters got the option of going back to our baptismal name, everyone said oh, that wild-eyed liberal will be the first to go back to Ann. No way. I had a pact with Joseph."

With that bargain kept, a page was turned in Jo Biondi's story and a chapter quietly ended. At the age of twenty-nine, almost unnoticed, several strands in her life had been woven together and knotted. I left her at that resting place and headed back into the freezing April drizzle, tired but engrossed in thought.

V

When Sister Josette and I met again, a southerly flow of air had closed another chapter: the winter of 1980. Gone was the bone-chilling damp of the previous week, and in its place appeared a hazy blue sky and the sights and smells of summer. From Jo's fifth-floor apartment, even the parking lot across the street seemed fresher, and the faint green of the hills beyond, while not yet lush, was emboldened. The raucous sound of the traffic below entered from an open window.

Jo's story, too, took on a new character. Gone were the sudden tragedies—a mother's death, the arrival of a disturbed stepmother, a father's stroke—that forced serious choices on her and made "doing good" seem essential to the survival of those she cared for. In their place came a gradual evolution (or so it seems, looking back) that led, choice by choice, to a place unimaginable as she began her thirteenth year of teaching in 1962: to this very apartment, where she is doing this work, living this life, and telling this story.

This apartment is a busy place. Though Jo blocks out time for our conversations, we are often interrupted by the phone, by soup boiling over, by students dropping off papers before an inflexible deadline. She likes to bake; the results are immediate and tangible, she explains. On this occasion she serves me homemade pastry and coffee and begins to tell how her life as a sister changed after a "turning point" in 1962, how she found "better ways" to be a sister. Whenever I ask a question, she studies it thoroughly, holding a finger over tightened lips, sometimes closing her eyes, challenged to find the quickest path to just the right words.

In 1962 Sister Josette was assigned to attend a three-day workshop on the educational use of closed-circuit television. Half the participants met periodically during the ensuing year; from these, the diocese chose a handful, Josette among them, for full-time television work. Producing programs for elementary school children, Jo traveled to Indiana University in the summers of 1964, 1965, and 1966 to obtain a master's degree in communications. The faculty promised her a scholarship if she stayed for the doctorate, and Jo's superiors agreed. She finished the Ph.D. in 1971. In the meantime, she broke another tradition by publishing articles, something nuns had not done, and became a regular writer for a Catholic newspaper. After receiving the degree, she obtained a position at a western university. She later became the first sister to host public affairs programs on a major radio station. When I spoke with Jo in 1980, she was on leave from the university and spending a year in the Midwest as a visiting professor, running workshops on the use of media, writing for the newspaper, and producing programs for the radio station.

In the 1960s, an enormous upheaval had shaken religious congregations. "It was right after the Second Vatican Council. We had been semicloistered, highly restricted in dress and mobility, and all of a sudden I was working with sisters, priests, brothers, and lay people in a common venture. I could see the extent of my influence wasn't restricted to a single classroom in a single parochial school but was very widespread." Subsequently, one-third of the sisters in Jo's order left; the number of novices diminished to a trickle. Remaining a sister became a matter of conscious, deliberate choice.

In large democratic meetings, Sister Josette's congregation gradually endorsed modifications in dress, a process that required historical research. "Our foundress was a wealthy do-gooder and never wanted to be a nun. She was very much aware of the plight of the poor Irish working girl, who in many instances had to do housework to support her family and in too many situations became a sex object for the master of the house. There was no recourse and no escape. Apparently one night a girl ran away from the house where she was working and went to our foundress and pleaded to be taken in. That was the beginning of a home and school for poor working girls. Our foundress soon gathered a number of ladies like herself together, and at some point the bishop prevailed on them to become nuns. Then she and her followers had to wear a significant dress. What they chose was a dress of middle-class Irish working women, so they would not be set apart from the others except for cross and beads. But when styles changed, the sisters' dress did not change because they had become an identifiable symbol. So if you go back to the spirit of the founders, it was to be someone who was not distinguished from the others. The concept was to serve, not to be set apart."

Living arrangements were also modified. When Jo moved west and rejoined her congregation in 1971, she was assigned to live with ten sisters teaching at a parish school. "At the time I was very aware of the Caesar Chavez boycott. I had done extensive reading and some reporting on it. At the convent we had a sister, a very, very nice woman, who was the buyer for the house. And we kept getting grapes and iceberg lettuce. On several occasions I told her what I had discovered and requested that she not buy the iceberg lettuce. She would listen to me and then go out and do the same thing. I'm not good at confrontation, and she was less good at it, but one day we just had to talk about it. This thing was driving me crazy. We could live without lettuce. And she said, 'No.' Chavez was crazy, and the sisters wanted lettuce, and she was going to go on getting it, and that was all there was to it. Well, I was absolutely powerless. I had no recourse, and I was not about to create a scene, but I began to realize that I was living with a number of inconsistencies, of which that was only one.

"Right around this time I went to a workshop on social justice given by a Dominican sister. She asked some very hard questions: Do you know what you are doing with your life, how much you are willing to take for what you believe in, who will stand by you in the crunch? Driving home in the car I announced to the other two sisters, 'As a result of this workshop, I'm going to be moving out of St. Margaret's Convent at the end of this year.' No further conversation. About two weeks later one sister came to my door and said, 'Jo, when you go, I want to go with you.' So we sat down and talked about what we thought it meant to be sisters today. We decided these things: first, we wanted a convent where people would live together with a genuine effort to be present to one another. We wanted to have some regular prayer that we could share, and we wanted to open our house to other people to share in what we are supposed to be experts at—prayer and concern for the ministry. And also if someone had a crisis, a person could come and stay with us, no questions asked.

"After the discussion I wrote up a philosophy and submitted it to our board of directors and the congregation, so they knew what we were about. We got permission to look for an apartment. Some time later, separate from us altogether, three other sisters, one of whom was the third in the car to the workshop, decided they wanted pretty much the same thing. Now, it turned out that a pastor had an old convent that had been unused for several years, and he wanted a group of sisters to live there to create a presence in the parish. We moved in, the five of us. We did the painting and wallpapering and tried to deinstitutionalize the building. We tried to build a community that would be durable. The original five are still there, and three more have joined us. It was an idea whose time had come."

The paradox of choice within choices: by way of the narrow passage of cloister, Jo Biondi had come to the place where every aspect of her life was open to question and needed a decision. "I think one of the most significant things about me is that I'm not willing to accept. I want to find another way. The sisters I live with have said that on my tombstone, if I have a tombstone, they're going to put, 'There's got to be another way.' I really believe that. I believe that part of my challenge is to find another way."

VI

Almost from the beginning of her sisterhood people have come unannounced into Josette's life, stayed for a while, and then left—only to return years later. "Ellen. I taught her in the fourth grade and went to her wedding sometime in the sixties. She moved to Illinois with her husband, had a lot of marital difficulties, and became very ill giving birth to a daughter. She left her husband, and they were divorced. She was living with a fellow, to whom she is now married, and in the time that she lived with him, there was a gas leak and their apartment exploded. Her little girl was badly burned and lingered for two weeks before she died—the final proof to the mother that there is no God. During that whole period Ellen would call me from Illinois in the middle of the night, just to talk for an hour or two. She was married last August, and she seems pretty much together again. For years she's resented God and has fought against any faith, but she has always loved me, and part of it is because I represent the faith that she denies. She never said that, but I know. In all the protestations of atheism, she wants to believe what I believe, and she's not going to let go of me.

"Ginny. One day in graduate school I was on my way to church, and I heard this person calling, 'Sister, Sister.' I turned around, and this rather attractive girl with a limp was coming toward me. He name was Ginny, and she blurted it all out, as I learned Ginny would do many times after that. She had had her eye on me. She knew that I went to St. Paul's, and she felt that she wanted to become a Catholic. Could she talk to me? Well, Ginny is the kind of person who bursts into your life and takes it over. Her own life had been hard. Her parents, who were alcoholics, had died in a car accident. She had gone through the courts, been brought up by a number of people, and was in college on a scholarship. For the next few months I helped Ginny with her religious instruction. Because she is bright, she forced me to look seriously at all the things I had taken for granted. She was baptized at St. Paul's, and I gave her a surprise party.

"Ginny is like a lot of people who have been part of my life for a period of their own personal need. All of a sudden someone will track me down, someone I haven't heard from in five or ten years, and he or she will be going through a crisis, and I will be there for a while, and then he or she will disappear. I never let them become overly dependent on me. I never let them hold on too long, and I always try to direct them toward people who are more capable of helping them.

"I heard from Ginny infrequently for a number of years. She married an alcoholic, arrested her career in favor of his, and was a secretary in some office. When I moved to my present community of sisters, she called one day and was hysterical on the phone. Could she please come and stay with me? I said, 'Come.' I hadn't time to talk to the sisters in the house, but that was one of the understandings that we had when we established the house, and I knew there would be no problem. I don't know how long Ginny stayed, two or three weeks, but in that period of time we shared a lot and I also put her in touch with some professional counselors. Her marriage was subsequently annulled as a result. She moved out east. I heard from her once or twice. She was back in school on a scholarship and was doing well. Then a letter I sent came back with no forwarding address, and I haven't heard from her in three or four years. But she knows where I am.

"Dan. On the evening of her baptism, Ginny and I were at the bus station waiting for a friend, and this young fellow kept walking back and forth, eyeing me up and down and making me a little nervous. I was then in a limited habit, but obviously still a sister. Finally, at one point when Ginny was not with me, he came and said, 'I saw you in St. Paul's today and I see you again tonight, and I think maybe it's a sign I should ask you for help.' As it turned out, his name was Dan; he was seventeen; he was living with an alcoholic grandmother who had thrown him out; he was sleeping on the floor of a doughnut shop. He was a tenth-grade dropout; he was without money; and all he wanted was a job. So I said I would do my best, and I gave him my number and told him to call me at eleven the next morning. By the time Dan phoned me I had spoken to someone who had found him a job at McDonald's. Then I began to tutor him in English. I paid his rent in an apartment across the street from where I was living. That began our relationship. Dan is now thirty, and I see him regularly and keep in touch when I'm not nearby.

"Dan sends me Mother's Day cards. His mother abandoned him and shows up when she needs him. He has told me, in writing and verbally, that I have cared for him more than his mother ever did. Dan is not expressive, but he has tested my constancy. This year he called me one night at eleven-thirty and begged me to go to him because he was going to kill himself. He was involved in his first and only homosexual relationship and it was falling apart. I think if I were to let Dan go he would commit suicide.

"Bill and Claude. Bill was one of my university colleagues, a brilliant teacher who intimidated everyone in the department except me. I began to reach out to him when I felt he was feeling rejection from other faculty members. He was living with a young man. I don't know whether the relationship was homosexual or convenience or what, but on one occasion I invited the two of them to our convent for mass, a dinner, and an evening of relaxation. He and this fellow Claude came, and they liked it. I invited them a second time, and I went out to dinner with them at their request and met Claude's mother. I knew a little bit about Claude. I knew that his father was an alcoholic and had rejected him. I knew that there were psychological problems and that he was in counseling.

"One morning, early, a student called me and said she had been at a class party that Bill was having in his apartment the night before when Bill got word that Claude had committed suicide. I called Bill right away, and I said, 'Bill, I just heard about Claude. Is there anything I can do?' He screamed into the phone, 'Come!' and hung up. It was a rainy day and traveling was bad, but I got a ride into the city. I spent the day with Bill and let him go through whatever grieving he had to do. He was hysterical. We went through Claude's things. There were magnificent black and white photos of fathers and sons, and they were just so revelatory to me. I was all choked up but clearly in control. Toward the end of this miserably rainy day, Claude's mother called. Claude was going to be cremated the next day, and they wanted me to preach the eulogy.

"How we ever got through the crematorium service that day, I don't know. It was a bitterly cold December day. It was my first experience in such a place, and I was overwhelmed by the artificiality. In the foyer they were putting up an artificial Christmas tree. We were led into a chapel where there were pews and an organ and some man playing a nondescript melody. Claude's body was in a box. Not a polished coffin, but a box. After the music stopped, it was my job to face this little band of people and try to make some sense out of this senseless tragedy. All I knew was that they invited me because I was Claude's only link with religion, and somehow they wanted me to lessen their grief and their guilt. I tried to communicate my faith in the resurrection, to let them know Claude as I—an outsider—knew him: as one who was tormented by an imperfect world and whose photographs showed so much of that. I can still see the faces of the people in that group. Bill was contorted with grief. Claude's mother was in a state of shock, red-faced and eyes blood-shot. His father was absolutely baffled. Claude's brother, whom I had never met, was there, and he looked just like Claude, which was scary. Whatever I said, whatever I managed to put together, I think helped a little bit in the healing.

"A fellow at the radio station had a son killed riding a bicycle. He was absolutely bitter against God. I had nothing smart to say to him, but I let him shout his anger at me. Eventually the hostility went, and he is warm toward me now. One of our school secretaries has a husband who is very close to death with cancer. Several times a year she has led me into a corner to speak about my belief in the resurrection. She said so many times that she wished she could believe in it. What I feel she is saying to me is, 'Tell me what you believe. I can't believe that myself, but it comforts me to know that somebody who is intelligent does believe it. I can't fully deny it as long as you're standing there saying you believe in it.' I've had that experience a lot of times.

"I've been the recipient of an awful lot of confidences. Just being in touch with the feelings that come from being a woman and from being human help me to understand a lot about love that is exchanged in excitement and betrayed, about rejection, and about loneliness. I think the confrontation with death, which has been a part of my life from my mother's time on and over and over again, has caused me to look deeply at the meaning of life. I think I represent a kind of stability. I don't fall apart. And I think that one of the things I inherited from my mother is a natural thoughtfulness, which has a way of expressing itself in sensitivity toward the pain of other people. I try not to allow people to wallow in self-pity. I try to bring them the understanding I think they need at a given point. In some way I can hold them when they need to be held and give them the courage to go out and be free."

VII

From time to time Josette spoke of making statements with her life, of standing for something through her choices, of being a representative, of bearing testimony. An example came when she spoke of her sexuality. "Other people simply can't understand celibacy. Maybe they can understand it in people who are cold and shrewish, but when a person is warm and appreciative and interactive, as many sisters are, it doesn't make any sense. The fact that I remain celibate without offspring or continuation of myself is a statement about my belief in the value of an individual life. I perceive myself as a testimony to the resurrection, which is a continued life. There are discouraging and lonely moments, but intellectually I affirm that a single life is in itself valuable beyond description. It doesn't depend on another life, on a spouse or a child, to justify itself. Now, the question has often crossed my mind: if an individual life is so valuable, why not produce more of them? I don't have a sure answer."

As a teacher, journalist, and broadcaster, Jo gives many of her waking hours to taking positions on the issues of the day—on the Equal Rights Amendment and women's ordination, on capital punishment and the draft, on nuclear disarmament and housing for the poor. She asks students, readers, and listeners to do the same. "I try to help people understand that the choices they make have consequences and that they should be ready to live with those consequences. I think it's important to present my students with a lot of alternatives. Even if they put energy into positions that I oppose with my whole intellect, at least they have explored the alternatives.

"Sometimes I have found it more comforting to invest my energies in works which have immediate results. For two years when I was doing part-time newspaper work and working on my dissertation, I managed to get down to a Catholic Worker soup kitchen on a regular basis, to dispense soup and bread to the derelicts who came in. These men came in off the street hungry. They needed food, and they needed someone to give them the food with a degree of warmth and humanness. That was very satisfying for me, sometimes more satisfying than taking stands. When I take a stand, I may very well be wrong, but I'm not wrong when I heal the broken body or comfort the person who is lonely.

"Still, I feel that the events of my life have brought me to a development of talents that may not provide immediate satisfaction but may have some wider effect. The opportunities I've had are absolutely outstanding. I made a decision thirty-three years ago to live my life behind closed doors as a nun, but I've traveled all over, I've had incredible opportunities to assess the human condition, to see the story of the rich man dining at the banquet and the poor man begging at the gate. Those opportunities didn't come my way so I could luxuriate in the intellectual consideration of them. I have to make a decision about what I'm going to do about them. Am I going to bury that information or find whatever way I can to spread it? There are many willing people who are able to do one-to-one work as well as or better than I, but everyone hasn't had the opportunities I have had to bring me to this level of giving, which is intellectually and ethically informed.

"Over the years I have had a lot of favorite Scripture stories—the prodigal son, the woman taken in adultery. When I got into communications a new one emerged. It was the story of the blind man who asked Jesus to heal him. Jesus bent down and spit on the dirt and touched the man's eyes with the clay that he made, and he said to the man, 'Do you see anything at all?' And the man said, 'I see people but they seem like trees walking.' Then Jesus repeated the process, and after the second anointing the translation that I favor says: 'And the man who was blind saw men as Jesus saw them.' I think I have had the second chance, that second sighting, over and over again. I think the second is symbolic for multiple chances to see people as Jesus saw them.

"The story gives me hope. It also says that there are a lot of people who don't see things the way that I do and who resent my vision. Maybe they'll be that way forever. Maybe I'm wrong. But there is always the possibility that they will be touched, and somehow that's related to my communications. The articles that I write and whose effects I never see, the words I speak on the air that millions of people hear on a Sunday, I don't know where they go, but somewhere in there, there is another touching."

She said that at our last meeting, a few days before she returned to the West Coast. With her teaching assignments over, her reflections were less hurried. She showed me a picture of Ellen, who had called and made plans to get together. She showed me letters and gag gifts she had received in the past. In the previous week she had thrown parties for students and friends and been given a huge bouquet of flowers and an "I Love Bloomington" T-shirt, which she had modeled on request. I had been to one of the parties and seen that she did indeed touch people— physically and emotionally. As she sat on the couch on this occasion, tears welled up as she thought of the impending separation from those she had come to care for. Unexpectedly, as if coming on a narrow clearing in the woods, she caught a glimpse of the road not taken. She looked long and hard at it, then chose her own path once again.

"I'm always the one who is leaving. I exchange a lot of life with people and feel part of them and care about them and all of a sudden I have to leave. I'm always going. I have probably had more farewell parties than anybody I know. I cannot bear it, and I hate it. I never go easily. I cry just sitting here thinking about it because I'm so close to it again.

"And I know the truth of the statement that in many instances you never go home again. I don't like to meet people after three years and realize that what was so strong just can't work anymore. With a lot of people I've offered something and I feel separated from the wonderful thing that was created. I lose it because I can't hold onto it. It slips like water through my fingers. I'm glad that the ties are not binding in a sense that would strangle, but I suffer loneliness.

"There is a man in my life whom I dearly love. I have for a long time. During the summer he and his wife came to visit me. I was thrilled to have the two of them with me and to show them this part of my life. We had a fine time, but there were moments. . . . We walked along, and they held hands, and I felt like the only person in the world. I see lots of ordinary things that I haven't had, and I sense the contrast. I can't help but know that there's a price to the life that I chose. It's not a thing you pay once. I mean, you can't walk through the world without knowing that it's preoccupied with the very things I've denied to my own experience.

"There have been times in my life when I have suddenly felt incredibly alone. It comes again and again: I realize I am the center of nobody's life. I am a nice convenience, and I'm helpful here, and I brighten this thing up, but if I were to die tomorrow, it wouldn't mean an awful lot. People would grieve, but I'm not sure there would be any profound sense of loss for a very long time. Sometimes I feel, God, I want someone to care more than this.

"But what is the alternative to not feeling the grief, the death of another departure? I'm not willing to accept it. The energy expended, the commitments made, the mistakes, the whole bulk of those experiences have fed into what I am today. People who have been a source of pain to me, they're part of the fabric of my life. They all live on in me. I do have a concept of the family of humankind. There's a prayer in the mass that says: 'Bless and unite all of your children wherever they may be.' I feel very much in touch with a lot of people living and dead who have meant something to me. Our love may not be exchanged in any physical way, but I sense connections. I sense a lot of unexpressed affection, and I know with a certainty that I have mattered."

INTERPRETATION: DEATH;
CARING FOR A CULTURE

Childless and in her early fifties, Josette Biondi nevertheless has a sense of posterity. "I know with a certainty that I have mattered." She is older than either Dorothy Woodson or Erzsébet Domier and has come by a different route to her present generative location. Dorothy's and Erzsi's lives were marked by deficiencies in nourishment, generative failures, and abrupt turns at the prospect of a second chance, Josette's by adequate sustenance, generative success, and the gradual climb from one type of fertility to another. Hesitant to speak at first, Dorothy and Erzsi relieved inner pressures as they told their stories. Although Josette's life was less dramatic than theirs and her narration less cathartic, her story shows how maternal caring can be sublimated and expanded beyond one's biological issue. "A Chosen Life" also reveals the presence of the shared symbol system we call culture and illustrates the role death plays in its transmission. This, I think, is its special contribution to this collection. People swim in a sea of meaning, but, like fish, they are rarely conscious of the water. A few, Sister Josette among them, become keenly aware of their symbolic environment and choose to take care of it.

Sister Jo adheres to a spiritual tradition that renounces childbearing in order to widen the scope of maternal concern. What she has done with her chosen life thus illustrates the generative potential in childlessness. Though she has never conceived or given birth, she has mothered, she has taught, and she has given voice to elements in an enduring meaning system. In other words, she has opened parental, technical, and cultural lines of transmission even as she has closed the biological. She feels responsible for the welfare of individuals who have walked "accidentally" into her life, and she wishes to uphold a well-defined but abstract set of religious and ethical principles. How did she come to feel that she was responsible for so much, that she—and no one else—would be the source of strength who "doesn't fall apart"?

DEATH AND GENERATIVITY

That death is as conspicuous as birth in stories of generativity should come as no surprise, for the turnover of generations is accomplished by death as well as by birth. "A Chosen Life" enables us to explore two ways death touches generativity: by sealing influence "taken in" from the past and by stimulating the desire to leave a mark on the future.

Josette's account of her mother's last months is a powerful story of identification with the deceased. Jo remembers defying her mother when she was sick and then being terrified as her mother pleaded hysterically with St. Theresa to make Jo a "good" girl. "I got good so fast!" Jo recalls, and well she might have, for a child of eight could easily imagine that the goodness her mother begged for was the only way to prevent horrible things from happening. Jo remembers with utter clarity the scene of her mother's death and in particular seeing a resemblance between her mother, looking peaceful and beautiful, and a picture of St. Theresa just above the bed. "Whatever that meant, I don't know, except it was a beautiful picture and she was a beautiful woman."

When Jo entered the cloister she became a "woman wrapped in silence" like her mother and St. Theresa. It is remarkable how often as a nun Jo reaffirmed that "doing good," no more and no less, was the purpose of her life. She had wanted to be a sister in order "to do the good things that Jesus did." At the time of final vows she gave a great deal of thought to a ring inscription and finally chose, "He went about doing good." Examining her religious order's origins, she discovered that its foundress was a "do-gooder." She stated in our conversations that she wanted to do nothing profound or extraordinary with her life, "just good as opposed to evil." As an eight-year-old, she had been terrified by the terrible things "being bad" did to her dying mother, and she had heard her mother beg a saint to make her daughter "good." Jo did not suddenly incorporate her mother's wish for goodness in the moments after her death, but that death confirmed a process already under way. In her memory, a single dramatic image of a daughter, a dead mother, and a picture into which the mother's essence seems to have risen condense a lifelong motif. It is a compelling picture of "taking in" the spirit of her mother's life and for this reason is vividly remembered.

A twenty-one-year-old woman once described for me a similar memory of "taking in" what her deceased parent stood for. She had been a rebellious teenager and was eighteen when her father died. A wake was held in the family home.

The night of the wake he was out in the living room, and I couldn't sleep. I didn't know what to do, so I got up and washed my hair. I came out, and the casket was there. I stayed away from it. I just sat there and said, "Well, you've got a lot of pull now, so do something. Send up signs. Do all these wonderful things." Then I'd say, "I'm really stupid! I'm sitting here talking to this dead body." So I'd run into the other room and I'd lie down and come back out, and each time I'd get closer until finally I was just there saying, "Well, you know you're going to be watching." And I had this great vision that he was going to be on my right-hand shoulder for the rest of my life. I thought, "Okay, I'm being watched over." Since then unbelievable things have happened. I used to run away from everything, but now I say that's not the way to do it. You face everything head-on 'cause you can beat it. Sometimes I feel it's unfortunate that he isn't seeing the progress. But he is. He's on my shoulder, every day, every night. I feel I'm so much of him, so much of him is me!

These two reactions to the death of a parent are not uncommon. Psychologist Peter Marris has described how widows gradually come to terms with the loss of their husbands by consolidating what is retrievable from the past and embedding it in the present.[1] The young seem to do something similar—and something more—with deceased elders. Some feel the continuing presence of those elders. If they fought them in life, they feel remorse and start to become what the elders wished all along. They make the dead live on by unconsciously taking their place or by identifying with the cultural ideals they stood for. Symbolically taking in the deceased, feeling "so much of him is me," they master loss and restore the continuity of life.

In Sister Jo's life, death does more than seal influence from her mother; it also stimulates the development of a precocious sense of responsibility. Some "existential debt" may have been created in her mind when her mother died, whether out of fear that she had contributed to the death or regret that she had failed to do something important afterward. Jo has a distinct memory of making the wrong decision about her mother's funeral. She should have resisted pressure and gone, she says, and she knew it from the moment she said no. In his autobiography, Gandhi makes much of his failure to be at his father's side when he died, "a blot I have never been able to efface or forget." Similar memories of regret are found in the autobiographies of other individuals who exhibit broad concerns for humanity.[2] What cannot be paid to a parent, they attempt to pay to the world.

Jo's position in the family after her mother's death only added to her sense of responsibility. Her father was destroyed, her sister helpless, and the stepmother who was to care for them was crazed. It fell to Jo to take her mother's place and hold her shattered world together. She had to be good so her parents would not fight. She had to go out in the cold to prevent the destruction of her mother's things. She had to take care of her sister and father. Every action of this young girl seemed to have enormous consequences. Being bad, in particular, made awful things happen. "When they fought, I felt it started with complaints about me. I always thought if I had been a better kid maybe there would have been less trouble at home."

At eleven she was removed from the scene of these burdens and sent to boarding school. At seventeen, however, she learned again that choices—even to "do good"—have dramatic effects. Stunned by her decision to enter the convent, her father had a stroke and nearly died. Jo canceled her plans, cared for him for a year, and then decided to leave his side. For the first ten years of her life as a sister, Jo lived with another debt that could not be paid. She had gravely disappointed her father, but he remained loyal to her. He was crippled, but she could not care for him as she wished. Remembering her frustration in cloister, she spoke of her father and humankind in the same breath, "There was so much suffering that needed to be relieved, so many people who needed to be talked to."

In the end the account was settled. Before he died, her father revealed that she more than anyone had been close and loyal to him. When he consented to see a priest, he at last blessed her choice and she experienced the redeeming power of a long-term stand of conscience. "St. Joseph kept his part of the bargain," she says of her deal with existence. All debts will be paid as long as she keeps his name and honors what he stood for.

Sister Josette bears the impress of these experiences with the death and near-death of her parents. Her generativity seems to say: I must give the world the compassion my mother showed and the "goodness" she wished for me. I must give it the care I owed my father—and I can never give enough. I will be the one who does not fall apart in the face of sickness, evil, and death, and I will be the one to realize that choices have deep and lasting consequences.

If death stimulates the younger generation to "take something in," it also stimulates the older generation to "leave something behind." I was surprised to find that a number of my storytellers had had close encounters with death. One woman whose life saw many expressions of generativity nearly bled to death when she was thirty-three. At the age of sixty-four she looked back and regarded her experience as a stimulus. "When you are there and conscious," she told me, "and you think you're almost gone, you really do think about the life you have led. You think that, well, you haven't got much time, there are so many things to be done. If I lived, I had better start. . . . I always say people should almost die once." Both Dorothy Woodson and Erzsébet Domier "almost died once," and their thoughts turned toward their children, one wanting to make every day count with her son, the other worrying about the scar a mother's suicide would leave on her daughter.

In this century, the prolongation of individual lives delays the time when people ordinarily receive reminders of death. It is not until the late thirties or early forties that the probability becomes high that one will lose an intimate to death, and it is not until this time—the noon of life, Jung called it—that individuals normally envision their own end. Various researchers have concluded that the fear of death is greater at midlife than later on and that a common response to it is the conscious creation of a legacy.[3] Jo Biondi, of course, is atypical in this regard. She has been aware of death from her early years and has met it time and again, both in religious reflection and in the personal tragedies of those close to her.

I do not mean to imply that generativity requires the awareness of one's impending death. People express their generativity quite unawares, particularly when they bear and raise children. What the prospect of death does is to make the process conscious and urgent. And it need not be death that triggers conscious thoughts of a legacy; the end of any capacity will do. A number of women who postponed childbearing until their thirties are now experiencing crises of biological fertility, as the end of their childbearing years comes into view. Some struggle with the decision over whether to have a child; others panic because they cannot conceive. Athletes who see the end of their playing days consciously begin to think of passing on their skills through coaching. Realizing that they will die, elders concede their wish for immortality to the next generation. They write wills and see to it that, although they will end up dead, they will not be a dead end.

Eventually those who hope to leave a legacy turn to culture, for the only bridge they can build in death is the same bridge the young will build to them—a bridge constructed of elements from meaning systems that both generations share. Material possessions alone cannot span the distance between the dead and the living; the possessions must contain some particles of shared meaning. To live on in the next generation, elders must attach their lives to the core symbols of their culture and in some way see themselves as testimony to those symbols. When they die, the bereaved will complete the process of attachment. They will seek answers to the mystery of death in beliefs common to both generations. They will eulogize the deceased by reaffirming the ideals his or her life represented. They will engage in rituals that bring participants to the culture's mythic center and its guiding ethos. When one of their own dies, communities become aware of the web of significance on which they live their lives.

CARING FOR A CULTURE

As Sister Josette currently sees her life, it is a "statement." She "presents" a paradox, "represents" a faith, "exemplifies" values, is a "reminder" of and a "testimony" to beliefs. She is often aware of standing for something. Her language reveals movement toward a rare form of cultural generativity. With the accumulation of years and anticipation of the end, certain individuals become, in George Vaillant's phrase, "keepers of meaning."[4] They identify with dominant cultural motifs and become mediators of those motifs for succeeding generations. Sister Jo cares for people, but more and more she is becoming aware of the need to care for a culture. She has to see to the well-being not only of individuals but also of shared truths and principles.

Like performers of classic works of art, mediators of a culture re-present and interpret ideas that underwrite a collectivity's symbolic life. Without a succession of particular presentations, the general symbol system would atrophy and die. In providing for its continued life, mediators symbolically partake of that which has more extension and duration than themselves. The music they play lives on through them; and so, in a way, they live on. The principles they uphold are passed on through their example; and so, in a way, they are passed on. Not all performances or ethical stands, of course, are "generative." The term is limited to those accompanied by a sense of cultural propagation. Such a sense ordinarily comes later in life, after seeing a number of performances of the same work or a number of tests of the same principle—and after realizing one's own mortality. In cultural mediation, different accents may be struck. If the stress falls on *my* living on, the generativity is agentic. If the life of the work or the principle is emphasized, the generativity is communal. Agentic generativity poses the danger of usurping a culture for self-aggrandizement—a development pushed to a mad extreme when the Reverend Jim Jones took members of his People's Temple off to Guyana and led them to suicide. His disciples had not existed to live up to Christian precepts but to be his clones. Jo Biondi's mediation of a culture, in contrast, is communal. She believes she is subordinate to ethical principles, and she guards the freedom of the people she touches. She wants to care for truth, not to be truth. The mediator with a communal orientation wants followers less for self-confirmation and more for the preservation of the principle or the classic with which the self is blended.

Sister Jo's cultural generativity may be traced to beginnings in her calling to be a sister. Already wanting to "do good," already possessed of a strong sense of responsibility, she found in that calling a cultural form to contain, activate, and channel her aspirations. She was connected to contemporaries with similar desires and given outlets to express them. She gained access to great figures from the past who possessed features identical with important dimensions of herself. As she said, "I wanted to do the good things that Jesus Christ did. . . . The sensitivity He brought to people is perfectly consonant with the humanitarian, compassionate qualities I received from my mother." Jo incorporated the spirit of Jesus, just as she had incorporated her mother's, symbolically "taking in" His body and blood in the sacrament of communion. The stories of Jesus, Mary, St. Joseph, and her order's foundress fired her imagination and connected her mundane activities to compelling mythical deeds in the past. These connections gave her senses of meaning and belonging in a collectivity of long duration. Embracing a cultural paradigm that matched the contours of her self, Josette formed an identity. Idiosyncratic strivings became a vocation. She received the kind of nourishment that only a culture can give and laid the foundation for her later mediation of that culture.

Sister Jo's generativity was first expressed as a teacher and a stand-in mother for grammar school students, "*my* children," she says. When she traded the classroom for the television studio, she gave up face-to-face contact for the promise of wider influence. But she continued to touch directly the people who sought her out in moments of crisis. After earning an advanced degree she returned to teaching, this time at the college level, and she found still other outlets in journalism and broadcasting. A strong maternal concern ran through all her contacts, yet not all of them ought to be called generative. Those that occurred in an intergenerational context surely do, as well as those that, with or without her knowledge, set in motion a chain of lasting influence. So too ought the final type of generativity to which she is heading: "I've had incredible opportunities to assess the human condition, to see the story of the rich man dining at the banquet and the poor man begging at the gate. . . . Am I going to bury that information or find whatever way I can to spread it? There are many willing people who are able to do one-to-one work as well as or better than I, but everyone hasn't had the opportunities I have had to bring me to this level of giving, which is intellectually and ethically informed."

Sister Jo has come to realize that the religious and ethical environments in which individuals live matter greatly to their well-being. In seeing to the health of those environments, she is similar to one who cares for the quality of air, land, or water. As such, she has an indirect yet critical impact on succeeding generations. Jo's freshening of the symbolic atmosphere of her religious order is illustrative of her cultural stewardship. Through the years she has asked what it means to be a sister in the contemporary world, and she has sought answers in the founding documents of her order. In the company of others she has pressed for modifications to bring the life of sister closer to the spirit of these documents. Finding "another way," she has cared for a culture as others have cared for the physical environment.

In the final analysis, it is her culture that has given Sister Josette Biondi the template for generative expression through childlessness. In this way she is different from the large cohort of men and women for whom lifetime childlessness is now predicted. The oldest of their number are now in their thirties, and few have had the advantage of a tradition giving meaning to childlessness. Will they experience dilemmas related to generativity and begin to develop such traditions? Will their lives be as fruitful as Jo's and, if not, will they have difficulty in their old age coping with the finitude of life? These questions cannot yet be answered. Some of the new cohort surely will discover "higher" forms of fertility, and the roads they take will remind us of Sister Jo's. Childless, they will know at the end that they have mattered.

7 · *In a Dream Castle*

S he seemed set apart as she entered the auditorium. She was a tiny old woman with an erect bearing, dressed in soft beige and wearing a rich fur tam. An antique lorgnette studded with jewels hung on a chain about her neck. The paleness and age of her features gave her an ethereal quality and made her seem like a vestige of another era, a link to an earlier time of elegance and culture.

She was escorted to a seat in the first row. By her side were a man as old and frail as she and two younger men, one bearded and one clean-shaven. Once seated, she raised her chin and watched a trio of musicians ascend the stage. The pianist, a tall, slender woman in pink and black, announced that the Tchaikovsky trio to be played that afternoon was first performed one hundred years before, almost to the day.

After the concert I searched the crowd for the old woman. I knew her reputation as an impresario and patroness of the arts, and I had asked her daughter, the afternoon's pianist, to arrange for us to meet. When I was introduced to her after the concert I asked to record her life history. What her reaction was I do not know, but within minutes, between greeting people who approached her in the foyer, she was dropping snippets of her story. "I've had a love affair with art." "My father was shot by the Communists." "I escaped under a load of coal." And, with a look of urgency: "I have to go to New York." She repeatedly asked my name and wondered if I spoke Russian. Her eyes were spirited and witty, but often they were faraway, as if in a dream.

Suddenly she asked if I had seen her collection of musical instruments and invited me to her home the next day.

I

I recorded Hannah Gordon's life story on some of winter's bleakest days. Her home was in a neighborhood of dark brick mansions set back from a winding, slush-covered street. Usually we sat upstairs in her study, and a maid would bring pastry and wine or coffee. Hannah would sit sideways in her chair and stare romantically into the distance. Her face seemed less pale now, and for the first time I noticed brown and reddish tints in her hair.

She was born in 1905 in the city of Odessa on the Black Sea, the oldest of five eventual children. "We lived in a large apartment which had a beautiful courtyard where children could play and be protected from any hazards of the street. We were entertained by various comedians who would come to the courtyard, put a little rug there, start climbing on each other's shoulders, and build a big column of human beings. We children were so cruel! We'd pull their hair or pull their jackets and the poor creatures would scream. I tell you that because I feel so guilty for having been part of those cruel children. I can see the faces of these miserable, demented creatures who would come and try to sing a song or turn a somersault, and then the pennies would be thrown from various windows.

"Odessa was a very beautiful city. Each holiday the caretaker of our building would put wires from one tree to another and then bring out lanterns and hang them. We children were so happy when he let us carry the lanterns from his little house to the street and hand them to him! In the city, the streets were lined with acacia trees, and in spring the smell was just heavenly. You could promenade on the boulevard or sit two hundred steps above the Black Sea and innocently spend the time seeing the fashions on the women. We also had a home by the sea, and we would spend the whole summer there. The beach had sand just like powder! I remember Father would come by train on weekends with bundles of chocolates and candies.

"We had a great opera house which was built exactly as the Paris opera houses. We had drama theaters, and on Saturday we would go to the theater and on Sunday to the opera house. That was just like a religion! We knew all the operas and all the plays, particularly Russian plays. My father was a painter who did decorations for the opera house. He had his atelier in the apartment, on the first floor. I remember his box of gold leaf. Certain designs had to have real gold, and he would take the tissue paper with the gold and put it on a very soft cushion made of chamois and cut the size he wanted. Everyone would stop breathing because the gold would fly in the air. I think he had to melt something for the gold to stick to, and then he would take a thin brush and rub it in his hair to make electricity and then, boom! pick up the gold and put it in place. You couldn't breathe. And then with a special brush he would wipe off the extra. He had assistants who did a lot of work. They were poor, young men, and on Fridays there was a lot of cooking and baking to do. The cook, with my mother's supervision, was busy for hours making cakes and cookies and particularly streusel, where the dough was put on a round table and then that wonderfully delicious mixture of ground almonds and honey and walnuts was put in. And all the assistants to my father, all the workers who prepared paint, would come from faraway ends of the city to drink some wine and vodka and to have all this pastry.

"We were brought up to be very quiet in my father's presence. He was an avid reader and would subscribe to all the magazines possible. He had tomes of Shakespeare with beautiful illustrations. Sometimes on a Saturday night he would be free, and he would let us girls take these beautifully bound books. He would stand in back of us, and suddenly we would hear a soliloquy of *Hamlet*. I'll say it in Russian: 'Imperious Caesar, dead and turn'd to clay, might stop a hole to keep the wind away. O, that that earth which kept the world in awe, should patch a wall t'expel the winter's flaw!'

"My father had a beautiful baritone voice. He was a handsome man, tall and lively, and he loved the women. I remember, very often, I would come home from school and our governess would say, '*Silence, silence, mes enfants*! Mama has a migraine!' She probably found out about some escapade of my father."

Hannah did not realize that she told the story of her father's escapades over and over, each time in the same formula, each time with the devil in her eyes. On one occasion her mind jumped to the tale of Eugene Onegin, the subject of Pushkin's narrative poem and later Tchaikovsky's opera. Hannah related how the heroine, a dreamy, innocent country girl, enters a loveless marriage when her feelings for the worldly Onegin are turned aside. After she moves to the city and reaches the pinnacle of society, Onegin at last falls in love with her. He makes advances but she refuses him, even though she desperately loves him. "Stupid!" Hannah exclaimed. That was her mother, she added—ever the dutiful wife though her husband went on "escapades." Hannah lit a cigarette and held it high in the air like an aristocrat. She began to speak of girlhood dreams of falling madly in love.

"I was just in the first year in the gymnasium, and we always had a tutor at home, and this young man, Peter was his name, was very handsome. I think he was in the eighth class in the gymnasium or already in the university. He lived in the same building, and he would come and help me out with my compositions, and my compositions were always . . . the highest mark was a five. You know how stupid girls fall in love. Well, the war came, and Peter was either recruited or volunteered, and then he came on a leave in his beautiful uniform. He came to take me to promenade. Imagine me with an officer! I don't know, maybe he loved me. I was already in the fifth class.

"I studied music with the wife of a famous Russian composer, and she had a son, Sebastian, who was in love with me. He was handsome, blond, blue-eyed, a real man, and oh, he could whistle! It was just sheer music. I used to come and take my piano lessons with Madame, and Sebastian would stay waiting. He could whistle, and you could be mesmerized by how beautiful it was!

"Our school was private. It was expensive, and the girls were all from the well-to-do people. Each class had a matron who supervised. She sat at her table, and the professors would come in. We would have to stand up and curtsy, and the matron would sit there until we sat down. Then the class went on. We had to take German and French and arithmetic, and then, of course, as you went to higher classes, there were physics and chemistry. There was Russian literature, which is really the most wonderful literature.

"It was eight years in the same school. It was very, very strict. We had to wear uniforms, and on Sunday we would be invited to a boys' school to dance. It was crazy—dancing waltzes, mazurkas, and polkas—but it was fun. It was all supervised, but we were glad to be out and to dance. I was one of the leading students. I graduated from the gymnasium with a gold medal, and the professor in literature sent me his book and wrote a dedication, 'To my precious pupil, the future writer.' I still have the book.

"We had all the luxuries. We didn't go to the store to buy dresses. We had a seamstress as part of our household. The magazines would come from Paris, and we would show her. 'I would like this dress.' And it was made. Looking back, it was perfect contentment. We followed the traditions without any pain, without any disappointment. It was happy, and we were gay, and we had all the freedom we wanted."

II

"Suddenly something threatening was in the air. You had to put shutters over the windows, and you peeked out. You heard that rebellious things were going on. 'The Communists are coming.' I don't remember where they were coming from. They were chasing out the White Russians, and then there was a period when the Communists were chased out by the French. Then the army of the Reds came again and chased them out.

"Every other week was—I'm trying to translate it—'the day of the free search of the government.' Money was confiscated. You couldn't go to the bank. So we had to leave our wonderful apartment on the second floor and move down to the ground floor, where my father's studio was. Each apartment had a deep cellar where you could keep wines and cognacs. All the liquor stores were confiscated by the government so you couldn't go and buy a bottle of wine. We must have had a lot of liquor in our cellar because Father, Papa, entertained people in the house, and the liquor came from the cellar. When the Communists took over, the big shots wanted some fancy drinks, and we had a cellar full of them, so they took them.

"Then we lived through the famine, which was dreadful. Nobody can really understand what it is to be hungry. It isn't that you say, 'Oh, I am so hungry,' and go home and find a dinner. There is nothing at home. When I was fourteen I went to the university, and they would give you a loaf of bread once a week, without a wrapper. The beggars knew about the day, so they would be ready with little knives to slice a piece.

"Now, how did I meet my husband? By chance, I remember now. I wanted to go with a friend of mine to see a play. It was a very important play, and it was very difficult to go and see. All of a sudden I see a young man come on a bicycle and give me an envelope of tickets. It was David's brother. David got the tickets for me. A friend of his was a boy friend of a very close friend of mine from the gymnasium. David heard all the tales about me, and he was very eager to meet me. So he sent his brother on a bicycle with a ticket, inviting me to go with him.

"I was a spoiled child, and independent, and I had an infatuation with a professor. I had Sebastian who was interested, I had Boris who was interested, I had Nicholas who was interested. I didn't think of a husband. Then came the famine, and David was always managing to get bread.

"And then I thought the young men I knew were all rich brats. They were handsome and interesting but impractical for the times of starvation. So you did not think of aesthetic things. It was just saving your stupid life. Here comes a young man who's bright, who's daring, and who knows how to make connections. He was a great manipulator, as young as he was.

"His father had a factory in the city, and after the war with the Germans you couldn't get any shoe polish. So he made shoe polish. Not that people had many shoes, but they still needed polish to cover up the damaged parts of them. They didn't have buttons so he bought all the broken records and melted them and made buttons. David was as inventive as his father. For instance, Russia at that time was very isolated from the rest of Europe. The country did not have typewriter ribbons or carbon paper because the supplies of these things from Germany stopped. David developed a way of making them so he was engaged by the government under the gun. The government would send a guard to take him to the Cheka. He didn't want them to have his formula so he would ask for materials that he did not need. Then he asked me, 'Would you like to see how I make it?' And then he said these extra chemicals had to be gotten out, so I put them in my bosom and snuck them out! If I were caught, they wouldn't think much to shoot me.

"He fell in love with me, but I was not in love with him. He proposed, and I left him for Sebastian. My sister Katya used to come and tell me he was weeping. 'Why don't you visit him?' I wasn't in love with him. Then David came and said he was leaving Russia. He didn't see anything promising, and he showed me his passport. So I kissed him good-bye and stole the passport. It was in his inner coat, and he was so involved in kissing me . . . . It was just that I didn't want him to go away because there was starvation in Russia.

"Eventually we got married. The reason really was . . . he could manage to get food and he was planning to escape from Russia.

"After we were married we had a room in a beautiful apartment of a very famous doctor. David always knew the right people, so we had our food. Once he managed to bring some meat and I made some hamburgers. And then my father came to visit because he knew there might be food. So he ate. My brother Stefan was about three years old, and I wrapped up a sandwich and said, 'This is for Stefan.' My father left, and we looked out of the window and saw him unwrap the package and eat it right in the street. Can you imagine a father doing that? It wasn't meanness, but the times were so terrible, there was no reason.

"Three of David's closest friends managed to get a boat to Constantinople, and they made arrangements for a sailor to come and smuggle us out. David was in the hospital with typhus when the boat was ready, and they wouldn't let him out. So we tied up sheets and he climbed out the window, and I pushed him to the railroad in a cart because he couldn't even walk. There were so many people in that railroad car! When we got to the boat, we were put under a pile of coal and a board was put over us.

"We had no papers so they took us across the Black Sea to Poti in the Caucasus. It took about a day to get there. We stayed in Poti until a boat came and took us to Constantinople. On the boat I shared a room with David and eight others. They were all Russian refugees. One was an opera singer. David and I were husband and wife so they put up two sheets to separate us from the others.

"We stayed in Constantinople about a year. I subscribed to *La Vie Parisienne* because we got it at home in Odessa, and they had all these risqué girls, so I would copy them on plywood. I made a little stand and painted the nude girl with the hat and the big hat box in front. And the Russians in Constantinople who used to stand on the corners selling pencils and I don't know what else were selling my art. We did have some money to pay the rent, but I really don't remember all the details."

III

"Certain things I would like to remember . . . flow away," Hannah said once, and the words apply to great portions of the middle of her life. As near as we could determine, she was married early in 1921 at the age of fifteen and escaped shortly thereafter. Over and over she volunteered the information that her father had been shot by the Communists, but she could not recall the circumstances of his death, and she had to think a long while before concluding that it took place before her escape. She remembers smuggling three things out of Russia: the paint box she used to paint her risqué Parisian girls, the lorgnette I had seen her wearing at the concert, and sheet music for melodeclamation, a dramatic reading of poetry with piano accompaniment. It was probably in the fall of 1923, when Hannah was eighteen, that she arrived in New York. She remembers that she and David lived with an aunt who ran a hotel on Coney Island, and she remembers that she got a job painting designs on china plates. She and David saved money to bring their families over from Russia, but Hannah cannot pinpoint the dates when they arrived. Nor does she mention an incident of blood poisoning in which she nearly died; this I learned of from her daughter. When she was pregnant with her first child, David left her to join relatives in Pennsylvania and start college. Sometime in 1926 she followed David to Pennsylvania, bringing with her a daughter, Catherine. Hannah and the baby lived with David for a while and then left his campus apartment and moved in with his father, who had just bought a small house. Neither husband nor wife seems to have minded living apart from each other.

It did not take Hannah long to find other Russian refugees who had been involved in theater and music. Many were now washing dishes and painting houses. David's father had taken up house painting, and on weekends Hannah and David earned money by hanging wallpaper. Saturday nights were set aside for singing, storytelling, and poetry recitation with other immigrants. The evenings often included Hannah's rendition of melodeclamation.

Her focus in her twenties, however, was on her daughter. Catherine was two when Hannah created a system of coloring keys and music and began to teach her piano. When Catherine was four, her lessons were taken over by a teacher at the conservatory where Hannah herself was teaching. Hannah never left her daughter's side during long hours of practice, and Catherine never balked. "She was the most accepting child, the most wonderful student. She practiced two hours a day and never wearied of it. No mistake she made was ever carried on." At five Catherine was giving recitals and accompanying her mother in performances of Russian folksongs or French storytelling. Every week the two of them dressed up and went to the symphony and then to a Russian restaurant where the orchestra's musicians congregated. Catherine played with that symphony for the first time when she was eight, and she became the subject of constant adulation.

In the meantime David had gotten his bachelor's degree, gone through medical school, and begun an eminent career as both a researcher and a practitioner. A son was born in 1929, and another son ten years later, when Hannah was thirty-four. The family moved into one of the city's exclusive neighborhoods, and Hannah began to collect Renaissance art and musical instruments. She met a German count who had fled the Nazis and opened an art gallery in New York. In the 1940s she began making trips to New York to buy art through him. Whether her split with David originated with those trips, whether its roots are deeper or shallower, no one is able or willing to say.

IV

The years went by. When she was thirty-seven, Hannah saw her teenage daughter abandon the piano to pursue a premedical curriculum in college. Upon graduation Catherine returned to music, married, and began to combine a career as a concert pianist with the raising of her family. In the meantime Hannah's sons were attending the best private schools and her husband was immersing himself ever deeper into his work. "I was a good wife," Hannah says, "but he did not appreciate what it was to have a husband and not to have him." His preoccupation with science gave her free rein in art. She obtained a master's degree in literature and began teaching Russian at a local college. As her collection of art and musical instruments grew, her world drifted apart from her husband's.

At some point she began inviting local chamber ensembles to perform for guests in her home. After one memorable recital she was approached with the idea of launching a concert series in a historic and recently renovated auditorium. It was 1955, Hannah was fifty, and she was about to enter the period of her greatest energy. Her recall of names and dates and places associated with that time is fragile, but the tenor of those two decades is conveyed by the vitality and intimacy of her mood. Over and

over she returned to the words, "I've had a love affair with art." Over
and over she looked in the distance and saw . . . what? "I made extremely interesting, creative friendships with the artists. They lived in
my home, where they were dined and treated like interesting, important
people. They had a bedroom, and there were always flowers on a little
table when they came in, and there was a big bowl of fresh fruit. This is
how I was brought up. If you have a guest staying over, you have these
accommodations. Hospitality is a great thing in Russia."

Because of the gaps in Hannah's memory, I turned to others for
impressions of her during her fifties and sixties. A dancer remembered
"how she came on stage in these wonderful Chinese gowns—the per-
sonification of everything that was cultured and right. And then the
executive in her little office, addressing envelopes, making phone calls,
getting publicity, arranging parties, selling tickets. She was on the job
twenty-eight hours a day. And then this motherly figure at her wonderful
home, providing these sumptuous banquets and treating everybody like
royalty. After a concert you're at your highest peak, and it's very depressing to have to go to a hotel room and go to bed. Here I did this
magnificent thing, and what does it all mean? Artists need to come down
out of that afterglow and meet their audience. And Hannah's parties were
a wonderful way of doing that.

"I would hear that somebody had come and stayed at her house
when they needed some time to think or to work, that she had given
people money or support to help them with their projects. She carried
on correspondence with artists and seemed to be in touch with their
needs. Artists are crazy people. They just need support and encouragement, and she had that intuitive faculty—maybe it was like
mothering—of knowing how and when to give them.

"The kind of world that Hannah came from was a world that started
when Peter the Great went to France and decided to bring French culture
back to the Russians. He wanted the Russian nobility to be as elegant
and refined and sophisticated as the French nobility. What we have in
Hannah is a spin-off of that: this love of beautiful objects, of music, of
theater, of culture. It all goes back to the period when the French ex-
ported their culture all over Europe. Hannah was the beneficiary of that,
and she brought it from the old world to this city." For twenty years the
cultural life of the city was shaped largely by her hands. And the careers
of young artists who have gone on to international acclaim benefited
immeasurably from her attention.

So the eulogies went. What Hannah's mind retrieves from the past,
however, is more modest: the sheer joy of contact with artists. "My
friendships were mostly with men. They were intelligent and alive and,

well, strong. I had a friend who was a German baron, and he had a great art gallery in Berlin. He was half Jewish so he had to flee Germany during Hitler's time. He was really the most interesting companion. He was a writer, he was a painter, he was a gourmet, he was a great connoisseur and . . . a great gigolo. An extremely interesting person. He introduced me to artists and writers and helped me buy paintings. Whenever I came to New York he would meet me and take me to the best restaurants. When I was running the concert series, I would dash off twice a year to engage artists, and I was dined and wined and treated royally.

"In New York I would always have a young man to go out with in the evening. I'll never forget one time there was a party for managers of concert series, and one young man said, 'Would you like to come with me?' I didn't like to go alone, but then to go on a bus with a group is not interesting either, so I said, 'Surely.' And he said, 'Well, before we go to this party I have to stop at the discotheque and meet someone at the bar. Would you mind?' I said no. So I was sitting there and the lights were crazy and the music was bang and bang, and one young man came up to me and said, 'Well, aren't you going to dance?' 'No, I'm waiting for a friend who is at the bar having a rendezvous.' Then I found out who that man was. He was an important person of the radio station, and he wanted me to go with him. We finally took him to our party."

Hannah's position as curator of the concert series ended in 1977, when she was seventy-two. Hannah had benefited from a sophisticated audience for most of her tenure, and her audience had benefited from her ability to engage outstanding artists. But in the 1970s the generation who knew music well enough to appreciate her work began to leave the city. The younger generation that was left behind preferred films and jazz to opera singers and chamber ensembles. Hannah no longer sold the number of series subscriptions she once did. Costs increased. Union demands became greater. Hannah was criticized for being out of touch with young people. Finally, a breaking point came and she resigned. "For twenty years I gave my time and money to run the series. I never got a cent. But the inconvenience and the encroaching on my ideas . . . . I don't think they acted right. I said, 'I don't have to take it.'"

V

"There comes to me now a great void," Hannah said of her present life. "I live with memories, and I feel terribly lonely." Her loneliness was momentarily assuaged when she took me through her house and showed me her collections. "I've always lived in a dream castle. I can go from one room to another and get an intimate feeling. Every time I go through it, it's just a love affair. I always fell in love with my paintings. It wasn't just because I wanted something on the wall, no!" In a dark, quiet room dominated by a Flemish masterpiece, she pointed to French furniture from the eighteenth century, a chest from the sixteenth, an ancient church pew she used to hold albums of medieval music. We stopped to go through scrapbooks of newspaper clippings that pictured her with ancient musical instruments from around the world. In another room she turned on lights over Renaissance paintings and played melodies on a harpsichord and a clavichord. Passing the grand piano at which her daughter practiced, Hannah showed me pictures of her family, which now stretched to four living generations. She pointed with pride to a sculpted head of her husband resting on the piano. It was the work of one of her grandsons. Then she found the sheet music for melodeclamation that she had taken from Russia, and that occasioned an explanation of the beauties of Russian diction. "It's a euphonious language—consonant, vowel, consonant, vowel—and I speak it very beautifully." She began to recite the poetry and was suddenly swept into a performance. Her acting was powerful and clear, her command of emotion stunning. None of the poetry had flowed from her mind. She remembered and dramatized verse after verse flawlessly. I learned later that she still gave concerts of melodeclamation.

In the foyer she stopped to show me her guest book, which contained hundreds of photographs, signatures, and expressions of thanks from the artists who had stayed with her. We passed a library of books on art and went upstairs to see tapestries and finely sewn Chinese costumes. We looked in quietly on the bedroom where visiting artists had slept. In another room I caught a glimpse of a portrait head of Hannah herself. She was angry that her grandson had not yet finished it. Then I was introduced to an astounding collection of musical instruments, hundreds of them packed into three tiny rooms. Hannah pointed out a Burmese harp, temple trumpets from Tibet, Spanish guitars, a one-string "trombamarina" from nineteenth-century Germany, a Persian spike fiddle. There were tiny drums made of human skulls and huge drums of animal skins. There were xylophones whose wooden bars sat on gourds and a portable "Bible organ" from the Middle Ages. Locked in lighted cabinets were dulcimers and lutes and harps and an intricately carved ivory recorder. When Hannah told me about her son bringing back instruments from his world travels, about visiting artists pleading with her to sell them a bassoon or a hurdy-gurdy, about schoolchildren touring her house, I could not tell whether she was referring to events thirty days or thirty years before.

At one point she retrieved a small wooden carrying case. "When my father gave this to me," she said, "that was the greatest gift I would want to have." It was nothing more than a battered box of old paints. Inside were dried-out tubes, dirty brushes, and a palette caked with layers of colors. It was the box she had smuggled out of Russia and used to paint pinups in Constantinople and china plates in New York.

Back in her study, which was warm and well lit in contrast with the museumlike atmosphere of the rest of the house, her mood became melancholic once again. "Right now I'm terribly depressed. Seeing how David is struggling. And then I think . . . to leave all this to my children. It is becoming now a great burden. I don't know what to do.

"It's not a joyous life. The few friends I had, they either moved away or died. I never had time to develop girl friends. I'd much rather be with men. When I go to New York to see my sister, I worry about how David is. I'm full of apprehensions about his health. He is a very secretive person and stubborn like a mule. I don't know what's wrong with him. Mentally, he is just as lucid as can be. I forget things, but he remembers to the slightest detail. The only thing he tells me is when he's angry with me. He says if anything happens to him, I'll have to fend for myself. I say, 'Don't tell me that. That's not the important thing!' I know he doesn't want to grieve me, but at times he can be very cruel. It's the cruelty of silence.

"I know he's in pain, but he won't let me take care of him. Sarah, the maid, takes care of him. She comes and puts drops in his eyes and drops in his ears. Sometimes I drive him around to protect him, but he resents it terribly. Sometimes I send Sarah with him, and then she becomes arrogant and impossible. Well, I just have to swallow that.

"David has a two-story laboratory full of machinery of his own design. It's being sold for junk now. People come by and offer him twenty dollars for something he paid thousands of dollars for. He doesn't have anything. He is trying to sell the building and I keep begging him. The paintings I could always sell and have some funds. I feel very pleased that I have something if he needs it.

"I never had a husband. He was always busy, and I always respected his inclinations. Fifteen or twenty years ago he separated himself from me. He went to another bedroom. We never shared the same bed and, after all, as a woman I did crave a man's attention. Well, that was his method. I just went wild, and he never stopped me. Maybe it was selfish on my part to give all my attention to the things I love. Now he kind of blames me for his situation.

"I always attracted men, but I was too stupid to take advantage. I was brought up with what is proper to do and what is not, so I was always scared. But I did find one man I fell in love with. I'm never going to tell you who. It was really love. Love is when you long to be with somebody. The torture of not seeing that person, the desire, the anticipation of the meeting: it is something that is very difficult to describe.

"I have opened my heart to you," she confessed at her sudden revelation. In a moment she deftly closed it again. In the brief interlude, her eyes watered, and she seemed a heroine of nineteenth-century Russian literature. Love as Hannah remembered it faced great obstacles. It was painful and intense, it engendered mutual understanding and inspiration, and it changed one's life forever. It was "the most beautiful part of a human being's life." Love today is "just going to bed." All Hannah added about her affair was how it ended: "Death."

VI

Wanting to know more about Hannah's life and wanting to learn of its impact on others, I visited her daughter Catherine. Catherine led me to Hannah's grandsons, the two young men I had seen at the Tchaikovsky concert. Nicholas, the clean-shaven one, had followed in the tradition of his grandfather and entered medicine. Alec, like his grandmother, was involved in art. It was he, in fact, who had sculpted the portrait heads that Hannah had shown me.

When I spent an April evening with them, it was as though I had stepped into the middle of a conversation that had been going on for years. I was unprepared for its intensity. Ever since their college days, now almost a decade in the past, the two had been doing what I was there to do: comprehend the influence of their grandparents on their lives. Alec described that influence in no uncertain terms. "Our parents were shocked when we first told them about the effect our grandparents had. I have a feeling that they had been very much aware of how dominating their own parents had been and that they said, 'Well, we are not going to do this to our kids.' They stepped aside. But that just allowed the lightning bolt to come straight through with no immunity whatsoever. By not bearing down on us, they allowed free range for the grandparents."

The influence came not from one but from four very different and powerful figures. On one side of the family was an emphasis on Judaism and success in the business world. On the other was a mysterious but deep-seated conflict between art and science, between Hannah and David, an intense man everyone described as a "genius." Nicholas recalled "little tiffs" between his grandmother and grandfather, but Alec remembered far more than that. "Once Grandpa and I went on a canoe trip for a week, and he just hammered into my head the entire time how much he hated Grandma. Whatever happened between them at whatever age, it created intense animosity. If Grandma represented something, he was against it. 'Why make art?' he would say. Nature was so beautiful that anything man made could not possibly compare with it. To be a scientist and to study nature was to imbue your existence with a beauty innately greater than anything man could make. And to spend your life thinking about anything else was a waste of time. He always said that. I'm thirty years old, and I can remember this from when I was five. I never had a normal conversation with him."

Most of the evening the grandsons compared impressions; though I was interested in their grandmother, her husband kept coming up.

Nicholas: "One time Grandpa said to me that all the conversations he ever had with anybody else were boring. All the parties he'd been to were boring."

Alec: "All the conversations. . . . He never had a conversation in my parents' home which had ever been worth anything."

"I couldn't believe it. I said, 'Wait a minute. That can't be true.' 'Yes, it's true.' But I think that's tainted by his old age and the fact that he's gotten so bitter as he's gotten older."

"Grandpa had us completely convinced that being a doctor was the only legitimate thing a person could possibly do."

"I remember spouting to friends in college things that came directly from his mouth. 'Why study literature? You can read it anytime. You have to study science.' "

"I used to paint when I was young, but one day in the sixth grade I made a conscious decision that I had to buckle down and study serious things. Doing art was just the most frivolous, irrelevant thing, so I just decided at that point to stop. That came from Grandpa. He was such a fanatic about science. My sculpture didn't really start until I was a senior at college, and it was not without a lot of trepidation and arguing. I had to struggle with what Grandpa said. Plus, art in Grandma's world was a very dead thing. I mean, you were respecting all these old masters, whereas you could go over to my other grandparents and see all these industrial giants shaking the world and moving. There life was surging forward, and here you had an ancient and monastic silence, a tomblike feeling of revering the art. When you're a kid you get the sense that if you go into the art world you're stuck with a withdrawn, hermitlike existence, whereas if you go into the business world, it's money and excitement. I still struggle with that feeling."

"An interesting story: Grandma went around Europe after the war, and she went to Picasso's studio. Picasso was there chatting with her, and he had this folio of ten prints which he wanted a hundred bucks for, and she didn't want it. She didn't like his work. When we heard this we started tearing out our hair! But if you offered her the same ten prints for the same one hundred dollars, she'd probably pass it up now. She just doesn't like the work. She doesn't like anything past 1800."

"Grandma had the potential to be an offsetting factor to Grandpa, but she was so withdrawn from the kids that you never got her propagandizing the fact to you that art was important. She just set up a general cultural ambience in her home. She established the fact that the sort of culture every normal person in America gets was not for you. What was for you was a much higher level of sophistication. To this day, if I'm playing a rock-and-roll station or a country station and Nicholas walks in the house, he walks over and turns the radio off without even saying anything!"

"I just played chamber music the other week with an older fellow who knew my grandmother. He said the musicians used to sign up for her series because of her parties. Otherwise they wouldn't have come. She would have banquets and these huge silver bowls of punch that bubbled over dry ice. They have pictures of us as little kids carrying dishes around. We used to toddle in there, helping them."

"One of the earliest memories I have is when they had these Russian sword dancers over. They came in the fifties, and there was probably not a damn thing to eat over there. Grandma would make this huge centerpiece with things you don't usually eat with your hands. And the Russkies came in and just wiped it out! Like locusts. There was not a single thing left! They ate the centerpiece—every orange, apple, pineapple, and banana!"

Back and forth they went, memories spilling over memories. Alec, bearded and bespectacled, stumbled over words in his earnestness. Nicholas's crystalline voice supported his brother but sometimes tempered his observations. Occasionally Nicholas left the table to serve tea or help out in the kitchen. After a time we were joined by his wife and infant son.

The two grandsons did more than reminisce. They puzzled. They formed and tested hypotheses. They examined now one side, now the other, of a question. Some of their impressions matched; some were discrepant. Both sensed that there had been an unspoken war for followers between their grandmother and grandfather. At one point Nicholas observed, "When Grandma plunked Mom down at the piano at the age of two and started practicing with her every day, it was a way of having influence over her that Grandpa didn't have. I really think that was part of it. I think Grandpa wrote off his son Jon. He speaks very little of Jon if at all. He wrote Jon off when he married a Gentile, much the way old Orthodox Jews used to say, 'You're dead.' When he talks about Jon the only thing he ever says is that he had very good hands and he should have been a surgeon."

"Plus, Jon had many of the same obsessions that Grandma does. He is very involved with the arts."

"Now, when their second son came along ten years later, he turned out to be a brilliant child. Grandpa must have been in his early forties when David was born, and he devoted an incredible amount of energy to this kid. Two winters in a row he took him out of school and they went on fantastic voyages down the Amazon. David was only in grade school at the time, and he would come home after two or three months at a shot and do all of the homework in one night. That's what Grandpa said. I don't know whether or not it's true. I think Grandpa put more effort into David than into anything in his life. That's why David went to the best private school, that's why he went to Harvard. And when David finally broke away and said he was not going to medical school, I'm sure that was a great shock to my grandfather."

"It was unbelievable. Oh, it was one of the most hideous traumas."

"Especially since he went into romance languages, which is more of Grandma's thing."

"I would like to find out when their marriage, which must have had some degree of love and affection, just dissolved into total. . . . The intensity of the anger Grandpa feels for her! In my private mind growing up, my feeling was that she must have had an affair with somebody and that was absolutely the most outrageous last straw to Grandpa and at that point he just drew up the drawbridge and retreated to the other side of the house. But no one knows."

"The most amazing thing is that when you hear Grandpa talk now, it sounds as though he was constantly trying to leave Grandma. The stories get jumbled, but as I understand it Grandma was in New York before the birth of Mom and Grandpa was in Pennsylvania. He was going to take off, and his father called Grandma and said, 'You better get here if you plan on hanging on to this guy.' And she hustled down here. That's one story I got. God knows whether it's really true. I think it was 1964 when he moved out of their bedroom complaining that the turning of the pages when she read at night was keeping him up. But I never thought . . . . It's really like something out of Chekhov. Just the other day I called up to say hello and Sarah was the only one home. So I talked to her for awhile. She is so entwined with all of this that she just begins to shout whenever she talks about it. She just screams into the phone. I said something like, 'You know, Grandma really needs more distractions, some friends,' because all of her friends have either died or moved away. Before I even finished she said, 'Yes, I told her if she quit having all those boy friends all these years, and started having some girl friends, she'd probably have a lot more people she could talk to.' I went, 'Boy friends?' I don't know anything about boy friends. Maybe I'm just totally naive. I have no idea. It would be a real shock to me to think if . . . . "

Near the end of the evening we came to the subject of Alec's art. The first head he ever did was of his grandfather, and he did it at the precise time when he was struggling for freedom from his influence. "When you do a portrait you examine someone else and tell what you think they are. And you're trying to get out of yourself whatever you feel you are. I was prompted to do him because it was a psychological necessity, almost. I mean, Nicholas has spent a lot of time with Grandpa now, talking to him about medical problems. But I also had the feeling you were talking with him because you're trying to come to terms with what he did to you."

"I'm thinking of the time when you were doing his head and I happened to come home and there is this great explosion, and Grandpa is all in a tizzy. Evidently he was sitting for Alec's head, and I guess he was just spouting doom and gloom the whole time until you got so mad you threw him out."

"It would get me. It was so depressing to have to sit and listen to him talk. It was profoundly demoralizing and actively crushing. But of course this has been going on since we can remember. From the very start of our existence, the same paranoia and a savage sense of pessimism and doom, incredibly strong. And I was trying to work, and when you work if you're tremendously depressed it is very hard because you have to concentrate hard. He was getting me so depressed I couldn't work anymore, so I finally told him he either had to shut up or he had to leave. I told him to get out, he was driving me so crazy."

"I think it's probably the best head Alec has done. I know Grandpa's personality and all the various sides of it, and I see them all in the head. You look at it from one way, it looks more optimistic, another more pessimistic, another side more serious. It really has a lot of feeling, a fire, an intenseness."

"Grandpa always looked like an avenging eagle to me. He has this tremendously intense stare, and he cranes his head forward like a hawk that's about to strike, but it's a completely defensive posture. He's looking and examining the environment to protect himself, not to go out and actually do something. So I was trying to capture that. I left the eyes empty, because he always had that deep, internal feeling about what he was to say."

"The last time we met, which was just a little less than a month ago, I asked him what it was like to be a Jew growing up, and he said it was extremely difficult. I said, 'Well, how did you even get into the gymnasium?' He said you had to pay. I don't know if it was a bribe or not, but he said you had to pay an incredible amount of money. Then for him to go up north to St. Petersburg, to the polytechnic institute, he said they had to pay thousands of rubles just because he was Jew."

"Once during the Passover service a couple of years ago, we were reading from a new Haggadah about the Jews in Russia, and they mentioned this certain pogrom which had been particularly savage. Grandpa happened to be reading at that point. He stopped in the middle of a sentence and said, 'I was there.' It just flashed in my mind: this picture of a five-year-old kid in little knickers or something, standing in the street and watching these Cossacks hurtling down the street, slicing people's heads off, slashing people to ribbons—all people he knew. He turned and said, 'The blood was running down the street just like it was raining.' So I'm thinking, if you are a five-year-old kid growing up in an environment where your life and the lives of everyone you know are threatened all the time, and you are powerless to defend yourself, that fact of life gets translated into an attitude which he has, that you're helpless to defend yourself against powers which are greater than you are."

Seven years after he completed his grandfather's portrait, Alec started on his grandmother's. "About half a year ago I started to do her head. She was incredibly enthusiastic about it. She was always saying, 'It's a miracle that you can do this.' When I was doing it, I was taping her stories. I was trying to get her history on tape, and there's no more perfect occasion than when she is just sitting there. So I worked and she talked. I was trying to get a picture of what life was like for her. When I wanted to find out what really happened I had to press her for very specific details. For instance, I wanted to know what the actual days and weeks were like when the Communists came to their town and her father was shot. I said, 'What exactly happened? Where did you find him? How did you find out he was shot?' And I found out amazing things I'd never heard before.

"She said, 'Someone came to our house and told us that a whole bunch of people had been rounded up and shot in a certain square.' I said, 'That must have been terrible!' She went, 'Yeah,' and I said, 'So what happened?' 'So we went down there and there he was. He was just lying on the street.'

"I said, 'Wait. You left the house, you walked down the street, you came into this square, and there was your father lying dead?' She goes, 'That's right. He was just lying on the street, shot. He was dead.' I said,

'Well, what happened then?' She said, 'Well, it was very difficult to get somebody to take him home.' But somebody—I don't know whether it was Gramp or not—got a wheelbarrow and picked her father out of the street, dropped him in, and wheeled him back to their house. I mean, that upset me, but she described it with this offhand sense of that was fate and that was life. They went out and there he was and he was dead. I mean the story was not a story that was told with a great sense of tragedy.

"I think Grandma's experience growing up in Odessa was that she knew Jews were discriminated against, but it wasn't a personal experience for her. For him it was a daily thing. Her father worked at the opera, and it was fairly pleasant. Maybe the generation before her had already assimilated to a certain extent and that was the value that was preached to her. I always had the sense of her trying to leap this wall of home life and religion that she thought surrounded her and lead her life on a plane which took her beyond that. Maybe there was a perception in her mind that being involved in the family was somehow a lower-class thing to do and that an aristocratic czarina type should be spending time at concerts with musicians and artists. So growing up with her I never had the feeling, which was a very intense feeling with dad's family, that she actively loved you. She had affection for you in some abstract sense, but never that sense that caring for her family and maintaining it, imbuing it with family spirit, was an important goal in itself. On family occasions like Passover, she would come, but you never had the sense that she was participating or that this was important to her.

"I have the feeling that somewhere between the Soviet Union and this country some gears which should have meshed didn't. She must have felt an intense need to hang on to what she had there, to continue her life as if nothing had happened. There was a very active attempt to create in Mom a personage who was a reincarnation of everything Grandma would have liked to have become in the Old World if Lenin had never come to power. If Grandma could have been an aristocratic lady who was famous in the arts and had a beautiful house and all these old master paintings, that's what she would have done there. And she created that environment here with her house.

"I wanted to put in her head this sense of remove, a kind of aristocratic remove from the world, and also a sense of pain, a feeling that somehow the world had betrayed her, that things have not turned out the way they were supposed to have and there is nothing that can be done about it. So you have in the turn of the head a projection of everything she imagined life was supposed to be, but then in the cast of the eyes and the features a sense of all that disappointment that things have not turned out."

INTERPRETATION: SILENCES;

HOW MEMORIES SPEAK

When I think of Hannah Gordon's last conversation with me in her study, I think of an empty stalk in an autumn field. The man she loved had died, her memory was fading, and she was left with "a great void." To understand her in this emptiness I had to go to the people and objects that would survive her death: to her daughter, to an artist whom she had inspired and helped, to the art with which she had filled her house, and finally to her grandsons. The first two women in this volume of life stories were approaching forty and looking upward to second chances at generativity. The third was in her fifties and at her generative peak. Hannah Gordon was in physical decline, and the circumstances of her life remind us of what remains *after* generativity.

And yet, when I recall my first glimpse of Hannah entering the auditorium where her daughter performed, and especially when I picture her giving her own concerts in melodeclamation (which she still does), I think of someone full of life. It is Hannah's culture—art—that gives her this life, and her identity is fused as thoroughly with art as Josette Biondi's is with religion. Hannah sees her life against a backdrop of literature and music, most of it from nineteenth-century Russia. If you were to ask about people in her life, she would recite a translation of *Hamlet,* or quote Pushkin, or describe a scene from an opera of Tchaikovsky. Whereas Sister Josette draws sustenance from identifying with mythologized religious figures, Hannah Gordon draws it from identifying with writers and painters and musicians and actors—with the doers of great deeds in her culture. And when she can perform in their medium she is radiant.

I chose to include Hannah's story in this collection because, as a great-grandmother, she heads one of the four-generation families whose number is increasing. Her living conditions—near, but not in the same house as her grandchildren—typify the circumstances of many of the elderly in the past two and a half decades. These circumstances, combined with longevity, create the conditions for unprecedented influence upon grandchildren, an extreme of which fell upon Alec and Nicholas. In their early thirties, they are still lifting the weight of that influence off their shoulders, and they speak of the process—"trying to figure ourselves out over the years," "getting an adult perspective on what they were saying to us as children"—the way others speak of separating from their parents. The power of grandparents is actually understated in "In a

Dream Castle," for the boys had to contend not with two but with four dominating figures. In some ways Hannah was the most remote of the lot, exerting her influence not through her person but through the atmosphere she created.

By the end of our evening together, Alec, Nicholas, and I began to realize that their grandfather Gordon had literally fought for possession of their minds against the subtle but pervasive influence of their grandmother. His battle was intensified by the defection of his own two sons, one of whom married outside Judaism and became involved in the arts, the other of whom refused to go to medical school and became a linguist. Having lost a war for successors in the first generation to follow him, he began another in the second. Competing now with two other grandparents as well as his wife, he propagandized his grandsons with the subtlety of a "lightning bolt." The conflict Alec and Nicholas felt between science and art can be traced two generations back to a personal conflict between David and Hannah Gordon, about which the boys are largely in the dark.

Because Hannah's memory is failing, and because she is unwilling to say more about the men in her life, her grandsons may remain in the dark. It is the darkness in their exchange with Hannah that I wish to address in this interpretation. I want to reflect first on the causes and consequences of silences like hers and then show how her spoken memories, incomplete as they are, shed light on the meaning with which she presently imbues her life.

INTERGENERATIONAL SILENCES

It was clear from the first minutes of my first conversation with Hannah Gordon that she was suffering from failures of memory. On some days she was able to recall more than on others, and she repeated herself constantly because she had forgotten what she had just said. Although conversations with other subjects unlocked fresh memories, nothing similar happened with Hannah, except, perhaps, when she made the fleeting revelation of her love affair. She seemed to recall the words with which she had encoded events, but she could not retrieve the events themselves. She would reiterate a sentence about her mother having a migraine or her father being shot, she would recite a literary passage that symbolized a relationship in her life, but she could not amplify beyond these formulas. In the midst of cerebral decline, Hannah had access to those parts of her life that had been stored in words, recited often, and spoken of recently.

But the silences in Hannah Gordon's story were not caused by memory failure alone. She could have said more about her differences with her husband and even more about her love affair, but she chose not to. Her reasons will remain her own, but their broad outline may be understood by a comparative look at silences that occurred in other stories.

These other silences fall into several categories. The most common was silence "for the record": roughly half the narrators came to a point at which they asked me to turn off the tape recorder. Then they acknowledged that their father had been in jail or that they themselves had evaded taxes, or they would vent their true feelings about the man their daughter married or disclose that their spouse had a drinking problem. I was a collaborator in maintaining these silences, and so they are omitted in the finished portraits in which more than a few people are not named and more than a few identities carry excessive disguises. Subtler silences—for me as well as for the record—occurred when a narrator closed the door on further questions with a quip, or revealed a less-secret secret to cover *the* secret, or attracted me away from one area of life by excessive talk about another—or simply declined to say more. It is entirely possible that some of these subtler silences resulted from intrapsychic repression.

Not all the reasons for silence were revealed to me, and even when they were, not all could be placed in meaningful categories. But I could watch the interplay between narrative on the record and off the record, I could listen to clues that accompanied silence, and I could study silences that were eventually broken. From these observations I noted that three kinds of material tended to be suppressed.

The first involved episodes of defeat and humiliation when individuals were overwhelmed by forces they could not control, when they momentarily *ceased to be actors* in the drama of their own lives. Several women chose not to name men who had kept them dependent and abused them. Men who bragged of sexual exploits were reluctant to bring up periods of impotence. Failures in work were also muted, and it was not failure per se, but failure that left one crushed in its wake that brought an end to words. The same was true of trauma. Horror itself did not induce silence; being numbed by constant horror or acquiescing in horror did. If a victim had been outraged by an atrocity and resisted in some way, if he or she had outwitted the victimizer, the episode was spoken of. Otherwise it was not. Even if individuals had words to carry their stories through times when they were helpless and out of control, their emotions were stilled. When an alcoholic came to an attempted suicide that culminated years of binges, her narrative became a deadened litany of the concrete: I got in the car, I went out, I had some beer, I got some gas, I tried to kill myself. It was a rendition shorn of affect and elaboration.

If silence shrouded events in which one ceased to act, it also covered episodes in which one acted, but *acted badly*—the second category of omissions. Though Dorothy Woodson and Erzsi Domier spoke openly about the damage they had done to children (and for that reason their stories are included in this volume), most narrators avoided discussion of the harm they had inflicted on others. Usually it was I who had to raise questions about important people omitted from a story, and I would find that regret, guilt, or grief had motivated the omission. Individuals acted badly not only by harming others but by violating the norms of their cultures. When stories were told, narrators were quiet both about their own transgressions and those of close friends and relatives. I had to guess about the nature of many hushed violations: conceiving a son out of wedlock, acting cowardly in war, experiencing and perhaps acting out homosexual inclinations, having an abortion. There were tendencies to speak only good of the deceased, to respect confidences, to avoid saying things that would injure relationships, to protect one's self-image, and to keep from children the knowledge that one had acted badly.

A third and rare kind of silence protected what individuals and families held most dear—the very holy as opposed to the unholy. This silence is exemplified by an incident I described when discussing the verification of life stories in Chapter 3. After seeing a draft of the biography of her family, a mother showed me two documents she had previously withheld. One was a meditative note written by her husband before his second surgery for cancer, and the other was a letter written by a psychiatrist after he died. Only the immediate family had ever seen these papers, and there was a feeling that one should not speak of what one saw. The messages they contained were spontaneous, not contrived, and spoke to the heart of what the deceased father meant to the family. They had been part of the family's "sacred center" to which few had access.

In view of these categories of silence, possible reasons for Hannah Gordon's suggest themselves. Although there never appeared to be a time when she was reduced by life to inaction, her affair was in violation of familial if not cultural norms. To speak of it now would only aggravate her relationship with her husband, who is old and infirm. It would destroy the picture of herself that she has cultivated in the minds of her children and grandchildren. And yet . . . Hannah may have acted badly in a different sense: her affair may not have measured up to her romantic ideal. Perhaps her love was not as grand and passionate as it should have been. Perhaps there was no single man or perhaps he was no Eugene Onegin. On the other hand, perhaps there was, and to speak of her love to an outsider, or even to her grandchildren, would be to defile it. Revelation would destroy her own sacred center, stripping away the romance that encases the affair in her memory.

Whatever the reasons for Hannah's reticence, her secret has affected her grandsons. Something has been passed on without awareness, a residue that I call a hidden legacy. In such a legacy there corresponds to the progenitor's silence a slow discovery in progeny that a secret has directed the course of their lives and must be found out. Alec and Nicholas have an easier task of discovery than Erzsébet Domier, whose parents' legacy was covered with lies, protected by the distance of an ocean, and eventually sealed by death. Though Hannah's story is slowly sinking into the oblivion of a failing memory, there is still time to ask her questions and make her legacy more explicit.

And that explains the urgency behind her grandsons' questions and their recording of her memories. Just as the anticipation of death can stimulate in elders a desire to leave a conscious legacy, so it can heighten in the young a desire to extract one. If the silence in a legacy is important enough, if the hints of what is there are compelling enough, if the sense is present that the secret is still affecting the person's life, the younger generation will increase pressure on the older to reveal. If revelation is not forthcoming, the young will fill the silence with their own projections. The sense of disappointment that Alec molded into his grandmother's sculpture was a statement about a period in her life, but it was just as much a statement about a period in his.

HOW MEMORIES SPEAK

Still, even with the silence it now contains, even with the gaps that invite projection, Hannah Gordon's story speaks, and speaks eloquently. For her grandsons, the trick is to know of what it speaks.

Psychologists who study memory have come to emphasize that it is a constructive process. Long-term memories in particular appear to be creations that depict what happened after a remembered event as much as or even more than the event itself. Elizabeth Loftus's well-known studies of eyewitnesses show that memory for accidents is shaped not merely by the perception of the original event but also by information gathered after the fact and even by the language used by interrogators who question the witnesses. All three sources blend into one "memory."[1] Ulric Neisser has suggested that the consistency in the structure of "flashbulb" memories (vivid recollections of hearing the news of historic events) results from the current requirements of narrative rather than from a "printing" mechanism that stamped the events in memory.[2] Hannah Gordon's early—and even her "first"—memories have the same quality. They are best understood as symbols of a sequence of events that took place long after the scenes depicted.[3]

What we call a "first" memory means different things to different narrators. To some, the first memory is the childhood recollection with which they open their life story. To others, it is the memory that is chronologically the earliest, the one that reaches farthest back in time. To still others, it is the childhood memory to which they ascribe primacy, that is, the one they see as a prototype or cause of other events. No matter which memory is designated as first, and no matter what meaning the designation has, I have found that it and other early memories are more than representations of the past. Very often they are metaphors for narrators' unconscious intuitions about major life motifs and about the present conditions of their lives. This is what early and especially first memories speak of.

The first three stories in this collection illustrate the power of first memories to condense into a single childhood event motifs that have lasted for decades. Dorothy Woodson's beginning memory of running lost and terrified through grass over her head, for example, represents her condition at critical moments later in life: she feels small, unnoticed, and frightened, and she does not know where to turn. (The memory is thematically the same as a memory from adulthood: she is lost in a blizzard, snow is flying over her head, and she cannot find her way.) Erzsébet Domier's earliest memory of sitting in the lap of a fatherly man and grabbing his pipe is an apt symbol, especially when taken in a Freudian sense, of her adolescent and adult life. Sister Jo Biondi, who has felt restless and confined from her novitiate days on, has a distinct first memory of being in a baby carriage and wanting to get out. Though these early memories depict childhood events, they are better understood as intuitions of major life motifs—as single, clear recollections seized by the imagination now because they have the capacity to condense and express perceptions of the route a life has taken.

Early memories also contain latent intuitions about the present condition of a life. Accompanying Dorothy Woodson's memory of running through tall grass, for example, is a cluster of early images filled with the fear of sickness and death that comes unseen. She eats a tomato and breaks out in hives, her brothers and sisters scream at a snake she does not see, she lies awake at night in dread of a fire that will come unannounced. These memories surface at a time when an unseen and potentially lethal lump in her breast is getting larger. Similarly, a man fearing a second and fatal heart attack declares his first memory to be of his grandmother's death. He remembers in particular how the family dog that had been lying on her bed stepped down the moment she passed away. Early memories often serve the function for individuals that myths of the world's creation do for collectivities. They explain and legitimate the present by relating it to founding events that took place "in the beginning."[4] In Alfred Adler's words, a person's earliest recollection is "his subjective starting point, the beginning of the autobiography he has made for himself."[5]

As the conditions of a life change, then, so will the content of the early images one can remember. "In so far as [an individual's] style of life alters," Adler writes, "his memories also will alter; he will remember different incidents, or he will put a different interpretation on the incidents he remembers."[6] When the subject of a forthcoming story recovered from alcoholism in his fifties, he discovered a number of pleasant memories from childhood that had previously been lost to him. I have even noticed that early memories reflect the changing climate of the teller-listener dyad. It was not until the end of her story, for instance, that Dorothy Woodson and I consciously reflected on her grace, and it was not until then that she revealed a childhood memory of a ballet teacher telling her of that grace. In Hannah Gordon's storytelling there was a continual parallel between the way she defined me and the way she described the men of her memory. Memories, in Adler's words, can be used to "stabilize a mood."

These early memories that change over the course of a life and even over the course of a life-storytelling often exist in contrasting pairs that are thematically related. Dorothy Woodson recalled feelings of beauty and grace along with feelings of ugliness. Erzsi Domier remembered an environment that scolded and terrified her along with a man who was an island of safety and warmth. Contrast often makes one particular episode stand out: it was the *only* time my father gave me a whipping, or (in a story to come) it was the *only* time my father paid attention to me. In interpreting first memories one must be aware that an opposite may lurk behind the memory that is presented. One therefore pays less attention to *whether* a memory denies or asserts and is very sensitive to *what* a memory denies or asserts.

How, then, do Hannah Gordon's memories, filled as they are with gaps, speak? And what do they speak of?

The most detailed of Hannah's memories are early images of Odessa, and these fall into two contrasting sets. On one side are recollections of the sordid side of life, and the prototype in this set is the one with which she begins her story. "Poor," "miserable," and "demented" entertainers are in the courtyard of her apartment, and she and other children tease and torment them. "I tell you that because I feel so guilty for having been part of those cruel children." Other memories in this cluster were passed on to me by Hannah's grandson. Hannah had told him of village idiots, of old men who peed in the gutters, and of gypsies who would steal your valuables if you were not careful. Hannah's mention of guilt in connection with her teasing is striking because guilt is rarely mentioned in her story.

I believe this cluster of memories represents Hannah's latent intuition about her own present condition. She had told me how dangerous it was for her to go to the city at night, and I later learned that she had twice been the victim of attempted street robberies. Thieves, like the gypsies she recalled, had literally tried to take away her valuables. Hannah identified with and felt compassion for the courtyard entertainers who, like herself, were unable to defend themselves. She felt guilty over teasing them as a child, and in her loneliness she felt as "poor" and "miserable" as they. Her description of them as "demented" is particularly poignant. I take it as an unconscious perception of her own loss of mental capacity.

Hannah's contrasting and by far dominant cluster of memories is typified by the incident she described when I asked specifically about a first memory. The memory she revealed was not first in the sense of earliest; it was, rather, a memory of first importance. Peter, the handsome young tutor who joined the military, comes one day in his "beautiful" uniform to take her for a promenade. "Imagine me with an officer!" Hannah exclaimed, as if she were once again walking that boulevard lined with acacia trees. It should be clear how often the central image of her first memory is reiterated in her story. It appears in her descriptions of her father, of the literature she loved, of the young men who admired her in Odessa, of a professor who infatuated her, of the older men who treated her "royally" in New York, and, fleetingly, of her secret lover. "A love affair is the most beautiful part of a human being's life," Hannah said once. Her dominant set of memories says it over and over again.

Hannah's cluster of romantic memories, then, depicts a major life motif, a statement she makes about the path of meaning her life has traveled. All these memories follow the theme of her very first: "Imagine me with an officer!" To be dreamily and painfully in love, to be in love as the heroines of great Russian literature were in love: this is the ideal that has always guided her, this is what gives meaning to her now, this is her lifeline to the collective symbol system we call culture. Memories that do not fit her ideal are falling fast by the wayside. The selectivity of memory is thus another mechanism through which the self is affixed to a culture. Though Hannah forgets the concrete details of her life, she recalls the literary passages and the melodeclamation that constitute elements of art. As the light of her memory continues to dwindle, it will focus ever more narrowly on her belief that only a love affair can give meaning to a human life.

In sum, Hannah Gordon's memories speak not by providing more detail about her past, but by revealing how she perceives herself as one who is becoming vulnerable and losing her mental capacity and how she yet remains attached to a sustaining culture. This is the culture she will remember at the end, and this is the culture for which she will be remembered.

Far from being lost on her grandson, the tension between Hannah Gordon's contrasting set of memories was captured perfectly by his sculpture. In her downcast eyes he injected the cold reality of her life as it currently was, but in the turn of her head he depicted her idealization of lifelong motifs. Though Alec still has questions about his grandmother's life, he has already sensed what her memories speak of.

PART III

The Stories
of Four Men

8 · Being a Daddy

We always met on the same street corner, a place where Robert Creighton feels at home. The first time I saw him I was waiting in a cafeteria and caught a glimpse through the window of a black man with a soft yet muscular physique. He was wearing a plaid shirt, Bermuda shorts, and sandals, and he carried a book. He entered the café, looked around, and stopped to chat with some of the patrons. Then he came over to my table, sat down, and started talking.

Our meeting had come about because of a newspaper story I had seen—a Father's Day article in which Robert reflected on his jealousy toward his wife during his first months as a father. "I wished I could breast-feed the child so he would gravitate toward me," he had said. Wanting to record the story behind that statement, I contacted Robert, and he agreed to meet me.

We had hamburgers and Cokes and talked about my work. Robert had a square, handsome face, little hair on top of his head, but a thick, closely trimmed beard. His eyes were dark and active. When we had finished eating, we went outside, crossed the street, and sat on the grass under a tree. There, once a week on sultry August evenings, against the sleepy roar of buses, the song of birds, and an occasional police siren, he recounted his life. As we talked, he was recognized, waved at, spoken with. I do not remember him ever standing quietly on that corner. Even now I can picture him waiting for me, head bobbing, arms thrusting, people reacting around him. Talking, he once told me, was his way "of getting a grip on the world."

I

Once into his story, Robert became loud and dramatic. Born the youngest of three boys in 1945, he grew up in Chicago apartments teeming with aunts and uncles and cousins. On warm summer nights, he said, rolling back and forth on the grass, "tons" of kids would run and holler in the streets while old people sat on the stoops and watched. Later, gangs replaced the kids, swarming "like locusts" over the streets, wielding guns and knives. "Gigantic" cops would appear, "millions" of them, and "beat up" on people. Robert jitterbugged from one incident to the next, amplifying his thoughts with gesture and rhetoric. He knew he was prone to "run off at the mouth," but he wanted to be sincere. He was in his element here, telling stories on a street corner, using words to get his grip on the world.

His founding memory—the one reaching farthest into the past—is of the time a tall, skinny man with the smell of mechanic's grease came heroically to rescue him. "I was sick. I don't know what was wrong, but my entire body had swollen up. My mother called it a spasm, so I guess I was jerking. I remember being a little butterball lying in bed with all these lights on me and all these adults standing over. And they said, 'Well, let's call Will.' My father's name was William, and he lived on the other side of town. When my mother called him, he came over in fifteen minutes. I remember him picking me up and taking me to the hospital in his car—a black, shiny Plymouth. Beautiful!"

All that followed in Robert's childhood was a betrayal of that memory. In the apartment where he lived, his mother had two small signs, and she still has them today. In glitter glued on blue cardboard they said, "God Bless Our Home" and "What Is Home without a Father?"

"I remember especially the times before Christmas. My father would ask my older brother, 'Willie, what do you want?' 'I want some engineers' boots and an Ivy League hat, and this and that and so on.' 'Robert, what do you want?' 'I want this, that, and the other.' And he'd say, 'Okay, I'll bring it.' And Mother always told him in front of us, 'Will, I told you never to make promises to these boys.' As soon as he left she would say, 'Come here, boys. Look, don't depend on your father. If he brings it, fine. If he doesn't, fine.' She'd caution us, but we cried our eyes out anyway. On Christmas Day, we'd be sitting in the house, listening. When is Daddy gonna call? Sometimes he never called. Sometimes he called and said, 'I can't come.'

"As I grew up I was much aware of not having a daddy. And people used to say, 'You're silly. You have a daddy. Everybody's got a daddy. How could you be born without a daddy?' They knew what we meant by not having a daddy. Other kids' daddies would come home. They would eat and smoke and get clean and shave, and then they'd go in their car and take their brood with them, right? Well, where was my daddy? He had his nice car. Kids would brag about their daddies. My daddy could do this and my daddy could do that. Well, where was my daddy? I better not say anything about my daddy—I didn't have one. And you know kids are often cruel. They'd say, 'Where's your father? You ain't got no father. I bet he didn't even marry your mother.' My cousins, especially the ones close to my age, would ask, 'Why your daddy's like that?' And, well, usually you defended your father. You thought that's what you should do. Everybody else defended his father. But the difference was you didn't live with yours, right? So I felt punished. Why me? You know, why can't I have a daddy?

"We saw him two, three times a year. Mother would take a vote. My oldest brother would walk out. My other brother didn't want to see him, so he said, 'Naw, don't let him come over. What does he do for us but cause us grief?' And I'd say, 'Aw, he's our father.' I was probably hiding my feelings because I thought you should love a daddy even though he was a rat. Maybe I was hating his guts, but I would say, 'Yeah, bring him in.' And he'd come over and get tough. 'Are you obeying your mother? Are you doing what you're supposed to in school?' And he couldn't care. He didn't want to be bothered with kids. The only way he could deal with little people was to get tough with them. 'Shut up, be quiet, sit down!' But he wasn't even sincere in that. It was phony. He could care less, and we knew it.

"I thought he was the smartest thing on earth. He built this car when he was a teenager, right? I remember going to his shop when I was twelve. Watching him and asking questions. I said, 'Daddy, could I come by every Saturday? I won't ask too many questions. Just watch you fix cars so I can learn.' He said, 'No. I don't want you here.'

"I used to do things to provoke him and make him whip me. Anything to get this man's attention. I would stick out my lip and pout. I would grumble under my breath, loud enough to make him say something. And he'd say, 'Who do you think you're talking to? I'm your daddy!' Pat phrases—that's all he ever said. And I'd make little smart remarks like, 'You ain't my daddy.' And he'd drop it.

"I didn't want him to drop it. I can remember his cigarette stains on the face bowl on the commode. In the morning I'd get up and I'd trace the stains, and I would smell the oil and the dirt. Anything just to get close to him. But he would not have it.

"Mother used to tell us that Daddy never grew up. That's what she always told us. And we knew his family was poor and they had eight children. He couldn't read and he couldn't see. He had lots of problems. He was hardheaded. He was a topnotch mechanic, but he couldn't get jobs. I don't think he particularly minded white folks, but I don't think he liked them either. He didn't know how to talk to people. Maybe he was bashful or conscious of his dialect when he was talking to white folks. So he got hostile.

"I think he could not handle the responsibility of what it means to be a daddy. Having somebody look up to you, for you to give guidance to. That's too much pressure. I mean, I got my own self to look after, how can I make sure this kid eats and gets home safe? Why be shackled with kids?

"We'd go to his mother's house every summer until we were fairly large teenagers. That was a meeting place. All the relatives would come, all of her sons, their wives, their kids, and my daddy. The house was little, and he was big. You couldn't miss him. And he would come in there and not say a word to us. And my grandmother cursed a lot. She always used the word nigger. And she would say, 'Nigger, if you don't speak to them, you get out of my house.' And he would mumble, 'Aw, Mama,' and say something to us. He would goof around a little bit and then he would leave. He could not *stand* us! I believe that's it: he could not *stand* us! He always came places and left early—in the middle of everything. Everybody's having a good time and he'd get up and say, 'I'm going.' I remember when my grandmother died and we were at her funeral—the three of us, my mother, my brother, and I. We hadn't seen him for *years*! He was sitting dead in front of us, two seats apart. You know, he never turned around. He never once turned around! His mama was dead, and black folks—not black folks, people generally—get together on funerals and weddings. He did not even turn around and look at us."

II

"My mother was a great lady. She came from the South sometime in the 1920s. I don't think she was quite thirteen. She lived with her great-aunt and with cousins and cousins and cousins. Before you knew it she was married and had three babies and there she was. I mean, that was her life. She's always been strait-laced—you know, keeping close to home, cooking, washing the kids, and not being too fast. Never really having a chance to live out her childhood. There she was shackled with these babies, and then she had to make sacrifices for us—which she did. People used to praise me about how good mother was. She was special, and everybody told us that."

"A lot of people in my area were on dope. They went to jail for various things. They were making all sorts of babies. Every young girl, it seemed, was pregnant, and the person that got them pregnant was out braggin', sayin', 'Hey, man, I got all these babies.' Gangs were roving the streets and fighting. I can't remember the names of the gangs, but they were ruthless. People with guns and knives would walk the street. When the black gangs didn't fight themselves they'd fight the Puerto Rican gangs. When the Puerto Rican gangs didn't fight themselves, they'd fight the blacks.

"My mother figured, well, this kid is gonna get in trouble. So every time anybody got in trouble she pointed it out to me. I mean, she used to preach all the time. That's the way she was. Talk, talk, talk. She pointed out when several white kids raped and killed this woman. They were smokin' reefer. That was a bad thing, them reefer. And she'd point that out to me. She'd wake me up in the middle of the night and point out gangs roaming the streets, throwing things. 'That's the kind of thing you shouldn't do.' I can remember stealing at the A & P. She made me take it back. I can remember stealing from a bakery—those little tags you get to wait in line. I showed Mother, and she said, 'Take them back.' I took them back, and the lady was so pleased she gave me some apple turnovers. People used to say, 'If your mother ever died, I don't know what would happen to you.'

"She used to have an old purse. You could smell the plastic, and we used to wrap it around with ties to keep it closed. When the insurance man would come we used to open it up and take out the dollars and give it to him. She never missed a payment. She'd buy everything with cash, or when she did buy things on time she did not miss a payment. I remember Tommy's Corner Store. She did all her shopping there. Every Saturday morning for years he'd come and beat on the door, 'Your mother said to bring the groceries. You boys wake up now and put the groceries up.' When she got paid from her domestic work on Saturday, she'd get off the bus and go by Tommy's and open her little purse and pay him.

"For the first ten, thirteen years of my life I was on ADC and she was doing domestic work. And she had to school us in lies, which she hated. 'When the case workers come by, don't tell them I'm working.' She recognized the impracticality of not lying. The domestic work was usually once a week on Saturday. Sometimes she would stay all night. She would always talk about when my second brother was a baby and she took him out to the white folks' house and she put him and the white baby in the stroller together and pushed them out in the street. And she would tell us that white Jewish people eat this way, they have this kind of religion, their house is this way. That was exposure for us. She used to point out the Jewish boys that were going to Cook County Hospital. 'Say, come here, look how he dresses!'

"I was really having problems because I was trying to work out this black and white thing and I couldn't do it. I was always embarrassed because we were on ADC and my mother was doing domestic work. Kids would tease me about it. You know, 'Your mother's a flunky for white folks.'

"We had a cousin who was always drunk. He hated cops. *Hated* cops, right? I think it had something to do with his daddy. He hated his daddy. Always ready to fight a cop. Man, he'd fight fifty hundred cops. He'd get drunk and he'd start fighting. And they'd call the cops and these cops— they were black cops, and I mean they were gigantic, all football players it looked like—they would just beat him on his head. He would be bleeding, and they'd handcuff him and they'd drag him downstairs and threaten to shoot him. And people from miles around would come and see it. This happened regularly, and it always embarrassed me—just this elemental quality of people. I always associated that with black people. I didn't know whites.

"I think my first contact with whites was with poor whites. I never knew people were as poor as blacks. I thought we were the scum of the earth. I remember I went to a store because a fellow named Jimmy worked there. He was a gang member, and he was older, and he had some 'in' with all the gangs, and I was going to him to say these people were gonna jump on me this afternoon, would you come and tell them not to? And this white girl walked in. She had on shorts and no shoes, and it looked like dirt was embedded in her skin. And she said, 'Give me a pound of hamburger meat.' Which to me is redundant. Of course, I didn't know the word redundant then. And I heard that with this twang, right? And then I saw where they lived, you know, and the children were dirty and the houses smelled, and they didn't have much money. I never knew people were that poor.

"I never saw those places where my mother worked, but I could fantasize about them, torn with jealousy because I'm thinking these people got money. That's the way we grew up. This is a white man's world, and you always got to fight it. And if a white person doesn't make it in this world, something is wrong with him because this is his world to begin with. That kind of thing was pushed into us constantly. Not by my mother, but in the neighborhood. A lot of parents were racists, and they did preach that. My mother didn't. In fact she preached against it. People are people. My mother always taught us to respect people regardless of their color.

"I remember one time a Polish kid was standing on the street corner. He was a patrol boy with an orange belt. I walked up to him and kneed him in the butt. Softly. I mean, it couldn't hurt a fly. He turned around and looked, and I cried. These blacks and whites are looking at me like I'm crazy, and I'm crying because he didn't do anything to me and I kicked him. I patted him and hugged him and told him I'm sorry. I don't know if the kid said anything or not, but I went home crying and I told Mother. I'd always tell Mother what I'd do, every little thing.

"I was imitating what was happening in the neighborhood, but on the other hand I was getting away from it. So far as gangs were concerned, I was glib, I could run fast, I always had bigger brothers or cousins who knew everybody and gave me protection. So I escaped that and associated with people who were not in gangs. I used to play a lot of basketball. Alley-ball, we'd call it. I was pretty good. Hang out in the alleys and play basketball and at night sit on the porch and drink beer and chase the girls. And I got into track, and I ran track maybe three years.

"I'd always get put out of school. I got good grades, but I had a big mouth. I wouldn't listen to anybody. When I was fifteen or sixteen, they were gonna send me to a school for bad boys. But I was too young for that so they sent me to a school where I learned something about blueprint reading. I stayed there for about three to four months, but to stay out of trouble I went to boxing. I boxed for about three months. I wasn't that good. I had three fights, and I won trophies. Years later, I read Ralph Ellison's *Invisible Man* and it reminded me of one of the bouts I had. We went out to the South Shore Country Club, which now is surrounded by black folks, but then it was all white. It was a big thing to go out there. All these white folks were sitting at tables around this ring in the middle. We were eating spaghetti, and after a while we went to the ring and we started boxing. I was conscious of all these white folks out there. And then years later I read *Invisible Man*, and they got a scene like that, where all these rich white folks in the South are looking to see these niggers kill each other. You got these two blacks mauling one another in the ring and I'm thinking about that and I'm angry. This whole thing about my mother being a flunky, about our being on ADC, about there being no daddy around, about there being so much chaos in the black community. There's rapes and there's murders and there's fights and all these young girls got babies, and if I don't be careful I'm going to go right to jail. All this stuff is bombarding me. And then this crazy civil rights comes along."

III

"Civil rights," I was to discover, referred not only to a period in our nation's history but also to a time in Robert's life from roughly his sixteenth to his twentieth years. In his life, "civil rights" was a period of uncontrollable anger, which was half of a mysterious "double conscious-ness." Robert claims the anger is now largely gone, but when he spoke of those five years, he had a look of intense concentration and his jaw thrust forward just as it had when he remembered his father.

It was a woman, a cousin of his, who introduced him to civil rights. Around 1960 or 1961, he got involved with church workers who were coming into the black community to try to stop gangs from fighting.

"I got into civil rights crazy as hell then. I was gonna make everybody free. I was still in high school, and I went down to the School Board and sat in. Got put in jail and got my picture in the paper. I started growing a beard and dressing ragged. I alienated myself from my family. I wouldn't eat meals with them. I very seldom would take baths because somehow I thought you had to sacrifice yourself to bring the good to the people, right?

"I just went all the way out. We'd go downtown and we'd sing and we'd make noise and we'd block the street and just all the cops in the city were out. I remember diving under paddy wagons. I can remember one vigil downtown. You know downtown Chicago. You got these big tall buildings. You stand in the middle of LaSalle and say one word, you can hear it all over the place. I remember tons of cops lined up along City Hall. Tons of marchers walking—we taking shifts, you know. I gave a dialogue. I was a nigger and I was a white and I was playing these roles, assuming different voices. Jumping up on the police cars. I just absolutely flipped out. And when I finished, I was sweating. I was shaking. It was as though I had delivered a sermon. I was just wiped out completely. They wanted to arrest me. My uncle was a cop, and he was there, and he wouldn't let them arrest me. This woman I knew, she and her boy friend said, 'Come on, man,' and they took me to their house in Old Town.

"When I graduated from high school and went to junior college, I'd never come to school. When I'd come to school, I'd stand up in the middle of the classroom preaching about civil rights. I mean, you can't do that, but that's the kind of thing I was doing. So they put me out after six months. I mean I was taking this stuff real seriously. In my recurring dream I was strapping bombs and bullets and hand grenades to me. I figured if I could end the whole world that would be it. Maybe if I killed myself through killing other people, that would be it."

The other half of Robert's double consciousness—what restrained his impulse to blow everything up—was the sense that somebody was look-ing out for him. When it wasn't his mother, it was a white woman named Ellen. "I met a few people who were starting a community

newspaper, and they invited me to come over. So I went over there and
worked with them. I was in production, and this white woman, Ellen,
was head of production. She was maybe seven years older than me, and
we just took to each other. She was married and had kids, but she was
real active in civil rights. She was like my mother. When I wouldn't get
to work, she'd cover for me. Half the time I'd be out walking a picket
line, and she would tell the boss, 'Just leave him alone,' and she would
take care of my work. She would feed me, take me home, make sure that
I was straight. I mean, she was really keeping me out of trouble. She'd
say, 'Well, I think you should be cool. I don't think you should do that.'
She was always there.

"I remember a protest in front of Mayor Daley's house. It was on a
Sunday night, and we walked around the neighborhood. People were
drinking beer on the porch, calling us all sorts of names. They had
gigantic dogs straining on leashes inside the fences. See, I'm getting
angry, right? And Al Raby and Dick Gregory sayin', 'Be cool. Don't say
anything to them. Let them say something to you, but you be dignified.'
And I'm saying that's nonsense, we got a right to defend ourselves. So
I'm going around cheerin' everybody on, right? So they got me arrested.

"And that's when I really felt bad. I mean—God!—here the leaders
are arresting me and I mean nothing but good. They handcuff me and
I'm so helpless. Ellen is in the crowd looking at me and she can't help
me. And nobody wants to hurt me. They're saying, 'Look, man, you're
ruining what we're doing. We've got to get rid of you.'

"So I go to court and there's tons of us, you know. We're standing up
talking, and my back is to the bench, so when the judge comes in, I don't
see him. The bailiff comes up to me and pushes me down. 'Sit down.' I
say, 'Wait. What you talkin' about?' When the cops see this, they think
I'm hassling the bailiff. 'Cause, you know, we gesticulating and everything, so they come, and the bailiff says, 'Get him out, get him out, get
him out!' So I'm walking to the door, you know, and I'm steaming. Just
millions of cops in the hallway and I get so mad—this is my recurring
dream of killing everybody—I just turn around and say, 'You cock-
suckers!' And just a million cops jump on me. Take me to the elevator,
handcuff me, smack me in the head with the back of a pistol, right? Not
hurtin' me, just scarin' me to death. Pushing me into the wall, taking me
out to their car. 'You black nigger, we gonna kill you.' And I'm just
shaking, right? They not gonna bother me, but I don't know that.

"So I went to the county lockup for thirty days. Ellen took me there
and kissed me and gave me money. Told me to take it easy. She wrote
and sent me books. The jail was a trip. I was totally different from
everybody in that place. I was a high school graduate. I had taught

myself to talk. I could read. I could write. They put me in with the young kids, not the old kids. So I was really big. I was a civil righter, so people respected me, and I knew Dick Gregory and they respected me. I'd been rubbing shoulders with all sorts of people who'd done all sorts of things.

"When civil rights first started I was really angry. I was bombarded with emotions I couldn't handle. I was young. Perhaps I was angry because I couldn't get into an apprenticeship program. Originally what I wanted to do when I graduated from high school was to follow the steps of my teacher and go to college and work on an industrial arts degree. Work as an apprentice printer until I got my journeyman's card and then come out and teach high school printing. But I couldn't get a job. Here I was aspiring to something that perhaps was beyond me. It was all mixed up. Perhaps if I'd had a mother and father, perhaps if things had been different for me, maybe I would have been able to control myself more in civil rights.

"I was frustrated, and I saw no real reason why things were the way they were. I said, God, it would be great if I could make a change, and the way I saw myself making a change was this bomb bit. But even concurrently I think I was saying, man, I just want to get away from it all. I don't know whether I got it from Martin Luther King or not, but he used to talk about going on the mountain. And for years my metaphor for getting myself together was to take my mother and my portable typewriter and sit on top of a mountain."

IV

Thirty days in jail with books and a journal helped calm Robert. His peaceful mountaintop fantasy came to the fore, and the vision of himself strapped with bombs faded. He was twenty when he left jail, and he was going to make the world right through thinking, not aggression. He got a War on Poverty job as a street worker who would control tensions between warring gangs. "I didn't care so much about their fighting, but I wanted them to *think*." The job lasted until funds ran out eight months later, in December 1966. Then another government program enabled him to enroll in a community college on a work-study program. He got a job at a YMCA and accepted Ellen's invitation to live in the attic of her house. He became more serious about writing. He kept up his journal and wrote short stories and essays about his experiences. His life began to have stability.

Then, in April 1967, standing on a street corner, he met another woman. "She was in a car with my boss, George. And George said, 'There's Robert. Hey, come here, Robert.' And I walked over, and I got kind of hip. I say, 'Yeah, I'm a writer,' and I start bragging about myself. Her name was Peggy. She was white, and she was running around with a group of black kids who were musicians. She was the impresario. She was taking these kids around to help them make contacts. That meeting was pretty much it until I saw her again on the street. Some black cat was trying to talk to her, you know, and she didn't want to be rude. She say, 'Well, I'd rather you not' and all that kind of nonsense, which to me was white folks' talk. And I say, 'Hey brother, get away.' I didn't get too tough, but I was firm. He walked away.

"She was a Joan Baez type with this long dress. I say, 'Hey, look, I get off at seven o'clock. Can I come around and talk to you?'

"It's the strangest thing. We took a walk around the neighborhood, we came back to the house, we sat on the couch and played music, and all I did from eleven to seven in the morning was talk. Talk, talk, talk—just like I'm talking to you now, in a tougher voice though. Then I had street language, you know, the black idiom. She just listened. She didn't have anything to say. She was quiet, and she had what I called white ways—very timid and shy—and I had what I called black ways—very aggressive. It was a complete clash.

"She had been in a nunnery, and she lived in a house full of ex-nuns. Crazy as hell. Religion never meant a thing to me. My mother and grandmother had been Baptists and sanctified and I thought they went a bit far with it. But here were these people all white, all Catholic, and all crazy. That's what I thought of them—nuts! And I cursed and I talked and I was rough. I had taken two courses in existential philosophy down at the Y, so I was full of it, right? I was just spouting. They thought I was absolutely nuts, and I thought they were absolutely nuts. We did everything different, talk different, look different, walk different. I was almost openly antagonistic to them. They had been white, middle-class girls that had gone to the nunnery to become nuns, and all of a sudden they left, just like that. And here they were holed up in apartment on the west side of Chicago trying to get their lives together. And they were having tons of problems. They were going to psychiatrists, and they would call them their shrink or their psych, and they would pay twenty, twenty-five dollars a visit. You know, it's hard getting your head to-gether, but that role was traditionally filled in the black community by preachers, by older folks, and simply by having an extended family. I was part of that. Even though I wouldn't seek help from the preacher, I would from the older black men and women. People ten years older than me would teach me to shoot pool, to talk to the girls, to drink, show me when the cops are coming. You would learn that way. Going to psychia-trists meant nothing to me.

"Slowly she began to talk. She was from Nebraska, and she was trying to deal with the problems of her mother and father being dead. Her folks died when she was a teenager. Her family was split up. She and her younger sister had to go to California, and her two brothers stayed in Nebraska. She didn't like the aunt and uncle who became her guardians. She was in a Catholic school so she figured her escape was the church. She ran out to be a nun. But she couldn't hack that. She got ulcers and left after six months. She went back to Nebraska and went to nursing school. She quit, she tried to commit suicide, she was hanging out playing the guitar and wearing sandals. Somehow she got to Chicago, and she was sort of on the edge of it—as I was, you know. She would cry and she would miss Nebraska and she hadn't seen her brothers and sisters. She was used to the country, and here in the city it was cramped. People were bugging her. People were making nasty remarks to her. And she was going nuts!

"I always talked about my mama. I loved my mama. That was my home base—the whole concept of mother. 'Everybody has a mother' is what I used to say. That meant everything. If you had a mother, you were all right, and everybody has a mother. Like in high school when I wanted to puncture the tires of my gym teacher, I said to myself, If it weren't for my mother and grandmother, I'd do this. If I wanted to do something evil to somebody, I would say to myself, How would his mother feel if I did that? That sort of stabilized me.

"I think Peggy recognized the love and the need for stability. After I was in school a while, I think she realized that I was serious about it and that I wanted to do something. We talked all the time, and it wasn't a game like I'm on top of the world and I can do anything I want. I had problems and I cried. I never hid anything. I never pretended. I mean if something would upset me and I couldn't deal with it, I'd cry. I recognized, too, that my talking was a way of dealing with a lot of my problems. She recognized it. I talked about why I talk so much, why I talk loud, why I talk incessantly. I knew why. It wasn't a way of putting others down or saying look at me, I'm good, I'm better. It was just a way of keeping myself from blowing up.

"She had heard tons of stereotypes about blacks, just as we all hear about one another, so she had to deal with my blackness. She had to deal with my maleness, too. I'm aggressive, I'm not quiet, I'm all over the place. It's hard to take me at times. But she went through it with no problems.

"We started seeing each other all the time, and Ellen was saying, 'Don't get involved living with a woman. You get her pregnant, what is going to happen? You don't want to get married. Look at you. You're just barely getting yourself together.' In the sixties, whites and blacks were going together and getting married, and she figured, hey man, that's faddish. 'You're just being caught up in a fad, and it won't do you any good.' She began to cry, and I got upset. I don't know if it was because Peggy was white or because she figured I was going to get shackled with a woman just when I was getting my head together. Finally, I moved from the attic and got an apartment with Peggy."

That winter, as Robert was finishing his two-year degree in the community college, he began to apply for financial aid to four-year universities. He was helped by a district head of the Office of Economic Opportunity to whom he had shown some of his writing. When Martin Luther King was assassinated in April 1968, Robert went out on the streets to calm people down. But when the Democratic National Convention exploded in violence four months later, he was in the woods of northern Wisconsin, completing three months as a counselor at a YMCA camp. Peggy had opposed his going, but Robert desperately wanted a last chance at boyhood. Every penny he earned was sent straight to her, and she put it with her earnings in the bank. By the end of the summer they had saved two thousand dollars.

During that same summer Robert was accepted at a university in Ohio. In the fall he and Peggy packed up the furniture and dishes they had been accumulating and left Chicago. Half a year later, in April 1969, they were married. Robert was twenty-three.

V

1970 was a landmark year. Enthused about writing, Robert took material he had been collecting and finished six short stories for a contest. He drew on tales an uncle used to tell over chitlings and beer. He drew on the advice he had heard all his life on street corners. He wrote about young black men learning from older black men and then replacing them in the pecking order, about a son who discovers that his father is a moral coward. He called the collection *Street Corner Philosopher*. It was not good enough to win a prize, but Robert had the satisfaction of knowing that he could produce and meet deadlines.

In June, Robert's mother came to Ohio to see him graduate from college, the first in her family to do so. In September he turned twenty-five and began the university's Ph.D. program in English, relishing the letters of recommendation professors had written on his behalf. Two years later, he had a master's degree. In the meantime Peggy earned nursing and bachelor's degrees and began part-time work.

Then, unexpectedly, Robert had a brief, sudden experience of coming apart. Perhaps he had been overinflated by the letters of recommendation two years before; perhaps he was out of his element in a white world; perhaps he had regrets over not applying for a writer's workshop; perhaps he missed Chicago; perhaps he was just working too hard. "I was unglued maybe a couple of weeks, and then I was back together again. Maybe it was a built-in warning system: don't get too cocky, you're a teaching assistant, you're the only black here, you're making it. I could see that as a warning that maybe I'd better start looking at myself in another way. School wasn't everything. I could do other things and get just as much satisfaction. My mother would have said, 'See, that was God talking to you.'

"For years we'd always wanted a kid, but we figured that being in school and trying to make it ourselves that it would be too much of a problem to have a child. I used to say, 'When I get my Ph.D. everything will be okay, Peg.' It probably wouldn't have, but that's what I was leading myself to believe. The emotional output that I'd have to have for a kid would take me away from that."

Just after his brief breakdown Robert and Peggy decided to have a baby. In March 1973, Noah was born; he was followed three years later by a second son, Matthew. Robert's mysterious coming apart turned out to be a premonition: he lost the ability to finish either courses or stories, and his work deteriorated to the point that in 1975 he was asked to leave the Ph.D. program. "I had washed out or flunked out, and that just bugged me because I had staked all my self-esteem on getting that Ph.D." Nevertheless, he continued to teach college courses on a part-time basis. In 1977 he added a job as a substitute high school teacher, and by 1978 he and Peggy had saved enough money to make a down payment on a large house in a neighborhood with deflated property values.

His failure to get a Ph.D. festered, but fatherhood put the wound in perspective. More important, it established a connection with welcome emotions, some old and nearly forgotten, some entirely new. "Noah cried from the day he was born to the day he was two, it seemed. Man, oh man, it was almost unbearable! I could not even think of this kid hurting himself without just feeling my heart . . . breaking, you know. I wanted to protect this kid from everything. I remember looking at him when he was on the bed when he was so little. His head was squished in, and he was grimacing because he had colic, and everything was wrong. You see this kid lying on the bed, and you're feeling so sorry for him. You know, what can you do? That's what it is to come into life. And I've never been able to release my emotions like that. Now I can hold him and I can kiss him and I can love him.

"You know, we would try to kiss Mother when she was young and she would push us off, like you can't get too close, you ain't got a daddy in this house, who knows what you boys are going to do? I think it was the way she grew up. Her aunt and her uncle had eight kids, and when she came in there were nine, plus there was always an extended family. I'm sure there was never much affection. It was all they could do to feed these kids and send them off to school and let them play and hope that they don't kill themselves. You know, so that you never learn to release your emotions. And I didn't either until Noah was born.

"Now we're always saying we love each other. Four o'clock, I say I got to go to school. They won't let me go without giving them a kiss. When Peggy leaves for work at night, I always say, 'Walk your mama to the door, so nobody hits her in the head, right?' Everybody's got to kiss. 'Oh, mama, I love you, give me a kiss.' I mean, five to ten minutes of this stuff. It goes on constantly.

"I learned to live and breathe the air and see for the first time. I could see that this world goes beyond me. And that's why I'm not so hung up now about that Ph.D. The point is that Ph.D. means nothing to these kids. They see me doing something, they say, 'You working on your Ph.D. now?' They don't have any idea what it is. 'How long is a Ph.D.?' They have no idea of what I'm talking about. And you learn, well, the world has to go on. You can't stop everything because the kids got to eat, they want to play, they want to go out. You learn to sacrifice, and you try not to do it grudgingly.

"One part of parenting that I learned from my mother that I don't like is this neurotic behavior. When Noah sets the table he puts the plate crooked and he doesn't put the fork right. He just does anything to get it over with. So I make him go back and make everything symmetrical. This is my neurosis. Sometimes I get so carried away that Peggy says, 'Hey, man, you don't have to do all this junk. Enjoy these kids.' So often Noah does something and I'm shouting at him and Peggy says, 'Wait a minute. This kid is three years old. You can't expect him to do it without your teaching him, and teaching him is just not saying it once and forgetting it.' 'Oh yeah, that's right. I forgot.' Part of being a father is immersing yourself in childhood. I never really lived a childhood. I was never able to immerse myself fully in things like so many people I see. They dance, they eat, they party. They get right into it, man. I'm a stiff person. I'm real uptight. I still don't play as much as I should, but I'm getting better at it.

"I consciously think of myself as a father 'cause I got those little kids. I always used to say, even before I had kids, that I'd never get a divorce because I always thought of divorce as a source of my problems, the problems I suffered because I had no father. I knew it was naive to keep saying I wouldn't get a divorce—I mean, if Peggy and I couldn't get along. But if that's the best we could do, I'd always say, like Mark Twain says about a dog and Pudd'nhead Wilson, that we'll cut these kids in half because you ain't going to take them all and I ain't going to take them all. I've been fortunate that I haven't had to deal with it, and I think if I did have to deal with it, I couldn't bear it.

"My wife is white, she's from Nebraska, and here I am black and I lived in the ghetto for most of my life, not understanding white folks 'cause I didn't know them except that I had a mother always saying, 'You can't hate people because of their color.' When Peggy and I got together she was totally different from me. But something was there, and we made it. In part it was personality and in part it was a hardheadedness in reaction to my father and hanging on to what my mother did,' cause she was always very steadfast. If she had to do something, she did it, and she lived by standards. When I was growing up, my saying when I wanted to do something mean to people was, 'Well, he or she has a mother.' That concept of mother . . . man, that was my metaphor for living. That meant everything. Just the idea that without that person to care for you, where would we be anyway? And it doesn't necessarily have to be a mother. It could be a father.

"The Christmas after Noah was born we went to a family party in Chicago. Peggy was there and the baby was there and my father was there, right? He had never met Peggy. Noah was a little baby, and he held him a bit, but you could see that he didn't want to. We ate, we were talking and milling around, and in the middle of the festivities he jumps up and he goes. That's what he did when I was a kid. So I start crying, and I say, 'God, he's never grown up. Maybe if I weren't there he would have stayed.' I cried then and I cried when I was a kid. It's just like you're there, you know, your kid, your wife, and your relatives, right, and you're having a good time, and all of a sudden he jumps up and says, 'Hey, I'm going.' You say, 'Dad, where are you going?' He says, 'Aw, I'm going. I'm leaving.' It's as though it's overwhelming—the fun, the being with people, the love. You can't handle it, you leave.

"I've always shied away from identifying the source of my anger. My brothers used to tell me, and my wife did too, 'Maybe if you stopped saying you like your daddy, you'd be all right.' But I never admitted to myself that I dislike him. I once bought him a present, and I didn't send it to him, and then I did it to be mean. Now I think if I buy him something or send him a Father's Day card, it will really hurt him because he knows this is mockery. It wouldn't be on my part. But to him . . . what have I ever done for this kid for him to say, hey, happy Father's Day? I think he'd just be overwhelmed. He couldn't take it.

"I don't know when the emotion that I felt toward my father went from hurt and pain to pity. I'm sorry for him. I feel sorry because now I think he is seeking us out, not me so much, but both my brothers. My mother doesn't particularly hear from him a lot, but she hears about him through the kids. They'll take the car down to him or he'll tow the car for them, or they'll invite him to something and Mother happens to be there. They'll see one another for Christmas. They're active in seeing that he comes by, but he also seeks them out, in his own strange way. He doesn't know my kids and he doesn't know my wife and he doesn't know me. I was thinking about inviting him here. But what would I do with him? He wouldn't come, first of all. He wouldn't know what to do. If he came here, what could he say to me? He knows his toughness won't work now, so what could he say? I think it's embarrassment and hurt on his part. All I can see is that he's an old man now, and as Malcolm X said about Kennedy, chickens come home to roost."

VI

Nearly two years after our first conversations Robert and I met again on the same street corner. He had a few hours before meeting his college composition class. Rain threatened on this warm, gray afternoon, but we decided to take a chance and sit outside. Robert talked as much as he always had. He was talking on the corner when I arrived. He called out to passers-by as the two of us conversed. He spent fifteen minutes catching up on news with a friend who happened to spot him. Yet there was a subtle change in him. I had never known him to ponder questions before answering, to use anything other than my last few words as a trigger for his remarks. This time, though, he seemed more relaxed. He would just as easily stop his flow of words as start it, turn it in one direction as the other. All he needed was the slightest hint that such was my pleasure. Perhaps he had not changed at all, and it was I who knew better how to talk with him.

He described himself at thirty-five as getting "into stride." He had moved into the "adult pattern of living" he had been hoping to reach. He had a firm contract with his high school and was teaching evenings and summers for the university. His writing was still in abeyance and so were his plans to finish his degree. He was determined to make up his mind about the latter. As a high school teacher, the degree would mean next to nothing financially. Either he would decide to let it go or sit down with an adviser and formulate a plan for its completion. As he thought about his neglected writing, he gave himself a homily such as his mother might have: "Write, write, write, all the time. You gotta keep writing, you gotta stay with it. You can never have a perfect setting to begin writing, and if you wait for it you'll never start."

He was a demanding teacher at a high school he described as hopeless. Discipline had broken down. In his first full year of teaching English he assigned students at least one paper a week, failed a quarter of them, and did not award an A or B. He argued that proficiency standards must be met before students are given diplomas. Students told him he was too hard, but he told them what lay ahead of them. His own son Noah attends a public school for exceptional children, a school in which Robert and Peggy are heavily involved as volunteers. A second grader, Noah reads on a par with some of Robert's high school students.

We talked about a workshop Peggy had organized for neighborhood children the previous summer. The theme was Africa, and the children studied, built huts, made costumes, and culminated four weeks of activity with a huge African feast. It had been a success, though Robert and she had sunk too much of their own money into it. Still, Peggy was planning another.

Then Robert dropped a surprise: his father had called. "After all these years this cat just gets on the phone from Chicago and says, 'Hey, I'm coming over. Something told me to come and see you.' I said, 'Okay, you can come.' I had mixed feelings about it, but my wife was furious, *furious*! She said, 'I'm not going to let him do to the kids what he did to you.' She didn't want me to be hurt, and she saw his coming here so suddenly and his having done nothing for us ever as maybe we're going to start this same thing in a new generation. My kids are going to say, 'Oh, this is my granddaddy,' and they're going to get hooked up with him and he's going to do the same thing. He's going to withdraw. And she didn't want that. She said, 'No, no, no, I don't want the kids to get to know him.' She was going to stay with some friends while he was here, but I convinced her not to because that would embarrass me. But she stayed in the bedroom the whole weekend. He's saying, 'Where is your wife?' and I'm saying, 'Well. . . . '

"We went on a drive, he and the kids and I, and I cried and told him what was happening. I told him about the hang-up of not having a father and about some of the quirky things he's done all of his life to us. And he said, 'Aw, man, forget that. You grown now, you got your own kids.' There was no way he could deal with it. He's an older man, and he's built up such a great defense that now he's not going to let anything penetrate. He's lived all his life with the notion of being a rat. That's what we called it. Not taking any responsibility for his kids, not even letting them know that he exists and that he cares about them. He wasn't going to get into that. I brought it up very briefly, and he just didn't want to talk about it.

"Finally I told him why my wife hadn't shown up, and he was fit to be tied. He was furious! He wanted to leave right then, that night. I said, 'No, wait until the morning,' and he finally waited.

"The following day he went back to Chicago, and he talked about it. He couldn't understand. He didn't even know my wife. How could she have anything to do with it? Certainly he understood how people could have feelings and want to protect those they love from being hurt, but the irony is that he had done just the opposite. He had said, 'Aw, forget those kids. I'm a man, I made three babies.' I'm sure he was bragging just like everybody else who never did anything for their kids, you know, street corner men. Now he's a little bit older and all of his children are grown, and he looks back on it and says, 'Hey, maybe it could have been different.' And it just hurt him that somebody could be that loyal, that dedicated to somebody else."

INTERPRETATION: REWORKING THE HERITAGE; AGENCY, COMMUNION, AND PARENTHOOD

Robert Creighton currently stands midway between generations. At thirty-five, he looks back at his father and realizes the man will always be lost in the distance. Slowly abandoning his hope for contact, slowly releasing his feeling of being punished, slowly converting his anger into detachment, Robert turns and looks ahead to his sons. He vows that he will make up for his father's distance by being close to them and by halting a tradition of negligent fatherhood. Robert's story is an example of the way individuals rework heritages, familial as well as cultural, before passing them on to future generations.

The new tradition of fathering that Robert starts comes from the interplay of maternal and paternal influences within him. His biography is not representative of the recently heralded "new fathers"[1] because the way he rebalances these influences is uniquely his own. But the mere fact that he is a man realigning motherhood and fatherhood reflects a facet of the demographic revolution. With families shrinking in size, with more women employed continuously and more men involved in the care of fewer children, the meaning of "masculine" and "feminine" in parenting is changing. Atypical in one respect, prototypical in another, Robert Creighton's life opens to view a key feature of generativity in its contemporary setting.

REWORKING THE HERITAGE

A naive understanding of generativity is that it means little more than passing on to the young what one has received from elders. The generative individual is seen as a conduit for the past's rush to the future. A more complex understanding, and one truer to the concrete lives of people, is that legacies do not flow smoothly through individuals. Received with a mixture of love and hate, owned and disavowed throughout life, they are blocked, added to, and redirected by each hand that touches them.

Nearly half the people whose lives I studied referred to deficiencies in their familial inheritance. Life had not dealt them an impossible hand, but they had been handicapped by poor or missing cards. Dorothy Woodson was overlooked by her mother and attributed the neglect to defects in herself: I received this hand because someone as inferior as I deserves it. Erzsi Domier was slipped a hidden legacy of deceit: lied to by her mother and abandoned by her father, she was disoriented, confused, and furious for most of her early adult life. Those chafing under deficiencies were among the younger of my subjects, still in the middle of life. Older narrators no longer wrestled with shortcomings in their parents. All who felt punished by a legacy expressed a wish to rectify it before passing it on, though some realized that it was too late and that they had already repeated their parents' mistakes. Those who successfully reworked a heritage, however, had the satisfaction of knowing their children would not suffer precisely as they did. Progeny, in fact, gave those standing between generations a way of mastering a painful past.

Robert Creighton felt punished by a gap in his inheritance. "Why me?" he asked. "Why can't I have a daddy?" His first memory of being carried to the hospital in a shiny black car is like the myth of Eden before the fall: in the beginning, it says, my father was a hero and cared about me. Even as subsequent disappointments and rejections left Robert bitter, he always hoped the hero would return. He defended his father; he wanted to open the household door to him when others did not; he asked politely for contact; he tried to provoke it. Each time his father walked out, Robert cried with anger and pain. The last time I spoke with him, his hope was nearly extinguished and anger had given way to pity.

The more Robert realizes he cannot change his history, the more compelled he is to rewrite it in a new generation. He has made it a cornerstone of his adult life to see that his sons are not hurt in the way he was. His deliberate reversal of a generational influence—his compensation and overcompensation for it—is the essence of what I call reworking the heritage.

Like second chances at generativity, opportunities to rework a heritage are opportunities to redo. In second chances, individuals attempt to make up for generative damage they have inflicted; when they rework a heritage, they attempt to rectify the damage they have received. When one reworks a heritage one does not merely turn it around in fantasy, undoing it, in the terms of psychoanalysis. The rectification goes beyond wishes; it is attempted in reality, albeit on substitute objects. It is true that being a good parent will never change the way one's own parent was. But a consistent theme in these stories of generativity is that when people feel something must be done about damage inflicted and hurt received, they act as if restitution were owed to something as broad as life itself and it did not matter which particle of life gives or receives payment. The emotions, in Freud's words, "displace," "sublimate," and "project." Undeterred by logic, they slide in and out of a variety of subjects and objects. Anger at one person is directed to another. Jealousy in me is attributed to you. If I cannot alter what my father was, I will take his place and become his opposite. There is no reason to these substitutions, but there is a good deal of rhyme. People derive a sense of closure, as when the last word of a couplet falls into place, when they play a painful record over—and get it right—in a new generation.

These intrapsychic substitutions personalize and deepen what would otherwise be common decency and give intergenerational corrections their sense of proper fit. Doing precisely those things my father never did vicariously does them for him (and I have long wished him to do them). At the same time, producing an extension of myself that is free from a specific scar vicariously removes it from me (and I have long wished it gone). Reworking a heritage, one masters pain and even executes a kind of vengeance on its inflicter. One stands cured in the reflected light of progeny and has a latent wholeness confirmed by them. Many kinds of emotional satisfaction are obtained from creating legacies of just those elements missing from one's own inheritance.

In the life histories I have collected, however, deprivation alone is insufficient to explain why a heritage is refashioned. Instead, in such cases I find histories of deprivation *and* nourishment—not just bad cards dealt by life but bad cards mixed with some very good ones.

In the story of Dorothy Woodson, for example, there is a recurring theme of not being heard. In contrast is a description of one central experience of being heard. Out of this clash of deprivation and nourishment, she formulates a desire, seemingly out of the blue, to help deaf people be heard. The urgency and rightness of this specific contribution to life flow from her hunger: others must not suffer as I did. The wherewithal to make the contribution and the model of how to do it come from her reception of sustenance: I will be a "soulmate" to others, just as my loved one was to me.

Without nourishment, people lack even a basic awareness of deprivation and may replicate it in the next generation. Nourishment not only empowers life projects of rectification by providing contrast and giving energy, it also offers a blueprint for action. Robert Creighton's father failed to provide for him, but his mother cared deeply and showed him how to be a parent. She became his model for fathering. Without her influence, Robert would not now be refashioning his heritage, no matter how deep his anger toward his father.

Although Robert Creighton's life is directed toward remaking a familial inheritance, it is clear that crafts and cultures undergo analogous processes. Jo Biondi, for example, has been reworking a purely cultural heritage. When her life as a sister became less restricted, she became aware of deficiencies in the "spirituality" she had been taught. She realized that spirituality had to offer more than regulation in order to sustain sisters in their contemporary work. Believing that her cultural roots were drying up, Jo delved into history and found the story of her order's foundress. That story provided meaning that could sustain contemporary activity, and it provided a model of how to act, starting with what to wear and where to live. The sharp contrast between then and now, between past nourishment and current deprivation, motivated the reshaping of her tradition. The meaning of being a sister was altered to fit modern life and to recapture her order's energizing beginnings.

The feature revealed in Jo Biondi's history appears as well in Robert Creighton's: deprivation alone will not prompt the renovation of a heritage. Robert was denied one card at the start of life, but he found another to play in its place. He learned how to be a father at the knees of his mother.

AGENCY, COMMUNION, AND PARENTHOOD

In studying Robert Creighton's life, I am struck by how his double consciousness corresponds to the poles that Jung and Levinson have

labeled the masculine and the feminine, and that I, following David
Bakan, refer to as agency and communion. Agency, the so-called masculine principle, encompasses a cluster of emotions centered on the assertion of power and the expansion of the individual self. Aggression, ambition, and the urge to master are clear manifestations of agency, but so are
isolation, separation, and the repression of feeling. Communion, the so-
called feminine principle, is expressed in contact, union, and the participation of the self in an interpersonal reality. Self-sacrifice and passivity
are part of communion, but so are openness, the lifting of repression, and
sensitivity to emotion.[2] I have often been impressed by the way these
antagonistic sets of emotions alternate in particular lives and how they
do so precisely as clusters.

Robert Creighton's agentic, or masculine, consciousness was ascendant in his late teens during his "crazy" period of "civil rights." In him,
agency is associated with his father and the street. Here are images of
repressive silence, feelings of alienation and rage, and the felt necessity
to survive and kill. In Robert's most despairing moments, agency became
a cancer. His recurring fantasy at these times was of himself wrapped in
bombs, bullets, and hand grenades, ready to blow up the world and
himself with it.

Robert's communal, or feminine, compartment contains feelings and
images associated with his mother and home: with caring and contact,
with talking instead of silence, with an emphasis on loyalty, morality,
and self-sacrifice. All these feelings mitigate agency and calm him. The
people who have released communal emotions in Robert's life have been
women and children, first his mother, then his mentor Ellen, then his
wife, and then his sons. When communion was at an ebb in his crazy
period, it was still visible in his fantasy of a quiet mountaintop where he
would retreat with his mother. The balance began to shift in the direction
of that fantasy when he met his future wife and talked the night through
to her. "She just listened. She didn't have anything to say. She was quiet,
and she had what I called white ways—very timid and shy—and I had
what I called black ways—very aggressive." Robert talked to her about
his mother and home, felt the calming influence of her quietness, and
learned that talking was a way of "keeping myself from blowing up."
Though he described his talk as "aggressive," I heard between the lines
the question, Is this a woman who can care for me? Robert's retreat into
the domesticity Peggy offered was relatively sudden. He seemed to
breathe a sigh of relief—as he seemed to in jail—that he no longer had
to exhibit bravado on the street.

When Robert began to fail in graduate school, he again turned to
domesticity, this time by deciding with Peggy to have a child. The birth

of that child marked Robert's conscious discovery of the communal side of existence. He eased up in his pursuit of a Ph.D., felt repressions lifting, and found tenderness. "I wanted to protect this kid from everything. . . . And I've never been able to release my emotions like that. Now I can hold him and I can kiss him and I can love him." With the arrival of children Robert learned that the world goes "beyond me."

I retrace this scenario because it differs from the course of agency and communion that several life-cycle researchers have postulated in men and because the difference is related to changing demographics of fatherhood.

David Gutmann, for example, has found that men in a number of cultures respond to parenthood in a way opposite to Robert Creighton's. When he became a parent, Robert retreated from agency and accentuated communion. Guttman's subjects did the reverse. Leaving the care of children to women, they amplified agency in the world of work and so provided for the family's physical security. Women, however, responded to parenthood by suppressing agentic feelings that might frighten or harm children. Amplifying communion, they became the center of affection in the family and saw to its emotional security. In the childbearing years there was a psychological division of labor that required men to suppress their femininity and women to suppress their masculinity. The suppressed characteristics were denied in oneself, projected onto the opposite sex, and lived out vicariously through them. Once children were grown and the "parental emergency" was over, there was a return of the repressed. According to Gutmann, "The sharp sex distinctions of earlier adulthood break down, each sex becomes to some degree what the other used to be, and there is ushered in the normal unisex of later life. Grandpa becomes sweet, affable, but rather vague. Grandma becomes tough-minded and intrusive."[3] In interview and questionnaire studies, Marjorie Lowenthal found that older men and women moved in precisely the directions pointed out by Gutmann;[4] using a biological approach, Levinson found that men at midlife were beginning the same reversal of masculinity and femininity.[5] Four decades before their work, Jung had compared masculinity and femininity to stores of substance of which unequal use is made in the first half of life: "A man consumes his large supply of masculine substance and has left over only the smaller amount of feminine substance, which must now be put to use. Conversely, the woman allows her hitherto unused supply of masculinity to become active."[6]

The life of Robert Creighton illustrates how the contraceptive and demographic revolutions in the United States are rewriting this scenario. Because we live in conditions of greater physical security, because we are having fewer children and devoting smaller segments of the life cycle to rearing them, the parental "emergency" is not as great as it once was. And the reasons for a sex-specific response to it have all but disappeared. Women as well as men are able to provide economic security for their families. In the 1980s more mothers are working outside the home, and their husbands in varying degrees are assuming the duties of child care.[7] Changes in child-custody laws have increased the number of divorced fathers with direct responsibility for their children. All this paternal involvement is coming at a time when the relative scarcity of children calls for unprecedented investments in each one of them. Among a growing minority of men, then, intimate contact with young children is eliciting rather than suppressing tenderness and nurturance. Though a biological imperative (the increase in testosterone) continues to amplify agency in young men, the conditions of parenting are tempering it. Agency and communion are beginning a new history in the male life cycle. It is not the end of parenthood in middle age that is prompting a decline in agency and a rise in communion; the reversal is beginning much earlier with the onset of parenthood. Complementary alterations are no doubt occurring in women.

There is a uniqueness to Robert's history, however, that forces us to go beyond changing demographics to understand his generativity. The nurturant impulses he felt at the birth of his children, and the femininity that he unabashedly reveals now, are clearly his mother's legacy, for while he passes on her kind of caring, he also passes on her "neurotic" fastidiousness. Her generativity was largely, but not totally, communal. "She had to make sacrifices for us—which she did," he says of her. The generativity of his father, which Robert rejects, was an agentic demonstration of virility: "Hey, man, I got all these babies." Though Robert's parental generativity is largely communal, he has not lost his capacity for agency. As a teacher, he is tough and demanding.

Robert Creighton has reworked a number of the legacies he received at birth: the meaning of blackness and whiteness, the meaning of being poor and having enough. The most significant change, however, may turn out to be the most general: the meaning of masculinity and femininity in parenting. It will be interesting to see how many men with different personal histories alter their heritage in the same way in the 1980s, how many discover new ways of "being a daddy."

9 · *The Message*

Ali Birri is spreading the message. In a well-lit church basement he faces an audience of more than a hundred people. They sit at long rows of tables, smoke cigarettes, and sip coffee from styrofoam cups. It is warm this summer evening, and Ali has taken off his blue blazer and draped it over a chair, leaving himself entirely in white—white shirt and tie, white pants and belt, white loafers.

Ali is a stocky man in his early fifties, with a round face, dark brown eyes, and a goatee. His manner is relaxed, but as he warms to his story, he begins to hitch his shoulder and stretch his neck rhythmically to the side. When he comes around to the front of the lectern and talks about "running terror," or when he says his problem was "mother," everyone nods knowingly. Events in his life, Ali declares, have unfolded "like the Big Book says." Time and again he has rediscovered "Step One" and "Step Three." Time and again he has been helped by a "Step Four" inventory. Most recently the key has been to "break dependencies," to "detach," to "let go of the Four Corners."

He talks for nearly an hour, and when he is finished he is radiant. He mills around expectantly and is not disappointed. Friends and strangers alike shake his hand or give him a hug. On the way home he drives his sports car fast and talks nonstop. "When I get up and give a talk, I say, Ali, get out of the way and listen to what happens. The energy just flows. You gotta give it away to keep it."

I

In the living room of Ali Birri's apartment there is a large L-shaped sofa with plenty of pillows. Tucked in a corner is an easel with a white metallic surface. It was there, more than a month before his talk, that I first met Ali. When I had called with a request to record his life story, he had agreed instantly. At our first meeting he settled into a soft orange chair, slipped off his sandals, and tucked his feet under his legs. That evening we broke our conversation only once—to watch an evening news report on the Israeli siege of Beirut.

Ali was the first of five children born to a Lebanese couple who immigrated to America in 1927. To the best of his knowledge, he was conceived in the old country and born in the new. Ali's father found factory work in Chicago but returned periodically to Lebanon to try to make a living there. He failed each time and had to leave. Early in his narrative Ali discussed his family lineage—that he was descended from a line of sheikhs, that he suspected insanity on his side of the family. "From what I hear, one of the founding great-grandmothers was a little flaky, and my great-grandfather healed her and married her. I think the whole family was a little crazy—well, not all the branches, because there were some branches that were not sheikhs." Ali seemed amused by the craziness he had inherited and even a little proud of it.

"I've been in Alcoholics Anonymous for thirteen years and only in the past seven or eight have pleasant scenes from my childhood come back to me. I remember one scene in which I was on the floor. I had a little red notebook, and I was trying to write the letter 'A,' and I was asking my mother, 'Is this okay?' I must have been four at the time, maybe younger. I remember just a little about kindergarten in Chicago, and then I remember being aboard a ship heading for Lebanon. I was six years old. I remember the tremendous storm we had—tremendous swells in the ocean. It was a frightening trip for some people, and yet to me it was fascinating. I remember getting to Beirut; it was all cluttered with people. And then we got in this old Model T or Model A, and it was a hard, tough road getting to my grandfather's house in Tibnin.

"The first impression I had of my grandfather was that he was an awesome man. He wore a turban, and he had a beard and steel blue-gray eyes. He had . . . in Arabic, it's called *wahra*. It's an awesomeness. I remember he presented that *wahra*. You knew there was power there. I saw an arbor of grapes on the roof of his house, and I said I wanted some grapes. My father immediately scolded me. 'No! You shouldn't ask for anything.' My grandfather said, 'No, no, let him. He needs some grapes.' So my grandfather overruled my father right away.

"My father wanted me to go in the tradition of my grandfather and be a sheikh. A sheikh is a religious leader of the community. It's a hereditary title, and the eldest son was expected to follow in the tradition. He was raised to read and understand the Koran and jurisprudence. Eventually he was sent to Najaf in Iraq. My father was a sheikh, but he was not trained. My grandfather had gone to Najaf. He was a schoolmaster, and he led the congregation in prayer. In Tibnin, my father hired my cousin as a tutor, and I learned to read and write Arabic pretty thoroughly. People would always refer to me as Sheikh Ali, so I knew there was something a little different about who I was.

"The older men in Tibnin would tell family stories. I especially loved it during the wintertime. People would come to visit us, and we'd sit around the fireplace on mats of papyrus reed and on sheepskins, roasting chestnuts and eating oranges. We'd all be huddled around the fire, and they would tell the stories. They would scare us with stories about the *dabaa*, which is the hyena. They told stories about how the Christians were protected from the Turks by the Moslems in Tibnin during World War I. Then when the French came in, the Christians returned the favor for the Moslems. During the period of Ashura, which is the commemoration of the death of Husain, the grandson of Muhammad, they would read and then they would sit there and cry. We all slept in the same room. They'd lay out mattresses next to each other, and the whole family slept together. I used to wake up at night, all hours of the night, and they'd be praying to Allah. I remember when my uncle said, 'Now's the time for you to learn how to pray. Come and stand beside me.' I started laughing, and he said, 'No, this is very serious.' So he forced me to stand and pray in the traditional Moslem style.

"Allah was an awesome figure. He became my grandfather, my father, and my mother. We used to get stories about how Allah would burn us in hell if we did wrong. If we were going to do something we would say, '*Inshallah*. If Allah wills it.' So He was part and parcel of our whole being. Whatever good befell you was from Allah. Whatever evil befell you was from Allah. It was all Allah's will.

"I liked life in Lebanon—being tutored under a fig tree, playing, going after certain plants you could eat. There was a natural well, and sometimes the women would bathe us kids there while they were doing the wash. Once I walked off by myself past a fort that was near the Christian part of town. There were hills there and a *wa'ar*, a brush-type forest. The ocean was way out in the distance. It was a beautiful summer day, and there was a gentle breeze wafting the clouds along. I just remember sitting on a rock and feeling as though I melted into all of that. The whole experience burned into my soul, and I've never forgotten it.

"When I was in Lebanon the first time I got typhoid. There was a little pond in the middle of town from which the cows and the goats drank. Sometimes the kids would go swimming in it, and as a consequence of that I got sick. There were two of us. The other kid died. I survived, but there were three months when I didn't know where I was.

"My father was already back in this country. At first, I didn't even know I was sick. My mother took me to Tyre, and I asked, 'What's wrong?' She said, 'You're sick,' and she took me to the doctor. At this doctor's some gal was on her stomach, and she had a hole in her back, and there was something in it. I was afraid the doctor was going to put a hole in my back. Then he told my mother that I had typhoid, and he told her what to do with me. Then the sickness took over. I was in and out of comas, I was burning with fever, I'd lose track of what was happening. I remember some of the older men would come over, and I heard one of them say, 'Well, why don't you brand him?' There's an old technique of branding a person with a hot poker on the head. 'That might help cure him.' I heard this, and I begged my mother, 'Please don't let them do that to me.' I'm sure they would have killed me if they had.

"I was in and out of comas for about a month and a half. I remember them trying the hot cups on my back. That wasn't too bad. I remember my mother making sure that nobody got near me or fed me because all I could eat was a little bit of warm milk with sugar in it and a little biscuit. One day I begged my sister, who was just a little girl, 'Please, give me some bread.' My mother had warned everybody not to give me any food. And I begged her. She said, 'No, I can't do that.' I begged her, 'Please give me a piece of bread.' And she did. I ate that piece of bread, and then my mother found out and beat the living daylights out of her because that night I got sick all over again. I mean I almost died, again.

"Then I got pneumonia and whooping cough. And . . . even when I'm talking about this it's starting to surface some feeling I have to deal with yet. But then, I remember, the fever finally broke, and I was like a little skeleton. My mother started to feed me a bit of pulverized raw meat to bring my strength back. It was three months before I was able to get up and move around."

I I

During the three months of his illness Ali's mother became his only link to life, and Ali construes that fact now as a symbol of all that went wrong with him. He speaks of his attachment to her as if it were an addiction. "Somehow or another in that experience I took it that I could not live without Mother. It was a deep dependency, a symbiotic relationship, one that has taken until just recently to break out of." One could not imagine a more capricious source of life. Ali's mother was both "powerful" and "crazy." "One minute I'd be on a pedestal and the next minute I'd be stomped. If I got into a fight and got beat up, I'd come home and get a beating. If I didn't fight I'd get a beating. Her attitude was always kick the shit out of the kid first and then tell him what he'd done wrong."

Ali returned to America when he recovered from his sickness and, except for a trip to Lebanon when he was nine, spent the rest of his childhood years in Chicago. His father was a strict disciplinarian, but Ali remembers being close to him, and he remembers his father's pride when he recited from the Koran. But when Ali began to act like his American friends and neglect his religion, his father became critical. "When I was thirteen my parents decided I should go to trade school. There was no way I was going to be a sheikh. I really didn't want to go, but they stomped me any time I objected. I hated trade school and became very lethargic. I started writing articles about man being depraved and rotten to the core. I knew I wasn't well. By the time I was fifteen I developed a case of fatigue. It got so bad I could go to the YMCA and watch my cousin and my buddy wrestle and get totally exhausted just sitting there watching."

Ali's first "purposeful" drink came at that time. A gang had gotten a bottle of wine, and Ali made a discovery. "It was a real turn-on. I suddenly felt free and loose and just happy. I was in one world at one moment and in another world at the next, and it was a very pleasant world. I even came down easily."

Ali persuaded his parents to allow him to leave school and work in the grocery store his father had purchased. At seventeen he obtained their permission to join the navy, and he entered just as World War II was ending. On the way to boot camp he was introduced to sex by a prostitute. Ali remembers some heavy drinking in the navy, and he remembers a false alarm when he thought his ship had been blown out of the water by a stray mine. "The first thought that came to my mind was, Oh, my poor mother. What's she going to think when she hears that I'm dead?" When the war was over his parents returned to Lebanon. Ali was discharged from the navy in August 1946 and promised he would join them there. "I went to New York to catch a ship, but they had a stevedore strike, so I spent a month in New York waiting for the strike to be over. I had a great time in New York, just fantastic. I lived at the St. George Hotel in Brooklyn. I knew the subway system, I was nineteen years old, I had it made."

III

"When I finally got to Lebanon, all of a sudden my parents wanted me to get married. They felt that if they married me off in Lebanon I wouldn't end up marrying some American who was going to call me a dirty black Syrian. They wanted me to follow in the tradition and marry a good Moslem girl. Well, I had found the red-light district in Beirut and gotten taken care of and I didn't want to get married. My mother came to Beirut and told me, 'I want you to see some girls I have lined up for you.' I said, 'No way.' She said, 'Yes, you will.' I said, 'No, I won't,' and she hauled off and slapped me. So I turned the other cheek. I said, 'Why don't you hit me on this side?' She started crying, and I said, 'Okay, I'll see who you wanted me to see.'

"So I was checking these gals out. Finally, my mother arranged to have this thirteen-year-old brought over. Her name was Ihsan. I see this little girl walk in, and she sees us and gets embarrassed and runs out. They bring her back, and my mother says, 'What do you think?' She had reddish-brown hair, and she was cute, and something within me. . . . Somehow or another I heard myself say yes. My mother felt really happy, and my father and his cousin went to ask for her hand in marriage.

"I'd go and visit her while my father was trying to negotiate. She didn't like me. She said she didn't like me. She was a terrified little girl. She didn't want to go through with this thing. And I was a little terrified too. What's a nineteen-year-old kid, wet behind the ears, doing married?

"At the wedding ceremony the women were in one place singing and dancing and decorating the bride. And the men were in another place congratulating my father. Finally, the contract was negotiated with the sheikh. Ihsan's parents wanted a thousand lire and my parents offered three thousand, so they couldn't say any more. The sheikh told me, 'If you agree to this, say I agree three times.' Then he went and negotiated with Ihsan. She balked, so they had her father come and agree for her. The document was signed, and a little bit later they said, 'Send the bride over to the house.'

"It wasn't a very pleasant experience because she was a virgin, and I was really frightened. I had to perform, and I didn't like it. It was about the closest thing you can get to a rape. I don't think she ever forgave me for that. It was a horrible, horrible experience. This is one part of my life I'm not very happy about, but we were both put in a circumstance we didn't like.

"We got married in February, and in May we were back in this country. She was seasick all the way back, but I was drinking and having a good time. I met this good-looking Greek-American girl, and we had a romance going throughout that whole voyage. I never wanted to get married. It was one of those situations in which the pressure was on and I finally agreed to marry somebody, but deep inside me I knew I wasn't ready for marriage. "When we came back we lived with my parents. Ihsan had no other relatives so she was forced to develop a relationship with me. I tried different jobs and couldn't stand them, so I went back to high school. Then I convinced my wife to have a baby, and we did. We named him Nasib, and he was a beautiful baby right from the beginning. My mother was ecstatic about him. My wife was fifteen and I was twenty, and I was about to start community college."

IV

"Two months later my mother had to go to the hospital for surgery. On the day before she was supposed to come home, I was visiting her and I lingered for a while. She said, 'What's the matter?' I said, 'Oh, I just feel like talking to you.' The next day I went to school. When I came home, I saw all these people in the house. They told me, 'Your mother is dead.' Evidently she had a blood clot that hit her brain and caused her to die instantly.

"I went into shock. I grieved a little, but mostly I went into shock.

"I was very depressed, and I barely got through my first semester. I was working sixteen hours a day in my father's grocery store and trying to go to college. I started to get up in the morning very tired. And then one night about a year after my mother died I went to a bar and I drank about five beers. I came home and went to sleep. Got up the next morning and went to the store. It was a hot summer day in July, and I went down to get a bag of charcoal for one of the customers. As I was coming up I felt funny. I said, I wonder how it'd feel to die. And all of a sudden I felt like I was coming apart and dying. I yelled to my brother, and he and my father rushed me to the hospital. I went into emergency, and I was telling them I'm going to die. A doctor examined me and started asking me questions, psychological questions. He said, 'This happens to young people your age. Just take it easy.' He sent me home, and right after I drove home I had a complete nervous breakdown. I was feeling nothing but hot and cold running fear. Terror. Lots of pain in my gut. I remember trying to find a way out. I even buttonholed a doctor at some doctors' convention. I was telling him, 'I'm sick. I need help.' The guy said, 'Buddy, you need help? Get yourself a bottle of whiskey.'

"It was a horrible experience, a deep depression that lasted about six months. I was on my own, and I didn't know what was happening to me. Now the Koran and the Bible became my friends. I couldn't sleep at night unless I was holding the Koran and the Bible."

V

That fall of 1949, Ali turned twenty-two and thought again of Lebanon. He persuaded his father to send him and his family there to finish his education on the GI Bill. Chancing on an unusually mild and sunny winter, he slowly worked himself out of his depression. He attended the American University of Beirut and got a part-time job as a reporter and translator for Beirut's first English-language newspaper. That job opened other doors, and Ali met wealthy industrialists, Egyptian movie stars, and political "big shots." He relished the power that rubbed off on him. "The Arabs," he added at one point, "are a people who look for a savior to do things for them. I remember being that way for a long, long time."

At the age of twenty-five Ali graduated from the university and returned to the United States with his family, which now included two sons. After trying several jobs, he spent four years as a social worker and four years as a probation officer. His family grew to six with the addition of a third son and his first daughter. But he spent little time with them. He was working long hours because, as he said, "I was going to save all of Chicago. There was gratification in that kind of power." Besides, he was giving his weekends to drinking.

"I rarely drank during the week, but I could hardly wait for Friday to come so I could go out and get bombed. I didn't drink for social reasons. I used to go out to get drunk, to release the pressures. I'd leave my wife and go bar hopping with my friends. We'd even go out chasing the girls. I'd come home at two or three o'clock in the morning all blown away. Maybe I'd drink Friday and Saturday, and Sunday I'd have to rest all day. I used to make promises to the kids, but most of the time I just was out of energy.

"Many of the people placed on probation had alcoholic backgrounds. We would threaten them with jail time and put them on a couple of years probation. 'Behave yourselves and don't drink.' And they'd go out and drink again. Well, I wanted to know what to do with these characters, so I managed to get a state scholarship to an institute on alcohol studies. It was a one-week institute in Kalamazoo. I remember a newspaper sent one of its reporters to cover it, and he was a lush. Kalamazoo at that time was a semidry town where you could only buy beer and wine at the bars. The only way you could buy whiskey by the glass was if you belonged to a private club—a key club. And somehow this reporter and I discovered every key club in Kalamazoo. We'd go out every night, and I didn't see any problem.

"The last night of the institute they took us to an open AA meeting and brought in an open speaker from Indiana. And this speaker gave one hell of a talk. I mean, one minute he had us laughing and the next minute he had us crying. There was a lot of energy shared. I thought it was one of the best talks I'd ever heard from anybody. I said, boy, that program is really great for *those* guys, little realizing that *I* had the problem.

"Then I started to run out of energy. I had a cousin who was a disabled veteran, and he managed to get ahold of some amphetamines. He told me about them, and I tried them. I got energy from them and started using them every so often. I found out now I could go out and drink on these and feel high and not get sick. I could drink more, and I could talk nonstop for three days and three nights if I wanted to. Then 1960 came along, and it got to the point where I was needing to take pills during the week—not drinking, but taking pills and then drinking lots of coffee with sugar in it. I liked the buzz I used to get from the pills. I didn't like coming down though, so at night I would take some beer and it would bring me down slower.

"Then I started doing something really crazy. I started going to the coffee houses and gambling, illegally, down in the basement with some of the shady characters in town, including my probationists. I'd be popping pills and trying to fill inside straights. I'd fill them, but I couldn't even see the hand, so I'd throw it in. I was losing money, and I would come home and cash bonds so I could cover my gambling debts. In the winter of 1962 it got so bad I couldn't stop anymore. At Christmas time my family bought me a coat, and I took it right back to Sears, got the money for it, and gambled the money away within two minutes. You talk about remorse. I'd like to have dug a hole, crawled into it, covered it up, and died. I didn't know what to do. I felt like I was caught in a whirlpool, and it was dragging me down. I was gambling. I was losing my self-respect and dignity. Everything was going down the drain. I could even sense that my wife had had it with me now and that she was about ready to take off with the kids.

"As my drinking progressed there was always the feeling that I was doing something wrong. I'd have to take two or three quick drinks to knock out my conscience so I could go on drinking. At this time I didn't exactly believe in Allah, but I was too scared not to. I had become an agnostic. But in spite of my agnosticism, I remember coming home after gambling away that coat and getting on my hands and knees with tears running down my eyes and saying, 'Allah, if you're there, please help me. I give up.'"

VI

Curled up in his chair and pulling occasionally at his nose, Ali seemed like a little boy, like someone who could indeed be utterly dependent on a mother or, in her place, on a holy book or even God. I could tell by his practiced phrases that he had told his story a number of times before and that he saw in it a pattern—more, the hand of Providence. He was spreading the message with his story, and spreading it seemed good for him, seemed necessary, almost, to maintain his vision.

He was a man fascinated by his inner life. To him, it was a force as mysterious and powerful as the ocean that had held him in awe as a boy. At the age of six it had plunged him into a coma, and now it could bring sudden terror or sudden ecstasy. Ali was vigilant about its swells and consulted them as he would an oracle. In 1963 and again in 1969 he had overwhelming inner experiences that he thinks of now as "theophanies." Both were triggered by a man he met two days after he got on his knees and begged Allah for help.

"That was a Saturday night. The next day, Sunday, there was a big snowstorm that went on all night and ended Monday morning. At that time I was a member of a committee that was supposed to meet at Cook County Jail. The chairman of the committee was Ed Chappell, the prison psychologist. The driving was treacherous, but I got there. When I did, they said, 'Didn't you get the phone call?' I said, 'What phone call?' 'Well, we told all the members of the committee not to show up because of the snowstorm.' So there I was with Ed Chappell, and he started showing me around the prison. All of a sudden he got a call that there was a violent prisoner who had fashioned a knife and was threatening people in his cell. Ed took me with him. I saw him walk in and talk this guy right out of the knife. I was impressed, and the next thing I know I started spilling my guts out to Ed. I sat there for about three hours, and I told him my life story. He sat patiently listening to me. When I finally sputtered out, he said, 'Well, we could help you. Your problem is mother.' Now, my mother was dead, of course, but I knew what he was saying.

"I made an agreement with him to be my therapist. Little by little I started revealing myself, and somehow or another as a result of meeting him almost daily, I found myself not using any more pills. I stopped drinking, and within six months I was clean of everything. And then one day I met him in a restaurant, and he said, 'Ali, we've reached an impasse. We're at a point where you're going to have to make a decision.' He drew a 'V' and said, 'You're here, and you've got to break through.' He didn't say what I had to do.

"I knew I had to take an action. I didn't exactly know what it was. I knew somehow it had to do with detaching from a dependency, and I knew it had to do with my mother. I narrowed it down to three choices. I could run away, just move out of the state. I could divorce my wife, who was a surrogate mother. Or I could leave my job, which was also a surrogate mother. The one about running I ruled out right away. The other two . . . . I remember clearly that it was a Sunday and that I was pacing up and down in my house. What should I do? What should I do? Finally, my eyes fell upon copies of the Koran. There were two volumes with Arabic on one side and English on the other. I said, maybe Allah will help me again. I've got four kids now. Do I divorce my wife or leave my job? I took the larger volume, and I prayed, and I asked for guidance. I opened up the book, and it said, 'Do not divorce thy wives thinking they are thy mothers. For it is thy mothers that bore thee not thy wives.' I had never read that before.

"I knew exactly what I had to do. The next morning I went to the office and typed up my resignation. I wanted to hand it to the judge before he went into court. But this morning he was busy and couldn't see me. I just sat there with my resignation in my pocket. I felt like something had been broken. Something within me had let go, and I decided I was going to trust Allah no matter what. All of a sudden I had a feeling that started off at my toes and filled my whole being. It was such a feeling of euphoria, and it was so absolutely beautiful, I could feel it fill the whole room. I'd never experienced any kind of high like that. No drugs, nothing ever did that. At that moment the court officer walked in with a young man for a presentencing investigation. I looked at this young man, and it was as though I could see an ectoplasmic form jump out at me. His whole personality jumped out at me. He was standing there, and I knew exactly what was wrong with him. Just intuitively. He sat down, and I asked him two or three questions, and he started crying. I wrote my report out and made my recommendations and sent him back. The court officer brought in a young lady. Exactly the same kind of experience. She sat down and started crying. All morning long I had people who would start crying. And this feeling was blowing my mind! There was a queasiness in the pit of my gut, yet the feeling was overwhelming.

"I called Ed and told him what had happened, and he said, 'Something had to happen.' I said, 'Okay, when do we start meeting again?' Then Ed and I started talking about things that were deeply mystical. The things we talked about and the images I had afterward were very mystical images.

"A year later Ed moved to Dallas, and I was left to my own devices. I still had this power, and it was quite a power. I became a guru. I'd have parties in my house, and I even built a room called 'The Room of Love, Romance, and Happiness.' It was a room with soft lights and music and nice carpeting, where we could sit around and talk. I attracted all kinds of sickies and started playing healer. People came like moths to a flame. Even my wife fell in love with me, and this is when our last child was conceived. The baby was the one child who was a child of love. We named him Isam Edward." It was 1963 and Ali was thirty-five when he had his first "theophany." He laughs now about his Room of Love, Romance, and Happiness, and he laughs too—but it is a different kind of laugh—at the simplicity of the way shown him by the Koran. How right that passage was, the laugh says. And how providential was the "chance" opening of a massive volume to precisely its location. Ali followed through on his job resignation but several years later found his power diminishing. For six years, as his five children grew up, he floated from job to job. When I asked about the concrete details of his life, he supplied them, but they were not the story he wanted to tell. What he wanted to relate was how he lost his energy again and how he turned once more to drinking and pills. When he got to three amphetamines with a fifth of Beefeater gin, he knew he was in trouble. It was March 1969.

"I put in a call to Ed Chappell in Dallas, and I told him I was in trouble. He said, 'I know. We've been waiting for you.'

"I decided to go to Dallas. I told my wife, and she said, 'Look, you go to Dallas, don't come back. I've had it with your therapy and your cures.' I got scared so I decided to go back to the Koran. What should I do? This time the message was, 'Moses saw the burning bush and said to his family, Tarry here for a while, while I go get some fire.' And, of course, that burning bush turned out to be his conversation with God.

"I took that as a clear indication that I had better go to Dallas. When I got there, Ed Chappell was waiting for me. He had a little cottage behind his house, and he put me there. The next morning he took me to different places. In one of them there was this gal who was one of the top commercial artists in Dallas, but she was heavy into dope and everything else. She was a seductive little wench. In between her trying to seduce me and Ed running interference on that, she suddenly asked me a question, a simple question. She said, 'Ali, are you an alcoholic?' There was no criticism in it. It was a matter-of-fact question that demanded a matter-of-fact answer, the best I knew. Suddenly I heard myself say, 'Yes, I think I am.' Just like that. And Ed's face. . . . He said, 'You make that admission?' I said, 'I guess so.' He said, 'Come with me.' He took me to one of her drawing boards and said, 'I want you to write down *I am an alcoholic*. In Arabic.' So I wrote it. It's interesting because I wrote the root word 'alcohol' instead of 'drunk,' *khamarji* instead of *sakarji*. Ed rolled up the paper and said, 'Are you willing to do whatever it takes to get the help you need?' I said, 'Yeah.' He said, 'Are you willing to go to AA meetings?' I said, 'Whatever.'

"Over the next few days Ed took me around Dallas and bounced me off every sickie he knew, and boy, did he know some! I could feel myself going right down to nothing. On the third day, we went to a restaurant with his wife, and the next thing I knew he took me on the side and said, 'Look here, you little son-of-a-bitch, I've been carrying you for seven years. You're an alcoholic and you better do something about it.' Well, this was the first time he'd ever talked to me like that, and I got frightened. All of a sudden this loving father was beating me down. We went back to the table, and I started crying. Then I heard him say to his wife, 'Maybe we should send him down to the alcohol rehab.' I hadn't had anything to drink in three or four days, and I didn't see why I should go, but they decided they would send me there. They brought in this husband and wife team, and I really started to break down. I became that little six-year-old boy that nearly died in Tibnin. I was terrified, and I was begging Ed for forgiveness. This couple put me in a car, and I swear I felt I was in the AA Mafia staff car. They took me down to the rehab center, and while the gal was talking to the director, this guy was sitting there talking to me. He was a loving and caring type, but I wasn't hearing what he was saying. I was more concerned with what was going on inside of me. It was a total regression. I was really frightened.

"All of a sudden while I was talking to him, it seemed as though a window parted and I saw my life pass into review. Quick sequences. I can't exactly remember what the sequence was, but I could see the conning, the lying, the gambling, the cheating, the whole works. I could see all the things I was holding onto. And the last picture that emerged was of my little son Isam, whom I love very much. Then a light went on in my head, and I could feel a cleansing. I seemed to dump all that junk right there. It was followed by an intense feeling of joy and serenity. It wasn't the kind of high I had before. It contained elements of that, but there was no strain to it. It was an experience in which I felt very loved. I can feel it now, in my blood.

"That night I slept in the tank with guys coming off of drunks, and I knew but for the grace of God there go I. I didn't sleep very well because I was so overwhelmed by this whole experience. I could see the Twelve Steps of AA written on the walls. I had read those steps many times, but they took on a new meaning for me. Then I called Ed and said, 'Hey, I thought you guys were gonna come down and see me last night.' He laughed as usual. He laughs a lot. He said, 'Oh, we lit a candle for you.' We lit a candle for you! I said, 'Well, I'm ready now.' So he sent somebody to pick me up. I didn't need to stay there. What had to happen, happened.

"I met him and some other people at a restaurant, and this power I had experienced years before was turned back on again. Boy, did it come on! It was really powerful. Ed knew that. He knew what had happened. And the remaining two days I was in Dallas, there were amazing encounters with people. I went with Ed to juvenile court. The director was a woman, and she wanted to hire me right on the spot. I hadn't said one word. I went to NCA, the National Council on Alcoholism, and this gal who was the director started asking questions and wondered if I would come and work for them. I wasn't even looking for a job. That's how great this power was."

VII

Rarely in recounting his life did Ali Birri bring up the subject of his family. I had to ask what they were thinking and doing during his college years in Beirut, during his decade of heavy drinking, and during the six years between his two "theophanies." When I did ask, I elicited admissions such as the following about the aftermath of his death-panic at twenty-one: "I don't remember what Ihsan was thinking at the time. She was pregnant with our second son, and she just carried the load." Ihsan was outraged by a brief affair Ali had with a nineteen-year-old, and she endured his periodic struggles with impotence. "As my alcoholism progressed she got the upper hand. I became suspicious and jealous of her. I didn't want anybody near her. When she wanted to go someplace I would saddle her with the kids, and if she enjoyed herself I would cause an uproar. That's one part of my life I really regret. Ihsan raised those kids." When Ali spent his week in Dallas in March 1969, he was forty-one, and the oldest of his children was already twenty.

What he regards as the final chapter in his life began with his return from Dallas and his introduction to AA. The beginning was anything but auspicious. "I called one of the kids and said, 'Meet me at the airport.' He met me, and I came home. I had a tremendous amount of power, but my wife didn't want to have a thing to do with me. The next thing I know, I begged her to take me back, and you know what happened? I lost my power, just like that. It went off just like it came on.

"I started going to AA meetings three times a day, seven days a week, but there was no power. Sometimes I'd go to midnight meetings just to stay alive. I didn't really accept the fact that I was an alcoholic. Even though I had written it down, I backed off of it in my own mind. I would say, 'My name is Ali and I'm a pill-coholic.' Finally I started to listen to some of the things that people said they did, and I started to see, hey, that's me, and that's me. Finally, I was able to say, 'Yeah, my name's Ali, and I'm an alcoholic.'

"I was out of work for three months, and then I got a job with the circuit court probation department. I was still going to two meetings a day. I'd catch a meeting, then do my field work, and then go to a meeting in the evening. My wife and I reconciled, and it looked like my life was starting to come back together. But I had ups and downs, jagged highs and lows. There was always a part of me. . . . I'd go to an AA meeting and I could hardly wait to get out. Other people would have coffee and associate with each other, but I limited my contacts. I made very few friends in AA.

"Around my second year I was getting more periods of depression and just not feeling right. I remember they announced my second anniversary at one group and asked me to say a couple of words. So I got up and said, 'You know, the first year was tough. The second year was even tougher. And right now I'm ready to send me back to the drawing board.' Just like that. I don't even know why I said that. A week later I collapsed emotionally and went into Sacred Heart Rehab Center, where Ed Chappell was waiting for me. He had moved from Dallas back to Chicago.

"At Sacred Heart I was whacko for about a week, until I got in touch with the fact that I hadn't accepted AA's First Step: 'We admitted we were powerless over alcohol and that our lives had become unmanageable.' I had accepted the first part of that step, but I had not fully accepted the second. I was admitting I was an alcoholic and I was seeking help, but I had not fully surrendered. In AA, it's called defiance. I was so defiant I wouldn't even pick up a drink. Most alcoholics will pick up a drink or a pill but I wouldn't, so I had an emotional collapse. I remember holding on not to go crazy, and then my energy just leveled. I was starting to ease off and feel a little better at Sacred Heart, when my father came to see me. Now, Sacred Heart is this old claptrap building, and I slept on a bunk in a dorm with seventy-eight other guys. Each of us had a locker, and that was all. I saw my father at the door, and he said, 'What the hell are you doing in a dump like this?' And I said to him, 'I'm here to save my ass.' He said, 'What do you mean, save it? Go home and take care of your family!' He gave me that order. I never had said no to my father before. I always honored him, but I had to tell him, 'No, father, I'm here to save my life.' I felt bad about that, but I knew I had to stay. I remember him walking out that door, very dejected."

In the decade that followed Ali never took a drink, but his energy—and his fortunes—fluctuated wildly. While he was still in Sacred Heart one of his sons was arrested for selling drugs to schoolchildren, and his wife emptied their bank account and fled to Lebanon. In 1973, after twenty-six years of marriage, he and Ihsan obtained a civil divorce. Two years later they finalized their separation with a Moslem divorce, and Ali jumped into a stormy relationship with a fellow alcoholic. In those years

Ali could not hold a job and collected unemployment compensation for months on end.

But in 1976, at the age of forty-eight, he entered a treatment program that addressed physical as well as emotional aspects of alcoholism. He went into training as an alcoholism therapist and got a job in a hospital. Since that time he has been steadily employed. Currently he splits his time between the hospital, a neighborhood services organization, and his own private practice, specializing in people with addictions. Normally, he stays with his clients for a year and then directs them to self-help groups based on AA principles. He has weeded most non-AA contacts from his life and declares that nothing, not even his family, is more important than AA. His entire life, from work to intimacy, is lived in AA "fellowship."

Ali has a simple explanation for his erratic energy swings in the 1970s. Whenever he "held on," the power clicked off. Whenever he "let go," it clicked back on. Ed Chappell kept drumming a lesson into him: he had to "detach," he had to relax "his tight grip on the universe," he had to sever "dependencies." "Dependencies" were emotional addictions as debilitating as pills and alcohol. Twice in his life Ali had completely let go of dependencies, and twice he had been flooded with a "higher power." But when he would revert to a dependency, as when he returned from Dallas and begged his wife to take him back, the power disappeared. Whenever Ali admits that he cannot handle things by himself, "the depressed person moves out and the power comes back on." In the aftermath of these surrenders, benefits come to him, even on the same day. In one case, he finds a job after months of searching; in another, he runs a particularly effective therapy group. "The key is surrender, surrender over and over again."

VIII

Surrender: it was the message Ali conveyed by telling his life story in a church basement, and it was the message he wished to convey to me. If you ask Ali why the fifty-fourth year of his life has been one of his best, he will tell you that the reason is surrender. Surrender, he explains, is expressed in AA's Third Step: We made a conscious decision to turn our will and our lives over to the care of God.

During one of our evening meetings Ali pulled the easel from the corner of his living room and drew an *I* on its shiny white surface. "It's time you heard about the Four Corners," he said, and enclosed the *I* in a large square. The *I* stood for the self, and each of the square's corners stood for a seducer of the self. In the corners Ali drew symbols of money, power, religion, and love. "The things in the corners don't have the power to give life, but the illusion is that they do. So I get the money today, or I get the love, but after the initial joy and pleasure I start to experience discontent. Eventually all this burns me up because it's not giving me life. Whatever energy I had now starts to run out.

"Alcoholics maintain the big I image. In the beginning it looks to them like they're walking on water." Below the box he drew a wavy line and sketched a figure on its surface. "They're walking right on top of the river of life. They've got it made. But as time goes on, that river starts to drag them down. Pretty soon they're thrashing around and yelling for help, and the next thing you know they start to drown. When they get down to the bottom, they see a bunch of zeros sitting around a table, an AA table." He drew the table as a rectangle with half a dozen circles around it. "If I come down here and I surrender and I become a zero equal with everybody else, I'm no longer the big I. And through the medium of the Third Step I'm given life. The experience of letting go connects us to that power which we call God. Then when I get the money, I get the power, I get the religion, I get the love, I can enjoy these things because they are no longer the source of my life. I will be content with whatever I get. Now, this process may take years, even after we come into AA. It may take a whole series of events like I've been describing to get there.

"This is the stuff Ed Chappell talks about. He keeps telling me I gotta separate from the corners. The toughest corner for me was the love corner, going back to the dependency on my mother. When I was six I took it that I could not live without Mother. Then, when she died, I also died. I really believe it was a death wish. And then I transferred my dependency to my wife. Even when I used to leave her on weekends and go out bar hopping and broad chasing, I was like a little boy running out and playing and coming home to Mama. When I left my wife and got into a relationship with this alcoholic, it was another transfer. It was like being addicted to heroin and then jumping to methadone—all part of the same lingering dependency pattern.

"I heard somebody say something the other day at an AA meeting that really got me in touch with how intense my symbiosis was to Mother. This gal talked about this guy she was married to. She said all he needed was him and his mother. She said they lived next door to her, and several times his mother even broke in and went to sleep in the same bed as them. Boy, did that hit me! The last several years I've been trying to detach from that kind of dependency. This last year I even gave up sex. I became celibate for a year. Recently there have been a couple of women, but I have no single attachment.

"Each time I was willing to let go of these corners I grew spiritually. Finally, something happened inside of me, which was my final surrender. I knew I had to detach, but I didn't have any more power to detach from the corners than I did from the alcohol and the pills. Finally, it sank into me that I was really powerless, that my life had become unmanageable, and that those are permanent conditions. I had never accepted the permanency of the conditions, at least for the second part of the First Step. That's when I let go and said, 'Hey, God, I can't handle this detachment. You're the one that's gonna have to pull it off.' Since then it's been happening. I'm feeling this freedom the Big Book talks about."

Ali had been anxious to get me to an AA meeting, and he drove me that evening to one in a run-down section of the city. He had dozens of meeting times and places at his fingertips, and he characterized this group as being on the young side with some bright "hippie" types. I met Ed Chappell there. He was a man of about sixty with piercing blue eyes such as Ali's grandfather might have had. He greeted me warmly and from time to time focused those eyes on me, as if they could read my inner thoughts. At one point he slipped me a piece of paper with a phone number, "if ever I needed help." To my surprise Ali told him that I was a candidate for Al-Anon.

Driving home, Ali said the evening had been an example of Twelfth-Step work. "The Twelfth Step comes as a result of all the other steps. 'Having had a spiritual awakening, we try to carry this message to other alcoholics and to practice these principles in all our affairs.' And what are the AA principles? They're love in action, as I see it. If you're really practicing AA principles you cannot *not* give love away. You can't contain it and selfishly say, well, this is mine. The more you give the more you've got to give. It continues to flow. From where? From a higher power.

"Some therapists understand the process of therapy, but they're not good therapists. They have book learning, but they don't manage to pull it off. What is it that some can do it and others can't? What is it that the ones who can are giving away? I believe it's God operating through people. Wednesday I know I touched a whole group. I know because they all came back and said, 'Boy, you were really right on. I wish we had tapes of that.' And I had given one of my standard lectures on the role of attitude change in recovering from alcoholism. It was a standard lecture, but when I let go and get out of the way, something happens. I touch people.

"Yesterday morning I was at the pool and I got talking to this young lady. I learned that she comes from alcoholic parents and grandparents. She drinks, but she minimizes what she drinks. She says, 'I don't want to quit drinking. I like the taste of the stuff,' which is one of the first things that alcoholics in their denial say. I gave her a look at what I saw happening with her. I told her about myself and suggested that if she wants to break out of the situation she's in, she might try an AA meeting. I said I would be willing to take her. It's as simple as that. Now she's ready to go to a meeting with me tomorrow. All we can do is introduce her to the fellowship of the meeting. It might not take for five, ten, or fifteen years, but when she's ready, she'll be back. Something happens at an AA meeting that doesn't happen anywhere else. She'll know where to go.

"I got a call earlier this evening from a young lady who had been one of my clients. She started as an Al-Anon, but we discovered she was really an alcoholic. We got her to AA, her life got changed around, but she has not surrendered. Yesterday I got her to commit to one thing. She came here, and I held her for about an hour. I just held her in my arms. Tight as a drum, still controlling, still being in charge, still not letting go. She was not ready to risk much, but at least she was willing just for me to hold her. We're going to help her eventually to let go."

When we drove through the city or went out to eat in the evening Ali would ask about my work and my family. Usually his questions were a prelude to his message, which was that I was searching for something and that to find it I would have to break dependencies and surrender. He alluded to various AA steps and to paradoxes that were no longer cryptic to me. When I mentioned that several relatives of mine had been addicted to alcohol he saw an opening and declared me a "co-alcoholic." Whenever I accepted one invitation to a meeting he was ready with another. But he never pushed. When I finally said no after the evening of his talk, he went no further.

It was on that evening that he mentioned a dream. "I have a fantasy about going to Lebanon someday and establishing an AA program there. For all I know, it might be an escape fantasy. There are days when my energy level is low and I'm in some pain. I still get very frightened at times. Those are the times when I would like to make a move. But somehow or another I still would like to do that. Lebanon has a severe drug and alcohol problem right now, especially as a consequence of this war. During the civil war the Christians were giving their fighting men pills and dope and everything else. Now they have a severe drug problem. Moslems too. Alcohol flows through that place like it was going out of style.

"When I was going to go there in 1975, my friends in AA said, 'Well, Ali, here's what you do. Once you get settled down, you put on a pot of coffee and you open up the Big Book before you and wait.' " Ali laughed at the simplicity of it all. "That's all you do," he repeated to himself.

"Just sit down, open up the Big Book, and wait. Don't worry. God will send the right persons to you." He looked at me once again. "It's true," he said. "People are put in our paths."

INTERPRETATION: THE TRANSFORMATION OF DEFECT; VALIDATING THE SELF

Ali Birri's life invites a variety of interpretations. Its fluctuations of energy can be explained biochemically, psychologically, religiously, and perhaps other ways as well. Each explanation assimilates the elements of his life into a specialized meaning system. Each places the life in the conceptual world of the interpreter, whether Ali wants it there or not.

I say this to bracket clinical interpretations that can rightly be made of "The Message" and to guide the reader to my own. I will even bypass Ali's own interpretation. Though he has hung his life on the framework of Alcoholics Anonymous, I will attach it to a different meaning system—to the theory of generativity that is unfolding in these pages. Doing so, I will adopt the perspective expressed by psychologist John Dollard nearly fifty years ago. In life history, Dollard wrote, "the person is viewed as an organic center of feeling moving through a culture and drawing magnetically to him the main strands of the culture."[1] From this perspective the story of Ali Birri has two contributions to make. First, it shows how the cultures to which people are "magnetically" attracted in their adult life permit defects in their past to be construed as strengths, thereby transforming the sense of wasted years. Second, it is an example of how generativity—in Ali's case, carrying the message—serves the function of preserving and validating a newly discovered self.

THE "RIGHT" CULTURE AND THE TRANSFORMATION OF DEFECT

In a fairy tale entitled *The Three Languages* an aged count becomes enraged with a son who squanders his schooling by learning the languages of dogs, frogs, and birds. The count orders servants to kill the boy, but they take pity on him and set him free in the forest. He wanders about and eventually comes upon a castle beset by the barking of bewitched dogs. Because he knows their language, he is able to release them from their spell and liberate the people of the kingdom. In gratitude, the king adopts the boy as his own.

When he grows into a man, the young count sets off for Rome. On the way he hears frogs croaking, and he realizes they are predicting the future. As he arrives in Rome the college of cardinals is meeting to elect a new pope. When two doves land on his shoulder, the cardinals take it as a sign and declare him pope. The count knows not the slightest thing about his new office, but he is able to understand the doves, who constantly whisper in his ear. Because he knows their language, he can take advantage of their wisdom and be spiritual father to the world. The animal languages that were a waste in his father's eyes have become the source of his fertility, and what was once stupidity has become genius.

The Three Languages illustrates a key motif in the lives of those who discover as adults a culture that is precisely right for them. Because the mythic substratum of the culture is exactly suited to their personal unconscious, it can transform their deepest defects into virtues and turn the virtues to reproductive ends. Often it is the culture's very outlet for generativity that effects the transformation. In the castle of his father (the "wrong" culture) the young boy is stupid and his languages useless, but in the new castle and in Rome (the "right" cultures) he is brilliant, and his languages are a resource. Throughout his adult life Ali Birri was desperately dependent on people and alcohol. In AA his dependency became a virtue; it became the source of his ability to surrender to a higher power.

Several narrators were conscious of similar transformations at the thresholds of new cultures. When Erzsi Domier stepped into the world of books and learning, the "trash" she had read as a girl became in her mind a valuable exposure to new words and new places that she could use in her writing. Her attempted suicide as a young mother became "material my kid can use." When Dorothy Woodson began to learn sign language and study the psychology of deafness, her painful memories of not being "heard" and her emotional "handicap" became the sources of empathy for deaf people. Similarly, the source of Robert Creighton's drive to be a good father is the pain he experienced at the hands of a bad father. As an alcoholism therapist said about fifteen years on binges: "I know what it's like to feel like a worm, to feel alone. To feel helpless, even hopeless, like there isn't a way out. I wouldn't trade that for anything. Now I can help patients see that a lot of negative things in their lives can be turned around to positive."

These expressions of transformation are in part rationalizations of a wasted, painful, or destructive past. At the same time they are reinterpretations of personal history used to confirm one's place in a new culture.

But they are more. The experience of transformation also contains realistic efforts at redoing that are made possible because *this* culture has the capacity that no other did: to sublimate *this* defect and channel it toward generative ends. In the new culture the very quality that once made the duckling ugly now makes the swan beautiful—and it is more than a matter of redefinition. It is a matter of energy that was once bottled up now being released.

There exists between Ali Birri and AA a "magnetic" attraction that goes beyond his desire to stay sober. Ali has not taken a drink for thirteen years, yet he devotes more and more energy to AA, seeing in it an inexhaustible mine of spirituality. If we look closely at the attraction, we will see a match between personality and culture that is more than "good enough." It is "just right."

In the founding memory of Ali's life, he is six years old, sick with typhoid, and terrified. Over a period of three months he lingers near death and learns a primitive lesson: only a single and very powerful source can save me. That source was his mother, and as Ali grew up he discovered that she was arbitrary, unpredictable, and beyond control. "One minute I'd be on a pedestal, and the next minute I'd be stomped." The only way to cope with her was to give in and turn his will over to her, to become totally dependent. Her caprice appears to have led him to a depressive episode of "learned helplessness"[2] in adolescence. Her will forced him into a marriage at nineteen. Then, suddenly and unpredictably, she abandoned him by dying. And Ali learned a second lesson: this single source of life can abandon me at any moment. Fearing he was going to die, Ali broke down emotionally and entered a deep depression.

As he came out of it he looked for something to replace his mother, a source that would not go away: the Koran and Bible, "big shots" in Lebanon, alcohol, pills, work, his wife. When they inevitably failed him, he reverted to the fundamental lesson he had learned as a child: surrender to a single powerful force. In one of the bleakest moments of his life, he got on his knees and prayed, "Allah, if you're there, please help me. I give up."

In the aftermath of that surrender, Ali met a man of power. Ali had always been impressed by men who had the *wahra*, the awesomeness, that he saw in his grandfather. He had always looked for saviors. Minutes after Ed Chappell showed *wahra* by talking a violent prisoner out of a knife, Ali was placing himself in his hands. When he told Ed his life story he received the preamble to a new interpretation: "Your problem is mother." Over the next six months Ali clung to Ed and found his condition improving. But when Ed forced him to make a decision on his own, he panicked. To make the decision he selected at random a passage from the Koran and gave himself up to its mandate. He surrendered again, but in a different way, to a "higher" power. He was rewarded with an intensely beautiful mystical experience that filled him with energy.

Then Ed moved away, and Ali was left on his own. After a few years he began to run out of energy and turned once more to drinking and pills. Again he surrendered to the Koran, placed himself in Ed's hands, and was rewarded with another mystical experience. The cycle repeated itself a third time: separation from Ed, loss of energy, return to Ed. For the last eighteen years Ed has been the man who is "waiting" for Ali when he hits bottom. Now, at a time Ali considers the best of his life, he sees Ed almost daily. A man of authority and charisma, Ed was the cultural gatekeeper who could activate Ali's wish for a savior. Now he continues as Ali's guide into AA's mythic center.

It should be clear how exactly the principles of AA fit Ali Birri's personality. AA's first three steps—admitting that one's life has become unmanageable, believing in a higher power, turning one's will over to God—merely prescribe what he has been doing all his life. To someone without Ali's past, even a fellow alcoholic, the concepts of AA may appear remote, empty, even alien. Entering AA would no doubt induce culture shock. But to Ali the concepts have always appeared rich and inexhaustible with meaning, possessing from the beginning an uncanny sense of the familiar. They were familiar because of his rearing in Islam, which is a religion that emphasizes submission to the will of Allah. They were familiar because he has always felt that an outside power was in control of his life, and though he tried to control that power—whether his mother or alcohol—he was never able to do so. In his most desperate moments he always gave himself up to it. The ideas of an unmanageable life that had to be surrendered to a higher power, then, fit Ali Birri. They recapitulated lifelong patterns and had somatic as well as cognitive referents. So closely did they match the contours of his personality that he felt personally addressed by them. He experienced the nourishment that this culture was capable of giving him.

And so his characteristic forming of addictive dependencies—his defect—was transformed into a virtue. It should be clear that AA does not break a pattern of dependency in Ali but carries it forward. His neurosis is not resolved but sublimated. When Ali speaks of "breaking" dependencies, he is referring to all but one: that on AA and the higher power that will never abandon him. He wishes that dependency to be total, and he wishes others to know about it. Hence he carries the message of surrender, being at last the sheikh he was originally expected to be.

Ali's entry into AA reiterates themes seen in other stories. His initiation began with a statement of identity: "I am an alcoholic." It took him several years to accept that statement, but now he articulates the familiar sense that his "new" self is really very old. In AA Ali was linked through the "Big Book," *Alcoholics Anonymous*, to stories of AA's founders, to the "great deeds" in the past that exemplify the ideals of AA and give hope that they are attainable. From the time he first "spilled his guts" to Ed Chappell, Ali has told and retold his life story, each time adjusting the fit to his culture's archetypal life patterns. At AA meetings, which are built around life-storytelling, he is exposed to other examples of rewritten personal history. When he hears something that "hits" him, when he sees his own life coming out "like the Big Book says," he gains confidence that he is indeed on the right path. Now he believes that everything in his life, including "chance" openings of the Koran and "chance" meetings with Ed Chappell, has been guided by God. None of the lives I recorded were as chaotic as Ali's, but no narrators were as convinced that plan and purpose lay beneath the chaos.

There is potential danger in cultures that magically transform defects into virtues, for any evil can be legitimated by a cohesive body of like-minded individuals. But self-help groups like AA have generally steered their members in a positive direction. In these groups the liabilities one has, the scars one carries, even the wrongs one has done become resources for others with similar problems. When people tell the story of how badly they abused their children or how compulsively they gambled, they are not only helping others. They are helping themselves by using a generative outlet to extract value from the wasted, defective years of their lives.

VALIDATING THE SELF

From no other individual I interviewed did I feel the recruiting pressure that I felt from Ali Birri. Others treated me as a generative target of one kind or another, but no one did so with the subtle constancy of Ali. His desire to bring me into Al-Anon was a variant of what I call the generative transference. Like anyone else who enters his life, I was seen as a recipient of the message.

Because the urge to proselytize was so strong in Ali, his story brings to the fore a theme common to many of the lives I recorded: how generative objects of all kinds—children, disciples, artistic products— serve the reflexive function of validating the progenitor. Generative objects define and contain the self, counter its centrifugal forces, and secure its footing in its present culture. They say the progenitor's place in life is the right one, that his or her life project is worthwhile. In some cases the containment and confirmation are symbolic and abstract and in others they are very real and concrete. As Erikson himself was aware, generativity (the seventh of his stages of life) sharpens identity (the fifth stage) as much as identity determines the outlines of generativity.

The validating power of progeny took many forms in the stories to which I listened. In one case, a child literally saved the life of his mother, who had taken an overdose of sleeping pills. In "Journey into the Lie," a mother's impulse to "exit" was restrained by the thought of a daughter who would have to live with the stigma of a suicide-mother. In "Mirror, Mirror," Dorothy Woodson saw in her son "a reason to fight for life" despite a lump in her breast. The validating power of followers motivated the competition of the grandparents for the allegiance of their grandsons in "In a Dream Castle." In accounts not published here the birth of a son forced a man to define himself as a homosexual, and the arrival of a daughter led a woman to live up to her "better" self. (Interestingly, on the six occasions when a specific child was mentioned in this context, it was always the youngest.) All these functions—keeping alive, defining, confirming—reveal the validating power of children.

The search for generative objects to validate the self is particularly strong when the self is vulnerable, as it is in a new culture, or when beliefs that protect the self are threatened. Leon Festinger's *When Prophecy Fails*, for example, reports a case of proselytizing that resulted, paradoxically, from a shattering of belief. A religious doomsday group had prophesied that the world would end by flood and that they would be saved by flying saucers before sunrise of a designated day. When the flood and the saucers failed to materialize, the group declared that the world had been spared because of their faith, and they set out to recruit new members. Proselytizing reduced the dissonance surrounding a belief badly shaken by reality.[3] When generativity of any kind is so clearly an attempt at bolstering the self it is rightfully called agentic: the emphasis is on the self and what children and followers can do for the self. Reflexive benefits for the progenitor are also evident in communal generativity, yet the accent here is on the progeny, not on the self.

Alcoholics Anonymous and organizations that share its philosophy are explicit about the reflexive power of new recruits. "If you hang onto your sobriety, you'll end up getting drunk" and "Get somebody to work on" are two of AA's well-known maxims. You carry the message to someone else as a way of shoring up your own beliefs, and when you see the Twelve Steps working with that person, your own belief in their efficacy is confirmed. The alcoholism therapist I referred to earlier had been sober for only two months when she was asked by a physician to do informal counseling at a halfway house for alcoholics. "I thought he must have some confidence in me if he wants me to go down there and talk to them about being sober," she said. "It made it more difficult for me to go out and drink on the weekends, when I was going to go down and talk to those men about sobriety on Wednesday nights. Now when I'm telling somebody about staying sober and how it gets better, I can be having a rotten day. But saying to someone new that it will get better helps me to remember, yeah, this is going to get better, it's going to pass."

In AA you tell your story because telling it is good for you. That is why Ali agreed so readily to tell me his. At initiation, life-storytelling is the medium through which one's history is attached to AA's history. But later on life-storytelling has a reproductive tone, as it did when Ali was spreading the message in a church basement and when he was recounting his life to me. At this point life stories begin to sound like the archetypal stories in AA's Big Book. They not only help to propagate AA by retelling its central stories, they also reinforce the storyteller's own convictions. The narrator has to live up to the story he or she tells.

Ali Birri is currently receiving the validation crucial to his well-being. When I saw him a year and a half after I first recorded his story, he described his life as more consistently serene. He attributes his present health to a deeper understanding of surrender and to his constant presence in the AA fellowship. I would add that he is also helped by the constant presence of his guide and the fact that his entire work life is now a vehicle through which he carries the message. Ali joined AA at the age of forty-one, but it was not until he was forty-eight that his recovery was stabilized. This is the point at which he began to pass his philosophy on through the medium of therapy. Between his clinical work and AA, he now has numerous generative outlets. What he said of the energy he feels when giving a talk is equally true of the "new" self he has embedded in the "right" culture: "You gotta give it away to keep it."

10 · *When the Wheat Was Green*

*T*he story for which Sarkis Hashoian will be remembered began on a beautiful spring day in eastern Turkey. Sark thinks it was in May because the wheat was still green. The year was 1915, but Sark does not say, "1915." Instead, he says, "massacre time."

Sark is seventy-six and one of the dwindling number of Armenians who were firsthand witnesses of the Turkish government's attempt during World War I to settle the "Armenian question" through deportation and extermination. He lives now in an inconspicuous bungalow not far from the cleaning store that he owned and operated for the last twenty-two years of his working life. Set on a street that has lost some trees, his home has beige aluminum siding, a tiny concrete porch with a brown awning, and just enough room for two lawn chairs.

I was put in touch with Sark because Armenian scholars I knew thought it important to record stories like his before it was too late, and because his family welcomed the prospect of having a single account of all the events of his life. I first met him on a sunny, cool spring morning reminiscent, perhaps, of the one in 1915. Tall and slender, he had a warm, pleasant face, wore glasses, and had thin white hair and a slight gray mustache. He wore a cardigan sweater that concealed a small waist-line bulge. His living room was filled with photographs and paintings, and every available window sash was covered with colorful glass knickknacks.

Before he began, Sark warned me that speaking of "massacre time" might give him the "shakes." In the beginning of his story, however, when he spoke of the years "before massacre," he nestled his head cozily in the shoulder of his chair. At times he bolted up like an ostrich and greeted a question of mine with a loud "Ooooh!" or "Yeeaah!" He wanted to tell his story as honestly as possible, and he proved to be an earnest narrator. Here is what he said.

I

"I was born in Turkey, and the village's name was Chanakhgee. My mother said the time was when we were doing noodles. Noodles, that was September. I said, 'What year?' She said, 'I don't know.' Heh, heh. I think maybe I could say 1905 or 6.

"It was mountainous around our village, and that's why they called it Chanakhgee. Chanakhgee means 'bowl.' I suppose that maybe couple hundred years ago some Moslems used to live in that village. And Armenians came and then these Moslems, these Kurds, they left. There were about a hundred and fifty homes in our village, and only two were Kurdish homes, and they were very friendly. We were all together nicely and didn't have no troubles. We were safe in the village because there were no Turks there.

"The houses were stone with a flat roof. In the summer it got hot, but inside, with those walls all stone, no heat would penetrate. We had a living room and two bedrooms, and then we had the animals in back. The barn was on one side and the cattles on the other, but there were walls between them. There was a cellar in the ground, and they had a door over it to keep it cool.

"The village, they were all farmers. Everybody had their own plots around the village and they plowed just like farmers over here. If I go over there, I betcha I can remember it. I could go and see all my plots, where they are. The plots were small. When the family had two or three boys and they'd get married, the father had to cut the plots and give to each one equal shares. So the plots got smaller and smaller, and the family grew, and there was no food to eat. So they had to come to America to work. They used to have grapes and all kind of fruits in the surroundings, but the Kurds, they used to come at night and steal everything. So they quit producing fruits and grew wheat, barley, cabbages, and things like that.

"I had my grandfather, my mother, and my two sisters. I was the oldest one. I don't remember my father. My father died in America. I just vaguely remember when I was small, my grandfather and I were sitting by the fireplace, and I went and cuddled by him. I was fooling around with the fire, and I felt a drop fall down. My grandfather was crying. I looked up that he's crying, and that's as much as I can remember. Later on they told me, 'Well, your father's dead.' He had a sore side and the doctors, they said he had appendix. He got operated on at eight in the morning, and he got pneumonia, and he fell from the bed and he died.

"I thought my grandfather was my father. My grandfather, he was crazy about me. He was a tall man and he was strong, and he had a face just like a stone, that face he had. His word was like law, and all the villagers, they used to respect him. My friends used to steal tobacco from him. See, he had these earthen jars, and he put tobacco in there to keep it nice and fresh. The kids used to get in the house, and they didn't see nobody around, and they took the jar and put tobacco in their pockets and put it back. And then my grandfather found out the tobacco was going down. 'I don't smoke that much. Something must be wrong.' One day he caught them and said, 'Don't you dare come over here to steal tobacco!' So they coaxed me to get tobacco, and I got caught. My grandfather said, 'You're not going to smoke?' I said, 'No, no, I don't smoke. My cousin told me to get it.' 'Well, next time, don't do it.' I never did it again. My cousin wrote a book in Armenian about our village, and he said that my grandfather was the village's mailman. He used to go to the main post office in another city and get all the mails and bring them to the village. That was his job because no one else would take a chance to go over there. Those Kurds, they came and robbed them. My cousin wrote that my grandfather was going to get the mail once and he saw that two Kurds were following him. So he figures out that these guys, they got something up their sleeves. So he gets to a little river in an isolated place. He takes all his clothes off, puts them on his head, and walks through the river and gets on the other side. These Kurds are following. He goes behind a tree, and they follow him too close, and he jumps on both of them. He grabs each one and hits their heads like this, and he ties both of them, and he takes them to the city, and he says these people tried to rob me. And the gendarmes, they took them. My grandfather didn't know what they did to them, but he got the mail and came back. That was before massacre.

"Turks used to come to the village. They had government suits on, and some of them wore fezzes and some wore—what did they call that?—just like a Russian Cossack's hat made from pure lambskin. They asked, 'How many cattles you got?' They counted them. They checked on your wheat fields, how many plots you had. The villagers that had guns, they hid them. Then all the elders went to the mayor's place, and the Turks figured out that so-and-so got so much, and so-and-so got so much, and they wanted taxes for all of that. I seen it but I was so young, I didn't pay attention.

"The church was in the center of the village. If I said the church's name was Sarkis, you wouldn't believe it, heh, heh. My name was that church's name. All the Armenians in the village, they used to go to that church and kiss those stones. They wore those stones out. We used to go to church every evening. The priest had eight children, and he had to work his own plot because the villagers couldn't help him. They went over there in the evening and gave him a couple of pennies. That wouldn't do with eight kids.

"We had a school right next to the church. Until massacre we would go to school. We studied arithmetic and geography, but the Turks wouldn't let them teach about Armenians. In wintertime, every child had to bring a bundle of wood to school to burn in the stove. Once they had snow for a whole week. It covered the whole house, and you couldn't get the animals out. You had to melt snow for the animals to drink. But just as soon as March came, the snow melted right away and you could see the grass grow.

"When spring came around, we had to do chores. My grandfather was too old to plow, and I was too small, so my grandfather brought Armenian orphan from another village, and that kid stayed with us until massacre time. I had to go with him and take care of the oxens. You gotta have three oxens. Two oxens pull plow and one you take to graze. Then an hour later you bring that one and let another one go, see? You exchange it. Once in a while I tried to hold the darn plow but I couldn't hold it. That sharp edge hit the oxen and cut their legs.

"In summertime the shepherd would take the sheep and go to the cottages in the mountains. There was a lake there with running water from the mountains. All summer long the animals would be all over those mountains. When the sheep had little ones we used to graze them. You had to bring them at noon when the shepherd milked the sheep and let them have a little nip. We drank sheep's milk and cattle milk and goat's milk, and then they mixed them together and they boiled it and they made yogurt out of it. From yogurt we got the butter and we got the cheese. Every fall they slaughtered one or two lambs for winter.

"Then they brought the wheat from outskirts to thresh it out. You had to bring it in with mules and donkeys and horses. They had a flat place, and they piled the wheat there. They had a board just like a sled, but they had a stone underneath that it cut the wheat. And on hot days the oxen pulled that damn thing and we had to ride it. We went round and round and round until that husk turned into fine, fine dust. When it was all crushed they poured it in a machine and separated the wheat. The rest, they put it in a barn for the animals to eat in winter.

"My mother was doing all the milking and doing housework, and then during harvest time, she had to cut the wheat all by hand. There was no male in the family to take care of chores, so she was doing them. My mother was very strong. Otherwise, during massacres, if you don't be strong, you die."

II

"And the massacres came, and one morning we heard the guns. I would say it was in May because the wheat was growing and it was still green. In the village people got together and sent a couple of guys to check up. They went, and all of the village was surrounded by Kurds. The Kurds told them, 'If you gonna resist, we gonna kill everyone.' Our elders came to us and said, 'You must leave the village. Go!' Even the priest said, 'Best thing is we get out. Let them come and take whatever they want. We go another village, and maybe in week or so, we come back.'

"We went out below the village, and the Kurds rushed in, oh, I would say about a hundred yards from us. That was the first time I saw those god-darned horses. Those horses, they come from farther east. And those people, they have those long white felt hats, and they put the turban around it, and one side hangs down like this. When they sit on those horses, you think that giants coming. They just drive right in. If you are underfoot, they step over you. Then they get the whip.

"They got in our place where we kept the cattles there. They broke the doors, and they took the cattles out and all our sheep and goats. But they forgot we had a horse. And my cousin said, 'At least let's go and get the horse so we can put some belongings on it.' While he was up there, a Kurd shot him in the leg, and he fell, and that was it.

"We had to leave, and we came to another village. There was Armenian house over there, and they let us in. We stayed there two weeks, and then again one morning the Kurds did the same thing in that village. They killed all the males, the ones that couldn't run away. They got the sword and pushed it through kids and just picked 'em up like that. I saw one of 'em's legs cut off. Then they killed my father—my grandfather—right on the steps of that house. His brother was lying out here, and my grandfather, he was on the second step, right against the wall, with his mouth open. I saw him with my eyes, and I got scared and I screamed and my mother grabbed me and said, 'Don't look, don't look!' Meantime, these Kurds surrounded us and pushed us to a larger space outside. They took my clothes off. One woman was standing over there, and this Kurd came and tried to take her clothes off. She was grabbing the clothes, and she went over to gendarme. 'We haven't done anything. Why do you do this to us?' And you know what gendarme did? He kicked her over the head. My mother, she had two dresses on, and she took one of them off and put it on me as a girl, because if it was a boy they kill him. Then this Bedouin grabbed my sister and said, 'I'm gonna take this girl to be my daughter.' And we all started crying. My mother pulled her, and that guy put her on his shoulder and took her. That was the end of it.

"And they picked up all those people and said, 'We're gonna send you into interior.' So we gotta walk, walk from that village. No food. Not a thing. The gendarmes from the village went with us. They were Turks, and they wouldn't say nothing to the Kurds. 'If you kill 'em, it's okay, but you gotta move these people out.' The Kurds figured that they take 'em out between two mountains so they can't run away, and then they start coming in from both sides and rob them and kill them. My mother saw large bush and while the people, about three or four hundred people, were walking, my mother grabbed me and my little sister. 'Get behind that bush!' And we stayed there in the bush till all the people went. Then we ran down to a ditch until it got dark.

"Night came, and it got cold. My mother and my sister and I, we were shivering. We had to hug each other to keep us warm. My sister had measles, and she was not feeling good. So what the heck we gonna do?

"Next day my mother carried her, and we went to a village close by our village. We tried to see what's what. We were hungry. My mother told me, she said, 'You sit over here. I go in that little village, get you something to eat.' So she went to Kurdish houses and said, 'How about giving us some buttermilk or something? My daughter is sick.' They got scared that this was contagious, so they wouldn't let her in.

"So my mother carried my sister, and we went to another village. We stayed with Kurds there about two days, and then some gendarmes came and told these people, 'If you have any Armenians, you better let us know, because if we find later on, you'll be guilty.' When my mother heard that, she put me behind the door. She said, 'Don't you dare come out, whatever happens. If they take me, I'll come back and find you.' And then she went out with my sister and said, 'I'm Armenian.' They took her. Meantime, I'm back there behind the door, and these people didn't say nothing. I didn't know what was happening. The lady gave me a piece of bread and put something on me just like a Kurdish boy.

"The gendarmes took my mother to another village. It happened that in this village there was an old Kurdish man who was very friendly with my grandfather, my mother's father. They were like . . . over here, the Indians, they used to say we are blood brother. My grandfather was a blacksmith, and this guy used to take everything over there, and my grandfather wouldn't charge because he was the blood brother. And this old man saw my mother and remembered right away. 'Oh, you are so-and-so's daughter!' And he told the gendarmes, he said, 'I'm gonna take this woman for me. I'm gonna keep her.' And, by golly, they let him have her.

"So my mother told this man, 'My son is in so-and-so place. I want to get him back.' So this guy sent two guys to pick me up.

"I came, and I asked my mother, 'Where's my sister?' She started crying. I said, 'What happened?'

" 'I drowned her.'

"You haven't got medical care, so what the hell you gonna do? My sister, she had her eyes blind and filled with maggots. My mother couldn't help her. She said, 'There was a little lake over there, and I took her there, and I took her clothes off and said, I'm gonna wash you a little bit.' She took her in the water and got out about this far and dropped her. But when she dropped her, my sister came back up and said, 'Ma-ma, what have I done to you? You gonna drown me.' My mother went back and picked her up and 'her flesh came all over me,' so she couldn't do nothing. She took her back out again and dropped her. My sister, she came up once again, and that was it. And then my mother sat down under a tree for hours. And this old man came and said, 'She's gone now, so forget it.' He brought her back, and she told me all that story."

III

"About a week later, another bunch of gendarmes, they came around and asked for us. So the man said, 'We got some neighbors here that might snitch on you. And I'm gonna be in trouble. I want you to go.'

"My mother said okay, and when night came, we ran away from there.

"We went to our village. The whole god-darned place was demolished. Everything was taken. We had nothing to eat, so my mother said, 'You know, I'm gonna take a chance and go to this Kurdish house.' She went over there at night, and this woman saw her, and she started embracing her. 'Why did it have to happen, this? This village was such a nice place. We were all just like brothers and sisters.' My mother said, 'Well, I don't know, but we are hungry. My son is over there. We haven't eaten for two days.'

"So the woman gave bread and gave buttermilk, cheese, and my mother brought it to me. She said to this woman, 'We'll come back and see you again.' She wouldn't take a chance and tell her where we were because, she said, 'You can never tell.'

"My mother went back, and this woman said, 'You know what I heard? Your brothers and quite a few Armenians, they ran away from massacres. They're in mountains. If you get a chance, you go over there and maybe they can do something.' So we went to the mountains, and we hid by our cottages, and it got dark, and we saw something moving. We thought it was a bear or something. And then my mother heard a voice coming. She said, 'I'll bet you that's my brother.' So we hollered in the night, and it was him. There were twelve of them. They ran away from massacre. At night they stayed in the cottages, and when daytime came they went in mountains. At that time, the wheat was just right. So they cut the wheat and took the husk out. They found a broken jug, made a fire, and boiled that and ate it.

"So my uncle told my mother, he said, 'Listen, there's no sense to stay here. We don't know what we're going to do. The best thing is you go to one of the close-by villages. You tell them you're so-and-so's daughter. You do their chores, take care of their animals. Maybe they'll keep you there for a while.'

"So she listened. She said, 'Okay, we go,' and we came to a little village. She told these Kurdish people, 'I'm so-and-so's daughter,' and, by golly, they let us in. They kept us over there that winter, and then this one Kurdish family wanted to come to Kharput. That's a city going west, about 150 miles away. 'Over there,' they said, 'there's not too much winter.' My mother said, 'Can we come with you?' They said, 'Sure, you can come with us.' In that time, everything was quiet. My mother was dressed as a Kurdish woman, and they gave me a little fez. It was so dirty that nobody wanted to look at it, heh, heh. So what are you gonna do?

"We crossed a river, and we came up to three mountains, and the middle is the highest mountain. All the villages surround that mountain. This one village was quite a bit higher than the rest of them. We came to the village, and we begged for some bread, and those people gave us bread and cheese and buttermilk. Over there they have a lot of cotton. My mother was good for making clothes, so this one villager, he said, 'Well, you come and work for me and you do this spinning.' So she was doing that spinning all day long, and she got a living out of it. In the next house they told me that I could come and take out sheep to graze and come and clean the barn.

"Then one day, accidentally, my aunt came. Where did she come from, I don't know. She said the Turks and the Kurds took them on a bridge and came in from both sides and started slaughtering, and she threw her child into the river. Then they pushed each other, and finally she ran away and that's why she came. She was all by herself.

"We were all right in the village because those villagers, they used to give us a lot of food to eat. They bought me a pair of shoes and gave me clothes. There isn't much winter there. It snows in the morning, and by noon it's all gone. So it was warm. After a couple of years, I slept in their house, and I was happy then, heh, heh. I didn't have nothing to worry about.

"We were there three, four years. We were not Armenians. We were Kurds. We dressed like Kurds. I played with Kurdish boys, and they didn't even know I was Armenian. I was Moslem at that time. At night I used to pray in Arabic. I just picked up the habit of doing it.

"In the evening I used to go over to my mother's and talk for a while, and then I went back to go to sleep. We had to talk in Kurdish. My mother, she said there was the same kind of massacre in 1895, but they didn't kill many people. The people went to homes of friendly Kurds in surrounding villages, and the Kurds came and took everything. 'In two weeks we came back to our homes.' She thought that was how it was supposed to be this time, but then a whole year went by and there was no hope. 'They want to kill us. That's all there is to it.' The Turks used to tell the people that the Russians are coming. 'We want to send you to interior so you don't get hurt.' The people don't know what the heck is going on. They take you to interior, take your shoes off, take your clothes off, and find any jewelry on you. They take it, and after that they kill you. That's all.

"My mother was a religious person, but sometimes she said, 'I don't think we praying does any good.' Every night we went to church, we kissed those stones, we prayed, and this happened. 'Why do you let the Turks do that to us? We haven't done anything to anybody.' She said the Turks used to go in the church and take the Bible and spit on it. They tore it apart and told 'em, 'Where is your Jesus Christ? Let him help you. Then we believe.' Nothing happened. 'The strong,' she said, 'have the swords.'

"But she did pray to find her daughter. She always did. All the time my mother said, 'Someday I'm gonna find your sister. I don't care, I can walk to end of the world, as long as I have hopes that I can find her.' "

IV

"My mother knew those Bedouins used to travel from east to west. When it got cold they went south or west with their herd and then they came back. My mother said, 'Maybe they'll come into these mountains.' There's water that comes right out of the high mountain, and it's green grass around there. Those people like that kind of place. They bring their sheep there and they make cheese and they take it to the city and sell it. That's how their life was.

"Some Kurdish fellow came over to that mountaintop looking for jobs, and we started to probe in his life, and he said he had been into Bedouin places where there were a few Armenian kids. So my mother asked him, 'Are you willing to take me over there to see if I can find my daughter?' My mother didn't know which group of Bedouins my sister was with, but she said, 'I'm gonna take a chance.'

"He said, 'If you give me something to eat, I'll help you.' So we gave him some wheat and about ten pounds of halva. They had a lot of mulberries there, wild ones that you pick up. They spread them under the sun, and they dry them out. Then they pack 'em together in a pan and put a stone on it, and that crushes it. It's very sweet. They call it halva. She gave him some of that halva, and he said, 'Okay, I'll come with you.'

"My mother told me what happened. They went to the first camp, they looked around, she wasn't there. They went further up and then she found my sister. But she wouldn't go near her. She wanted to know exactly that that was her daughter, so she just watched the reaction of her. The Bedouins didn't know my mother was Armenian. She wore the same type of clothes that all the rest of them had, and she could speak fluent Kurdish. They thought she was just ordinary person come to buy some cheese or butter. She slept right outside the tent. In the morning she would get up and tell those people, 'I can do the chores for you. Just give me a piece of bread.' She told me they used to feed her. They're good that way, you know? Anybody hungry, they feed 'em.

"Little by little my mother went over to talk to my sister. My sister could not speak Armenian. She forgot everything. Finally, my mother told her, 'I'm your mother. I been looking for you for four years. I want you to come with me.'

"My sister didn't want to go because she didn't know my mother. My mother said, 'You got aunt, you got brother. I want to take you with me and get you out of this misery that you're in.' My sister figured what difference it make if I stay here or go somewhere else with this woman, so she agreed. And then that Bedouin wouldn't let her go. My mother said, 'This is my daughter I came after!' The man said no. He thought my mother had money to give, but she said, 'I haven't got no money. You know that we were robbed. But this is my daughter, and I want to take her with me.' And the man said no. So she said, 'Well, if you don't let her go, I'm gonna go home.'

"She said that so he wouldn't be suspicious of her. When night came and she heard that everybody was sleeping, she went into the tent and told my sister, 'Come on, get up. Let's get out of here.' Early morning, they're gone.

"Meantime, it's about two weeks, we didn't hear nothing. My aunt says, 'You know, they might do something to her, kill her or something.' By golly, end of two weeks, there she comes with my sister.

"When my sister saw me, she recognized me. She said, 'You're my brother.' She said it in Kurdish. She came and hugged me. She didn't even remember my mother, but she remembered me. Then she said, 'This is my family.' "

V

"Then my aunt went down to another village and stayed with a woman who had been in this large city, Kharput. This woman told my aunt there was orphanage there. This orphanage, they picked up all these young kids, Armenians, and they took them and kept them.

"So we went down there to find out what's what. We came to Kharput, I would say, between 1920 and 1921. I was maybe fourteen, fifteen years old. We put my sister in orphanage, but they wouldn't take me. I was tall for my age, and they said, 'He can go out and work.'

"My mother said, 'Well, you know, there is a place where you can learn weaving. I'm gonna take you over there.' She took me, and the guy said, 'Sure, come on in and learn, but for two or three weeks we don't pay nothing. You bring your own food and you just learn.'

"So I got a job weaving. They pay you by the yardage. So many yards you weave, that's what you're going to get. I wasn't, heh, fast enough to do it. Maybe a couple of yards a day. I thought this is no good. I can't make nothing out of this. So I went to the place where all the shoe-makers were, and I saw some guy who was speaking Armenian. I went over there, I said, 'You're Armenian?' He said yes. He was the head of that shoe shop. I said, 'Is possible if I come over here and learn shoe-making?' He said, 'Have you ever done any shoemaking?' I said, 'No, I want to come over and learn.' So he said, "Come tomorrow morning.' So I went over there, and they taught me how to do the top, the facing, and all that, and they gave me—how I say that in American money?—would be about twenty cents a day.

"We rented a little house in Kharput. My mother and my aunt, they were going in surrounding villages and working there all day. They got, say, half a bushel of wheat, barley, whatever. We lived close by the orphanage, and every Sunday my sister used to come and stay all day. At that time it was safe in Kharput. The Turks wouldn't bother us no more if you were Armenian, see? They even had Armenian church in Kharput, and my mother started taking me there. Little by little, it came back again, our language.

"Then my aunt brought us a rumor that the Turks were gonna trap Armenians. See, the Turks were smart. They said we're gonna draft the men regardless of what nationality are you. They catch you on the streets, they wanna know how old are you, and they say, 'You gotta fight for your country.' They take you, and that's the end of it. You're gone. If you're Armenian, they kill you. Nobody knows.

"My aunt had a friend, he said, 'The best thing for us, we better run away from 'em. There's a Kurdish fellow, he's been in Aleppo two, three times, and he's taken some people over there. He wants ten gold pieces to take you there.' Aleppo is about three hundred miles away, in Syria. They didn't have no massacre there.

"My mother said to me, 'If you get a chance to go to Aleppo, you go.' We found the guide, and my aunt made the arrangements. We didn't give that Kurd no money. When I got to Aleppo, the Kurd would have to bring a letter from me, show it to my aunt and mother, and then he gets his money.

"There were six of us, five Armenians, and one Greek. This guide was making big money—ten gold pieces from each person. He told us we're gonna have different kind of clothes, Kurdish clothes. 'You gotta salute like that, and you gotta learn the language. Make mistake speaking it and we all get caught and that's it. We be chopped off. Your name is Kurdish this, the other guy's name is Kurdish this. Don't give no Armenian names.' My name was Hussein, just like King Hussein.

"My mother was in a village working so I said good-bye to my sister and my aunt. Those days, there was no such thing as you gonna see them again or not. That's life, that's all. I said, 'Just as soon as I get to Aleppo, I'm gonna write to United States. I have cousins there. They gotta send me money and then maybe you will come.' "

VI

"So we left. We used to walk at night and sleep daytime. When we got short of food, the guide went and bought some bread and brought it to us. One night we slept outside, and I got sick. I must have caught pneumonia, you know? I got so bad I couldn't walk, and I said, 'Leave me here. Go.' He said, 'No, if we leave you here, somebody comes over, asks questions. You might snitch on us and then we'd all get caught.' So they grabbed me. 'Once in a while you sit down and once in a while walk.' Finally, we got some place where they had a fountain with water coming out, and they grabbed my head and they pushed it in that water to shake me up. In the meantime, this Kurdish guide, he saw a flock of sheep. 'We gonna catch one of those sheep.' They milked it and gave it to me, and, by golly, I felt better when they gave me that milk.

"We came on this wide river, the Euphrates, and we had to get across. So this Kurd went into the village and got a couple of guys to come over. We had to pay them some money. They had a sheepskin raft. The air is in there like a balloon, and that's why it floats. They have a long stick, and they just push it until you get on other side.

"Then we came to this large city, Malatia, they call it. This Kurd knew a couple of Armenians living there, and so he took us there. I was still sick, and they tried to feed me and bring me to life, you know? We stayed there five days, and next morning we started walking.

"That son-of-a-gun guide, he knew what he was doing. Once in a while he put his head down on the ground and said, 'There is people coming. Let's get out.' Because at night you don't know and you suddenly see somebody is right ahead of you. So we would move out and get under a bush and sure enough there would be four or five horses. One place we got so close to 'em. The road was here and we got in a ditch. You don't move, you don't talk, you don't cough. They came and just went by. We didn't know who they were.

"Five days we walked. We came to the city that is the home town of our guide. That was halfway to Aleppo. Summertime, all the people, they go to the cottages. Nobody was in the city so we were safe there. He took us in a house and said, 'I'm gonna go to the cottage and I'm gonna bring you some food.' So we stayed there three, four days. He came back, brought us some food, and he went again. Then we heard some footsteps on the roof. It's a flat roof, and they have a little hole in it to give light. One of our guys, he was smoking a cigarette, and this guy was walking on the roof with someone and said, 'What is the smoke coming out?' He knew that nobody was supposed to be here. So this guy walked down, came to the door, and tried to open it. Well, what are you gonna do? It was too late now, so we figured out that if this guy opens the door and comes in we would never let him go out. You gotta kill him. So we stayed behind the door, and he hit it with his foot. He left, and we thought he was going to bring some other people to investigate. He didn't come, thank God. When evening came, our guide came from the cottage, and we told him all about it. 'Oh, man,' he said, 'we gotta get out of here tonight. They're suspicious. This is my house, and they know what I am doing. You don't know when they're gonna come, and we're all gonna be in bad shape.' So we just got out and left.

"Two days later we found a little peninsula with water all around it. The land was high and the water was, I would say, fifteen or twenty feet below. Straight down. It was so thick a place nobody could see you. They had these bamboo things growing. We figured out that we can hide here daytime and then move out. Came noon, we got thirsty, but we didn't have a chance to go out and get some water. The village kids, they were all around there playing, and if they ever saw us they would go and notify the gendarmes. I said, 'Jesus, we can't stay here like this without water. It's so damn hot.' So we figured out what to do. We cut some bamboo down, and we cut notches in it, and we tied the bamboo with leaves so they don't get no air. Then we shoved it down in the water, and we started sucking. We sucked the water right out.

"We came to . . . Antep, they call it. It is about one day's walk from Antep to the boundary of Syria. They have two mountains, and the road goes right in the middle. There's no trees, no bushes, nothing. Bare sand. So this Kurd told us to go up the mountain and he was gonna go in the city to get some bread. Boy, when the sun came out, that damn thing was hot! We couldn't even talk, our mouths were so dry. Then one of the fellows said he saw trees far away. He said, 'Maybe there is water there. Let's go.' So he coaxed me to go with him, and we walked down from the mountain. We got close to the trees, and this guide was sitting there. He turned around and said, 'You better go back or I'm gonna shoot you.' So we just turned back again. No water. Nothing.

"That evening he came and fixed us up. He said, 'You know, this is a very desolate place. If anybody sees you, they kill you. That's why I told you to stay up there, so nobody on road sees you.'

"That night we came to the boundary. This guide said, 'This is crucial place. If anybody don't see us, we're free.' The moon was out, and we saw some reflection—just like a gun pointing at you. So we got behind the bushes and told the guy there's something going on.

"We started creeping to the boundary and then we saw train tracks. We never thought that those tracks would reflect the moon like that. The guide said, 'We're okay. Jump over to the other side.' So we did, and that was it. We were singing that we are free now."

VII

"After that we walked daytime. Now it was all desert. You see heat waves go like this, and it's dry. One of our guys, his shoes were too tight and he got blisters, so I had to give my shoes to him, and I had to walk barefoot for two or three hours, and then he'd take them off and give them to me. We wrapped his feet with rags so he didn't get hurt.

"We passed some Turkish gendarmes going home from Aleppo, and they almost caught us. We said good morning, but the Greek fellow saluted the wrong way. We walked quite a way, and all of a sudden the gendarme said, 'Stop! Where do you come from?' So the guide told the Greek fellow, 'Goddarn it, we told you don't open you mouth.' They were suspicious because Greeks speak different dialect.

"So I went back and said, 'What do you want?' They said, 'That man over there, he's a Christian.' I said, 'No, he's not Christian. He went to Istanbul and he's got that dialect in him. We ordinary people here.' They said, 'Do you swear that you're telling the truth?' I raised my hand, and I said, 'Yes.' So they said, 'Okay, go ahead.'

"Then we gave hell to the Greek fellow. 'From now on when we go in any village you walk and go outskirts and sit there.'

"When we came to Aleppo, we gave the guide the letter that he's supposed to take back and collect his money. One of my partners wrote in Armenian about the hardships we had and everything is okay, and the guide came back with the letter and told him, 'Hey, what hardships did you have that you wrote about in this letter?' The guide read Armenian! We were flabbergasted. Then he told the story about his family. He said, 'My great-grandfather was Armenian, and the Kurds, they just massacred anything there was, so he turned to Moslem.'

"It took twenty-eight days to get to Aleppo. When we came there we went to Armenian church and slept on the floor. The next day we found out about Red Cross, so we went to Red Cross, and they gave us some shoes and clothes. A couple of guys that came before us, they took us to a little two-by-four place they used to rent just to sleep in. And then about three, four months later, we heard that the government let all the Armenians go, without any trouble. They could leave the country. So every day we went to the market to watch. A lot of Armenians used to come in there. Finally, I noticed my mother sitting on a wagon, and I ran over there. 'Oh, my God,' she said, 'finally we find each other!'"

"My aunt was there too. I wrote to my cousin, and I got money by telegraph. I rented a house, and my mother and my aunt, we went to the house. And then, I would say about a month later, we heard that some of the orphanage was coming. They would put 'em in a train and bring 'em to Armenian church. Finally, I found out that whole orphanage was there, so I went to look for my sister, and I noticed her and got her. She said, 'By golly, we never thought we would be able to see each other!'

"We stayed in Aleppo about seven months. My aunt, her son in St. Louis made arrangements that bring her to United States. I had an uncle in Canada that I sent a letter to him, and he made an affidavit for my sister, my mother, and me. So we came to Canada. My sister and I came first. We went to Marseilles, and from there we went to Paris. We stayed there three days, and then the agent said that certain day the boat came to Cherbourg. Cherbourg is, I would say, about four, five hours by train. From Cherbourg we came to England, and then we came to Canada. We were in third class, way down in the bottom! They wouldn't even allow us to go up to the second floor. 'Your ticket says you're going to stay.' We looked through the portholes, and all we saw was water, nothing else. And then, that's why I don't like macaroni. Because in that darn ship, every day, that macaroni! I got sick and tired of it.

"When I came to Quebec, I spit in the ocean. No more, I said, I don't want to go to the other side of that ocean. They give me gold, I wouldn't go. I got enough, way up to here."

VIII

Sark and his sister reached Canada in May 1923 and took a train to the small Ontario town where his uncle lived. He worked in a shoe factory for four or five months and then got a job at a foundry. About that time his mother arrived from Syria. A marriage was arranged between Sark's sister and an Armenian living in Pennsylvania. When Sark's mother visited her daughter shortly after the wedding, she met another Armenian and, around the age of fifty-five, married him. Sark left his uncle's for foundry jobs in Windsor and later in Pennsylvania. "I was worried about my stomach, nothing else. There was no such thing as fun. You just worked, made money, and rested, that's all." He moved to Detroit, met a tailor at an Armenian coffee house, and decided to learn the clothing business. In 1928, at the age of twenty-three, he entered a partnership and started his own dry cleaning business. He sold it early in 1929, just before he got married.

All during Sark's story his wife Anne had listened from the next room, and several times she used the occasion of serving coffee to interject her own version of events. She was a domineering woman, and every now and then Sark would angrily rebuff her. This was his story, not hers. He told it with a practical efficiency that reminded me of his mother's. Clipped expressions—"What are you gonna do?" "That was it"—held back tears and moved him swiftly from one event to the next. Every now and then he would begin but break off a cry of incomprehension and rage.

Once we came to the subject of his courtship, however, his tone changed, and he willingly passed the ball to Anne. Anne was the sister-in-law of the tailor who had introduced Sark to the clothing business. When I asked Sark about his first impressions of her, she characteristically shouted something from the other room, and Sark said playfully, "From there she can tell you all the details!"

"You better tell because I wouldn't even look at you!" she shouted back.

"Oh, get outta here. You...."

Anne came in the room. "I was only fifteen when I met him. I had to marry an Armenian, and he was the best-looking Armenian I saw. Like I tell my grandson, Sark was very handsome. He had spats on, and he was really a sharpie."

"Stetson hat. No glasses. She says she fell in love with my spats and my dog."

"And you had a car."

"Yeah, I paid $800 for this Whippet. We used to go for rides in it. The dog, I would put him in the back seat."

"We would call each other and meet over at my sister's. Her husband was born in Chanakhgee, so they helped Sark out as much as they could. Sark wouldn't dare come to my house. My folks disapproved. Freshwater immigrant, they called him."

"Nobody had a car. I was a good taxi. 'How about driving downtown?' She didn't want to get a streetcar. Once I took her over to the theater with her girl friends. She hated me for that because I didn't buy her ticket. 'Go to heck,' I said, 'I drive you over here. Get your own ticket!'"

"Fifty-two years ago, you're talking about! You remember that just like. . . ."

"I remember because you told me so!"

"I told you you were cheap and that stayed with you."

"That stayed with me good." Sark paused. He would give her an inch but no more: "Well, I thought that she was the only one. If I get married, it's her. Otherwise I wouldn't look at nobody. I didn't know what the heck was going on. It just happened accidentally."

"Some accident. We had to run away because there was disapproval. My folks had already picked somebody for me, and I figured no way because he was a short, dumpy guy. Here I got a tall, handsome one. When he said, 'Let's get married,' I said, 'Yep.'"

"I bought the ring, and you know what happened then? I put it in my coat pocket. I still had the store, and I hung my coat in the store. Next day I was gonna take it and give it to her. I went over to give it to her, and I looked and the ring was gone. Somebody stole it from my pocket."

"He had to buy me another one."

"I got a cheaper one, heh, heh."

They were married at a minister's home in February 1929. Sark had just sold his business, so he withdrew all his money from the bank, and the two set off on a trip to Pennsylvania. A telegram informed Anne's mother of what had happened. Then Sark sold his Whippet, and he and Anne went to Toronto, where he got a job in a dry cleaning plant.

"The Depression came, and I had a job over there, and over here people were on welfare. I never had any government handout." In 1934 Sark and Anne returned to Detroit with a four-year-old son, and Sark got another job in dry cleaning. Two years later a daughter was born.

In 1939 he bought a lot and built a house on it. "I looked around for the style of house, and the cheapest way possible to get it. This house

cost me $3,800. The lot was $350. This was first house on the block."
After the mortgage was paid off, he bought another lot a block away,
built his own dry cleaning shop, and called it Atlas Cleaners. Sark was
forty-four when it opened in 1950; his son was twenty and his daughter
fourteen. Anne was his full-time partner. "He had his department, and I
had mine," she said, "and we never interfered with one another. I used to
press two hundred dresses, and I had to be real good because that guy
there was the inspector. Everything had to be just so." Sark's son married
in 1954 and his daughter two years later. They gave Sark and Anne
seven grandchildren. The dry cleaning business flourished in the 1950s
but did less well in the 1960s. In 1972 it was sold, and Sark and Anne
retired. He was sixty-six.

After one of my visits with Sark, I drove by the building that was once
Atlas Cleaners and is now a VFW Hall. A single-story structure with a
flat roof, it has cinder-block walls and a windowless front of dark red
brick. It stands alone on its block, surrounded by a few trees, a small
parking lot, and picnic tables. The thought of it does not make Sark
nostalgic. "I said to my son, 'Go to school and learn some other trade.'"

IX

Sarkis Hashoian has been married to the same woman for more than fifty
years, and he has lived in the same house for more than forty. "I'm
gonna die here," he told me at our last meeting. "I don't wanna move
nowhere." When he built the house he hid five hundred dollars in a
block in the foundation. The money is still there, just in case he has to
leave quickly.

Though we had talked of many events in his life, it was the story of
massacre time that came back at the end. "I get dreams lots of times.
Even the other day I woke up panting. The Turks were taking me
somewhere high in the mountains and telling me to jump down."

The perspective of half a century has not tempered Sark's feelings—
quite the opposite. This affable man who refuses to budge from his home
is angry.

"When you're young, you don't realize things like when you're older.
We played with Turkish kids and Kurdish kids. We just grew up with
them. If you're hungry, and the place you go are all Turks, and if they
beat you if they know you're Armenian, what are you gonna do? You
gotta get along with them. Then, when you get older, you ask, why this
happen to us? I think now, the Christian world, they didn't help us at all.
When they were killing a million and a half Christians over there, where
were you? Where was your pope? Where were your Frenchmen, British,

Germans, all those guys to say, 'Why do you kill those Christian people? They haven't done anything.'

"The other day I was talking to this fellow. He was, I would say, about twenty, twenty-one years old when massacre came, but he was a shoemaker, see? That's why they didn't kill him. They took him and said, 'You better sew shoes for us.' He said to me, 'We were bunch of sheep. We were gonna get killed. Why didn't we kill one Kurd at least?' He said, 'It's too late now. I wish that what I got now I had then. Then I would have killed one or two or three of them. If I get killed, I get killed.'

"One fellow was telling me about this entirely different region. The priest told the villagers, 'Go and be sacrificed to Jesus Christ.' He didn't come out and say, 'Stand up, fight for your rights. You haven't done anything.' He said, 'Go, be sacrificed to Jesus Christ.' And they did. They be sacrificed. When I heard that, I got so god-darned burned up. I said, 'How stupid can we be?' If I was young and knew that I was gonna get killed, at least I kill somebody.

"One village, oh, a couple of hours away from us, stayed and fought. Their priest told them, 'Where are you going? Stop! Stay here, we fight. We gonna die sooner or later.' Some of the people said, 'Maybe they'll just take us away for a couple of weeks, but then they'll send us back here, like 1895.' That one priest said, 'This is gonna be different.' He stayed and fought, and he died with six people. After they killed them, these Kurds, they took and buried them. They told each other, 'These people have a right to be buried honorably because they fight for their rights.'

"What can we do? The past is past. I spit in that ocean. That land belongs to Armenians for thousands of years, and today they want those lands back. United States not gonna give one inch. As long as the United States give the Turks billions of dollars a year, you think they're gonna give us our land? United States takes my tax money, my earnings, and gives it to them. The Turks killed my ancestors. Why should they take my money and give it to somebody who is my enemy?

"My mother was in her nineties when she died, and she would always talk about my younger sister that she threw in the water. She always talked, and then the tears came out of her eyes. Probably she dreamed about her. She closed her eyes, she thought that she's still over there. That voice coming from the water, that 'Why do you do this to me?' She would hear that young girl crying all through her life. That's all written in her life.

"She was with us when my son's little daughter died. She wanted to go to the funeral parlor, but I said, 'No, don't go over there and see the poor kid, dead. That's gonna stay in your mind.'

"I used to talk about it to the kids. I've got a map upstairs. I brought it down, I told my son, 'See, I started from here, I came over here and came over here.' The kids don't eat their dinner, I say, 'You be fussy about it? In my time, if I had a little crumb I would be thankful.' Every day that I live I thank God that I live that long. I never regret that I should have been this, I should have been that. You give me three square meals a day, a place to sleep, that's all I need. You know, a lot of people over here say, 'Oh, depression's going to come. We are out of work. What are we gonna do?' I say, 'Goddarn it! We were over there. We didn't know where it would come from, our next meal.' See? I can go and get a bottle of buttermilk and piece of bread and sit down and I'm satisfied.

"The stories should never die. I don't care who says, they should never die because it could happen here. It depends on whoever goes in Washington. You know during Japanese wars? In California they got all those people in concentration camp. Those were poor people, innocent people. They were born there, they lived there, their sons went out to fight for their country, but still they took 'em and put 'em in concentration camp. They could do it to anybody, any minority. See, that's why I said there should be stories written so the younger generation doesn't think it's not going to happen here. Nobody ever thought it was gonna happen in Germany, but it happened over there too."

INTERPRETATION: THE TELLING OF TRAUMA; "GOOD" STORIES AND GENERATIVE POWER

In Sarkis Hashoian's life story, the seven years from 1915 to 1922 stand out of all proportion to the remaining sixty-eight. I was first referred to him to hear the story of that time. Those seven years were the ones to which he hurried when he began his account, and they were the ones that most absorbed me. When the time came to commit his life to writing, the events of "massacre time" and his escape to Syria flowed naturally, not because Sark had gotten his story straight from telling it often (actually, he was vague and inconsistent regarding many details), but because the underlying structure of his experience made it conducive to narrative. The story told and wrote itself. And it is no coincidence that the years of Sark's life that fell so naturally into narrative are also the years for which he will be remembered.

More than any other story in this collection, "When the Wheat Was Green" explores narrative as a medium of generativity, as a vehicle that carries the meaning of a life from one generation to the next. My interpretation of the story postulates a kind of natural selection that combs experiences for those that made "good" stories and eventually brings the best of them into a community's mythic storehouse. I will develop the interpretation by asking why Sark speaks of trauma when survivors of other atrocities often do not and by examining the generative power that accrues to good stories like his.

THE TELLING OF TRAUMA

Survivors of the Nazi Holocaust during World War II and of the Turkish massacres during and after World War I are currently the subjects of numerous oral history projects. For the survivors the projects represent a very special case of legacy-making and can pose a very special dilemma. As they reach old age, they feel a mounting pressure from successors to speak of the horror they endured. A record must be made so that punishment or restitution or at least acknowledgment can be compelled from perpetrators, so that genocide will never again be tolerated. The survivors are the last living witnesses of the crimes and yet, despite all the encouragement to speak, they often stand mute. The effects of trauma—confusion, embarrassment, disgust, terror, guilt, defeat—shroud their experience in silence. Why, they ask, should we traumatize the children with what was done to us? Why burden them with our humiliation and loss and anger? What good can come from it? Further, the very nature of sustained, relentless victimization often precludes words. The extremity of a death camp overwhelms language and obliterates shared systems of meaning. In Henry Greenspan's summary, "Survivors' experiences [are] imprinted into their awareness at a time when they have been compelled to suspend most of those ego processes providing continuity and mediation."[1] To ward off the threat of annihilation, to stave off the process of surrender, victims become numb to the deadly significance of the situation. How can they now speak the unspeakable, give meaning to that which has none?

Against this backdrop of not telling, Sarkis Hashoian speaks, and speaks with full affect. What is it that enables him to respond almost eagerly to my request for a record of his experience?

The main reason Sark is able to speak lies in the nature of his experiences. During massacre time he saw evil, but thanks to his mother, he was always a step ahead of it. It did not engulf him hour after hour, day after day, year after year, as it did survivors of concentration camps. He fled roving bands of murderers, not the systematic, scientific—and unimaginable—machine of the "Final Solution." Sark was never forced into circumstances in which he acted shamefully, nor did he ever do anything that engendered embarrassment or guilt. True, there were silences in his story. In his oral account he failed to convey the extent to which he had once "become" a Kurd. I had to figure out how long he had passed as a Kurdish boy and how thoroughly he had done so, even praying at night in Arabic. I had to make sure the written story contained these features; they were not part of his spontaneous narrative. Though Sark understated the extent of his identification with his victimizers, he seems never to have collaborated with the enemy and certainly not to have betrayed fellow Armenians. In other words, his experiences were such that actors could continue to act well and eventually escape from evil. He was confronted with horror but never overcome by it.

Further, when I visited Sark, there were timing features in his life that made the telling of his story especially right. His longstanding anger has grown over the years with the realization of how the events of 1915 fit into a pattern of attempted genocide. Now he looks back, admittedly from the safe distance of an ocean and the secure span of half a century, and says he would have responded differently to the criminals: he would have fought them to the death. But he cannot change history, and so the best he can do is cooperate with those who want to make a public record of the crime. In some way, being a witness moves Sark in the direction of finishing the agenda set by his anger, of making things right within himself, of giving himself integrity as he reviews his life in old age. Awareness of death, I believe, adds consciousness and urgency to his task. And though I do not want to downplay these "deep" reasons, I cannot overlook everyday motives that impel his speaking. These were the motives of all the retirees I interviewed: they simply wanted someone to talk with, to take them seriously, to relieve their loneliness, and to enhance their status in the household that was rapidly becoming their entire world.

Not only was Sark's telling right for him, it fit naturally into the flow of the Hashoian family history. Sark had both a predecessor who was a model of speaking and successors who wished him to speak. His mother was a constant talker. She told Sark about his sister's drowning immediately after it happened, she told him of previous massacres, she told him of her constant prayer to find his sister, and she told him later how she finally led her from the Bedouins. When she came to America she always spoke of the horrible thing she had been forced to do to her younger daughter. On one occasion she told Sark's wife Anne that she couldn't sleep because, in Anne's words, "All those pasts would come to her and she would hear the young girl crying." Sark told me that story of the drowning twice, each time speaking the words of the girl in the same deliberate, reverent way: "Ma-ma, what have I done to you?" I could tell he had heard the words many times and spoken them many times. Without a ritual for relating them, he would have broken down. The girl's words have stood at the core of his mother's story for two generations, and I expect they will occupy the same place, and be spoken of the same way, for generations to come.

Sark's son was anxious to have the complete version of his father's life on tape before it was too late. He and his children had heard pieces of that story over the years, and now he felt it was time to bring them together into a coherent whole. He even volunteered to talk to me about the impact of his father's experiences upon himself and his children.

If personal and familial timing was conducive to Sark's telling, so was cultural timing. Corresponding to his need to speak was an urgent need in the Armenian community to reach the last living survivors of the massacres and make a record of their testimony. Because Sark's story spoke of crimes committed by Turks, because it spoke of bravery and shrewdness in Armenians, it was what the collectors of oral history wanted to hear. Another Armenian whose history I took down had fled a different area of Turkey than Sark. He and his family lost home and possessions, but they did not suffer atrocities. Near the end of his account he expressed the fear that Armenians who read his story would condemn it for not being damaging enough to the Turks. In contrast, Sark knew that his story was one the caretakers of his culture valued, one they wanted to record, and one he could tell with pride and righteous anger. It concretized for subsequent generations an enduring theme in the history of his people.

In the development of personal, familial, and cultural histories, then, the timing was right for Sark's story. Telling it connected his past and present and tied him to a network of other storytellers. Sometimes he would just as soon avoid them; but, according to his wife at least, he does talk with other Armenian survivors and takes special pleasure in reminiscing about the time before the massacres. To make a record with me of the events between 1915 and 1922 took the waste of pain, suffering, and loss and transformed it into something useful for others. "The stories should never die," Sark said. "They should never die because it could happen here." Sark's experiences happened to be those that could be fashioned into memorable narrative, into what I call a good story.

"GOOD" STORIES AND GENERATIVE POWER

What Sark and others, including myself, have done with seven years of his life illustrates a kind of natural selection for narrative. By *natural selection* I mean a process whereby individuals and collectivities filter lives for elements that fall into meaningful stories and then pass the stories from one generation to the next. Certain experiences, in other words, naturally make for good stories, and good stories make for generative power.

I am of course speaking of a very specific kind of story in a very specific context. I am not discussing fiction or various types of experimental narrative that literary elites write for each other. I am talking rather about the stories that families and communities tell about what took place in their members' lives. Sometimes they talk about the entire life of a particularly important person, but more often they select episodes from a number of lives like Sark Hashoian's.

The episodes they select are naturally good stories. Good stories have powerful central figures who behave in accord with values shared by teller and listener. They have, in other words, actors who act well. The stories also have a linearity that we, at least in the West, look for in normal narrative. That is, they have a beginning, middle, and end; they have tension and uncertainty followed by resolution and clarity; they go somewhere. The leading actor of Sark's account was his mother, a clever, cunning, and courageous woman, who never ceased to resist and outmaneuver her victimizers. No doubt her strength and her capacity to act well have been enhanced with Sark's telling of the story, but it is true that she survived an attack on her village and a butchering of her relatives, that she lost one child to kidnapping and had to drown another, that she stole the kidnapped child back, that she arranged Sark's escape to Syria and later followed him. These events constitute a natural, even archetypal, story of deliverance. What is more, it is a story in which the moral order of the universe is first destroyed and then restored. A mother must kill her own child, but she receives a "second chance" and snatches another who has been lost from the den of iniquity. Although evil is not conquered in the story, it does not have its way. It touches but does not defeat the story's principals. Because deliverance and restoration occur, the story can be told. Even more, it can be heard.

Good stories have generative potential for several reasons. One is that they are memorable. That is, they are aligned with the distortions that memory normally makes in creating personal history. Psychologist Anthony Greenwald has compiled laboratory evidence that in remembering past events, the biases of "egocentricity" and "beneffectance" are present.

Egocentricity is the tendency to distort personal history to make oneself more a cause (and also a target) of events than one really is. *Beneffectance* is the tendency to recall successes and take credit for them while forgetting or denying responsibility for failures. Without these biases, says Greenwald, the ego would not survive and personal history would not exist.[2] Memory, in other words, looks for events of which egocentricity and beneffectance can be predicated, of which it can be said that there were actors who acted well.[3]

It works out that the very biases that protect the egos of the older generation and make its experience memorable foster the creation of stories with which the young can identify. This is another reason why good stories have generative power. Humiliation prevents one elder from speaking of the time in his life when, ceasing to be an actor, he was reduced to helpless dependency. Guilt causes another to skirt moments when, acting badly, she violated her culture's ideals. Intrapsychic mechanisms thus filter from life-historical recounting helpless or evil figures whom the young could not emulate, who could not even assume the role of a story's protagonist.

In good stories there is ambiguity in the midst of definition. Alongside characters' stated motives there are unspoken thoughts and feelings that allow listeners to insert their own, to enter the story even as it enters them. If there is trauma, as in Sark Hashoian's story, it is presented obliquely, with a measure of remove permitted to listeners. Because their faces are not rubbed in horror and because they learn it can be escaped, listeners do not distance themselves from the account. Projecting themselves into it, they incorporate it.

Naturally good stories have room, too, for the gradual injection of mythical elements. Myth makes good stories better. The presence of religious myth is obvious in Sister Josette's life story and in Ali Birri's. Literary myth is equally obvious in Hannah Gordon's and will be seen again in the one to follow. In Sark Hashoian's narrative the mythical element is present as an archetypal story of deliverance to which his own conforms, as the ideals of persistence, courage, and intelligence to which his heroine measures up, as a shared anger which his people feel toward their oppressors. The latent elements of myth are already prized by those who hear Sark's story; hence these elements give his bare facts a special tonus and power.

Good stories become better, then, if they restate one of the abiding myths of a culture or if, at a time of cultural change, they provide a new variant of the myth. If a new culture is coming into existence, that story will emerge as a prototype that establishes a myth capable of energizing future adherents. In their mythic storehouses collectivities preserve classic stories, archetypal charts of the life journey. Anthropologist David Plath calls such charts "cultural pathways." They are "ideas that we can draw upon to plot where we are in the tangled currents of change and to project where we yet may go . . . what a contemporary anthropologist would call an ethnotheory or folk theory of the life course and its transitions."[4] These pathways do not exist as abstract essences but are embodied in thousands of concrete instances, in thousands of stories like Sark's. Those that happen to be added to the collection will be the ones that already fit an existing archetype or alter it in some badly needed way. In telling a good story, one retells one of the culture's enduring stories.[5] One provides a particular for the universal and ensures thereby that the culture will carry on.

Silences enter life stories when a match between the real and the mythical, between actual events and the culture's archetype, cannot be made. If too much of a life is lost to silence, a search will begin for other lives whose actual contours match more completely the idealized blueprints of the culture—lives about whom less silence is needed.

Little silence is needed about Sarkis Hashoian's life between 1915 and 1922. Almost four years elapsed between my first visit with him and the time I mailed him the manuscript of "When the Wheat Was Green." His eyesight had faded during that time, so the story had to be read to him by Anne. When we got together, Anne brought out an old map of the Middle East on which Sark's journey of twenty-eight days had been marked in ink with a dotted line. We retraced his steps, and I learned that Sark had first told his story over this very map to his grandson. The occasion was a high school writing assignment more than a dozen years earlier. The grandson chose to do a paper about his grandfather, consciously exploiting the fact that he was writing at the same age at which his grandfather had escaped. Point by point he compared his own life of ease with his grandfather's life of hardship. In difficult times later in life the grandson went back to his grandfather's experience: "If he got through that, I can get through anything."

Sark's family is extraordinarily proud of his role during massacre time. When I spoke with his fifty-four-year-old son Ralph, I learned that as a young father Sark had said little of his experiences. When he spoke of them, he selected a single episode to drive home an admonition to his children. Eat your dinner—look at the crumbs I had to be thankful for. Don't make trouble in the neighborhood—"they" will come and get you. As a boy, Ralph tired of the lectures and recoiled from modeling himself on a man who spoke broken English and dressed strangely. But later on he "rediscovered" his father and he "rediscovered" Armenians, thanks in part to a wife who became intensely interested in Armenian history.

Sark, it turns out, had been stunned when I approached him with the request to record his story. He was not accustomed to being in the family's spotlight. Now Ralph was pleased that his father was at last getting his due, and he was grateful that his memories had been pulled together into a coherent whole. It had taken only several weeks for the Hashoians to distribute copies of "When the Wheat Was Green" to all the children and grandchildren. Said Ralph: "I'm proud of his survival."

There, I believe, lies the idealized meaning this story will have for the Hashoian descendents. *Survival* is the concept around which history and myth happened to join forces for them, giving generative power to the "great deeds" of their forebears. Only the strongest survived, Ralph says; the weak were weeded out. The Hashoian family has a good story to reinforce that conviction for future generations.

1 · The Cup

_T_here came a moment when he slowed down in his story, when he started seeing long stretches of his life in mere instants. With a mild insistence he suddenly said, "There's a story I have to tell you."

He was an old man who could have been Santa Claus but for his smooth-shaven face and the neat trim of his white hair. He had thick wrinkles, a large red nose, and soft blue-gray eyes. In a hoarse Italian accent, he had been retracing the path of his life, when he slowed down and then stopped. His grin broadened, and he moved to the edge of his chair, resting his round belly on thick, sturdy legs.

"This story was told by my dad. Once there was a godfather that stood up in a baptism for his friend. And this little godson grew up without knowing his godfather. No fault of the godfather, but sometimes you see somebody every day, and sometimes you don't see them in a lifetime. So this godson, one day, he got to visit his godfather. When he introduced himself, he said, 'I'm your godchild. I heard about you, and I was in the area, and I came over to see you.'

" 'By golly!' the godfather said, 'I wouldn't have known you if I woulda seen you on the street, and you wouldn't have known me because when I stood up in your baptism you was a little baby and I was a young fellow. Just think how many years elapse without us seeing one another!'

"Well, the godfather brought a loaf of bread and some cheese and some olive and they broke bread together, and they talked many things, and then the godchild told him, he said, 'Beside coming over to see you today, I got a favor to ask from you. You know, I need a hundred lire, and I thought while I'm here, I'm going to ask you for that hundred lire, and see what you like to do for me.'

"The godfather said, 'You see that cup over there on top of that high dresser? Get that cup and bring it over to the table.' It was a cup that you eat broke-up bread in, with coffee and milk, that they use in the old country. The godson went and got that cup made out of porcelain, and there was money inside. They counted the money and there was a hundred lire. The godfather said, 'Is this what you need?'

" 'Yeah.'

" 'Well, it's yours. Take it.'

"So the godchild, he took the money and he put it in his pocket and thanked his godfather. He said, 'As soon as I have the money, I'll bring it back.'

"The godfather said, 'It's up to you.'

"So a few months went by, six months, eight months, ten months, and he came back to see his godfather. Again, they broke bread together, they talked many things, and then the godchild said, 'You know, I need a favor. I need a hundred lire.'

" 'You see that cup over there?' said the godfather. 'Go and get it.'

"So he went over to get the cup, and he said, 'Are you sure it's this cup?'

" 'Yes, that's the cup.'

" 'But there is nothing in this cup.'

" 'Well,' the godfather said, 'there is supposed to be a hundred lire.'

" 'But the last time I was here, you gave it to me. I took it, and now there is nothing.'

"So the godfather told him, he said, 'You get back what you put in! I had a hundred lire, and I gave it to you, and you didn't bring it back. How can I give it to you again?' "

Whenever he told a tale like that, he seemed to be hearing it himself for the first time, wide-eyed and open-mouthed. The tales were woven into his own life story, which he told with delight and utmost seriousness. Our conversations were always prefaced with offers of wine and cheese and fruits and vegetables. My visits were an occasion, and he wanted them to last as long as possible.

I

Chris Vitullo's life began in 1905 in a fishing village on the island of Sicily. The people were poor, but Chris's earliest memories are of riches—of being fed and clothed and loved. In those memories he finds coins and buried treasure and feels sources pouring sustenance into him. Children worked hard, but they also swam in the sea, played on sandy beaches, made toys, and pretended buttons and peach pits were money. Chris loves to dwell on his early years, and he does so with an infectious glee that turns suddenly to tears at special memories of being cared for.

When he was born, his father, like many men in the village, was in the United States trying to earn money for his family.

"I guess my mother and dad had about ten children. They lost the first one, and then they had three girls. And then they started having boys. There were some lost because we were seven altogether, three girls and four boys. I was the littlest one of them all. I can visualize this little boy, Chris, which is me, with this little dress on. It was plaid, greenish with red. I must have been less than three years old to wear a dress.

"The first time I saw my father, he came from the United States. I could have been maybe four years old. My mother told me that he was gonna come and we were gonna go on the road about three, four blocks away, where this horse and wagon, like a bus, was gonna come by and leave my father. She was excited, and she said, 'Come on, you're gonna meet your father, and don't forget what you're gonna do.' I was supposed to kiss his hand and . . . I'm getting the goose pimple now, see, talking about it . . . she says, 'He's gonna grab you and he's gonna put you on his shoulder. He's gonna hug you and he's gonna kiss you. That's your father!' And he did. He did just what she said.

"I kissed his hand, and I asked him to bless me. '*Sa benedicta, padre.*' Naturally my dad, he picked me up and he put me in his chest, and then he put two fingers in his vest pocket and he got couple big coins, silver coins. They were dollars, and he gave them to me. Just think how tickled I was, huh? Oh, boy! The first time I met him, he gave me two coins made out of silver, two silver dollars. He kissed me. He was so happy. I could see his blue eyes with tears."

Like his father, Chris had fair skin and blond hair, a "head of wool," according to the dark-skinned villagers. Chris remembers helping his father in the lemon orchards, vineyards, and onion fields surrounding the village, and he remembers admonitions about *l'ubbidienza*, obedience, and *il rispetto*, respect. When Chris was six, his father returned to America, taking along some of Chris's brothers and sisters. "Those brothers, when they got in this country, they wrote my mother, 'Tell my brother to dig under the last bush of the cactus by the wall and see what he finds.' And I find bags of buttons and peach pits, just like I find a treasury of gold!

"My mother used to write letters for the fishermen's wives. They brought the letters they received from their husbands or their sons in the United States, and my mother would read the letters to them. They would say, 'Now, are you going to write me a letter for my husband?' 'Yes I will. You think it over a couple days, and then I'll answer the letter.' I watched them come back. Day or two later, those people brought us fish. My mother never charged anything, and so they thought they were obliged to her, and for the respect they brought her some fish.

"My mother was something else, bless her. She had a very lovable disposition. I wanted to stay close to her as much as possible. When she was not around, I would ask, 'Where's Mom?' My sisters would say, 'Somebody took your mother.' I would get panicky and start screaming and looking for her. And they have to tell me that they tease me. My mother would say, 'Why did you tell him that?'

"I cried when I first realized that I didn't have her picture as a young woman. I wanted to find out how she looked in her young life, when she married my dad. I asked her, 'Where is your picture?' She said, 'We didn't have any.' There were not too many pictures in those days in Italy. I said, 'I want to know what you looked like when you were young.' She was surprised, I guess. She tried to please me in telling me she was the same. But she wasn't the same. She said, 'Well, that's the way I am.' I was little, and I cried because I couldn't see her when she was young.

"She really worked hard, poor lady. She made practically all our clothes. She was washing and cleaning all the time. She talked little things when she had her hands full. She used to tell me about my father. He was a handsome guy and from a good family. When you were engaged in those days, you didn't go and see your girl friend and take her out for a walk in the park. You went over and visited the family and there was your girl. She didn't sit on your lap, and she didn't give you no kiss. She had to hold her composure, and she would have to behave like a gentle person, and you had to do the same. Respectably you greeted the family. "Hello pop, hello mom, how's everybody, nice day.' You sat down a little bit and maybe they offered you a snack or something, and you stayed an hour or so and then you wished them a good evening. And this was your girl friend! There must have been a way of loving people without touching hands. And my mother would say that when my dad left the house, she would go at the door and watch him until he would turn the corner. At the turn, my dad would turn around too, to see if she was watching, and he would run into the building. One time he scratched his nose! So he must have really loved my mother, to turn around to see whether she was watching for him.

"So they married. They were very happy people together. And then my father was unjustly accused of some crime that happened in that little particular city, which cost him quite a bit of money and quite a bit of time until he was proven innocent. The losses brought him to the condition that he had to go out of the nation to make a living. He had to sell all his dairy farm, maybe twenty, twenty-five milking cows. My brothers and my father had to leave Italy and look for some work. He'd go away three, four years at a time to make a few hundred dollars. This is a story I was told by my mother, and my mother is a very honest person. My mother would say that where my father put his feet on the ground, she was not worthy of putting her face. She would tell that to the kids and to the neighbors and to the friends. Just think how much she loved my father!

"She told me so many things! The first story that she told me, it was a little story just like one of those fairy tales, about the little mouse that he live in a warehouse full of cheeses, so happy and content with all this enormous amount of cheeses. And one day he decided that he was going to take a trip and go visit some of his ancestors that live in the country far away. And on his long journey he met another little mouse, and it was a surprise between those two little mouses—one was so beautiful and fat and one was so frail and thin. And they talk it over, and the way my mother would say it, I could practically see those two little mouses talking to one another. "One says, 'How come, *compadre*, you so skinny? By golly, I could count your ribs. What are you eating?'

" 'Oh,' he says, 'there is plenty of food over here. I dig *parazzi*, these wild onions. I eat them. I enjoy. I live. I'm all right. But by the way, how come you so beautiful? You so fat, you have beautiful hair, nice and shiny. You look all dress up, glowing like sunshine.'

" 'Oh,' he says, 'you ought to see what I have. I have a warehouse full of beautiful cheeses. Every day they come and take some out and they put some back. I'm the boss of the cheese. When I want to taste one of them I dig a hole into it and I eat. That's my food!'

" 'My God, I would love to come over and see it!'

"At this point I would wait for my mother to finish the words. I would look at her with my mouth open expecting her to tell me more, and she would go on and finish up the story. The mouses, they went on the journey back to the warehouse. Just before they got to the premises, the city mouse told his *compadre*, 'You know, I never told you, but at the door that we're going to go in, they got a hole for a cat to go in and out. There is nothing to worry because this cat is blind from one eye, and she usually puts the blind eye toward the hole so she won't be disturbed by the light, and she sleeps all the time. We have to watch out that the cat is sleeping, and we slip in. When we go near the hole, you go in.'

" 'No,' he says, 'I'm not going to go in. I'm a stranger. I don't know the cat. I don't know my way around. You go in and lead the way.' And they debate back and forth until they decide that the city mouse was going to go in. And he did. And that cat had the good eye on the hole, and when that poor little mouse come in, she grab him and he start squeaking, and the squeaks sound like *zio, zio, zio*. And *zio* in Italian means uncle. The little mouse from the country, he heard him squeak and squeal *zio*, and he says, 'And it's your uncle. Just think what he would have done to me! I'm a total stranger.' So he decides in his own opinion to go back at the wild onions and be happy thereafter.

"I thought I wanted more from my mother's story, but now I'm thinking that my mother was telling me that it's not what you would like to have, it's what you actually have that counts. If you could be happy on the wild onions, good. If you're looking for beautiful cheeses, you could get in trouble. So why not live happy where you are at?"

II

"My brothers in the United States, they begged my mother, 'Send our brother to learn the barber trade. Over here in this country, the barbers are dressed in white. They look like doctors, and they make money inside the roof, not outside the roof. The customer comes in and brings him the little coins, and they live happy. They don't have to go in the railroad tracks to work. They don't have to do any factory work.'

"My mother was glad. She said, 'You know your brother Charlie and your brother Tom, what they want you to do? They want you to learn the barber trade. I know the old man that used to cut the hair to my dad, and I'm gonna take you there.'

"I was about seven years old. I said that if this is what my brothers think would be good for me, I will go. So my mother took me hand by hand. I was nervous a little bit, but she was holding my hand. She introduced me to him. She said, 'Maestro Antonino, this is my son. His name is Christopher.'

" 'Oh, nice. *Come sta?* How are you?'

" '*Sta bene.*'

"My mother was telling Maestro Antonino, 'My husband and my children over in the United States, they like to have this boy learn the barber business, so I'm going to give you my son to teach.'

" 'Oh, good, good,' he said. 'Good, I need you.' He was a nice old man. He had been a barber for many, many years. He was just like a doctor. He knew how to bleed people. He knew how to pull teeth. His wife, she was a pretty old lady too. I remember them just like I would see them today. They were a little hunched. In the wintertime they would have a little open fire outside, and when the smoke would dissipate, they would bring in the charcoal in a little stove made out of copper, with a handle. Enough to take the chill off the house. He would light up something that would make a little smoke, and he would inhale it. He must have had something like asthma, to my imagination of the poor guy.

"He would receive some of his customers, and toward the evening we used to go out and find customers in their own home, when they came back from work. We would walk two, maybe even a little bit better than two miles, to shave a customer. Can you imagine anybody doing anything like that? For nothing! They would pay three times a year, for Christmas and New Year holiday, for Easter holiday, and for one of the Blessed Mother of that little city, which is September the eighth.

"Every day, seven days a week, I used to go and shake little pieces of cloth. Pieces of pants, pieces of shirts, pieces of junk clothes—they would cut them up and make pieces he could wipe his razor on. He put them all in one basket. I would shake the soapsuds with the whiskers out and I would wash these little cloths and hang them up to dry. If he wanted to buy something or if he wanted to tell some people that he was waiting in the barbershop, I would go and do all of these little errands for him.

"He would ask me to watch him. 'You doing anything? Why don't you watch me cut hair?' He showed me how to hold the comb. You cut the hair over the comb and make sure that the scissor doesn't slip under. You figure out how many inches you want the hair off the scalp, you get the hairs, you put them in between your fingers, you cut them all around the head on the top.

"Whenever I started making the suds for lather, he would say, 'Rub it real good. Rub it real hard.' The soap was in paste form. I would get a little piece of that soap, put it in the brush, dab the brush in a little warm water, and then I would start to lather up the customer's face. And put the basin with water right under his neck so any dribbling would go in the container. You understand what I'm talking about? Then Maestro Antonino would say, 'Did you rub it real good? I'm gonna see if you did.' And many times that he tried with the razor, he said, 'You didn't rub it good. I can't even cut 'em. Give me that brush. I'm gonna do it myself and show you how you rub it.' And he would show me.

"The first time I lathered somebody, I was not that tall so I had to go on top of a little stool. I put the soap in the brush and I started going around. But I was amateur. I was not perfect yet. I smeared the soap all over his eyes, in his nose. I was apologizing to him. 'Oh, I didn't mean to do that.' 'That's all right, that's all right. You're gonna learn. You'll learn, you'll be all right.' It was words of encouragement. The people were nice.

"I had to learn how to strap the razor. I had to watch how he would hone it. He would put a drop of olive oil in the stone and then he would hone the razor back and forth and try it on his nail to see if it would stick. I had to keep an eye at what he was doing. 'Keep on watching me and pretty soon, before you know it, you're gonna shave people.' Later he asked me to shave, and I thought I was not yet ready. I was eight and a half years old. I said, 'I don't know. I'm afraid.' He said, 'Oh, you shave now. I told you what to do. Put the razor flat. Don't put it on an angle. Put it flat with the face and glide. It'll shave.' By golly, it was too. The way he was teaching me was the truth.

"I think the first time I shave, my father's brother came over. 'How's Chris doing? Do you think he's going to be a barber or what?' 'Yeah, yeah, he's going to work on you. Give your uncle a shave.' And I started shaving him. I finished the cheek and then Antonino finished it up. He said, 'You think he shaves all right?' My uncle said, 'Well, I couldn't even feel that on my face. He's got a light hand, you know, the hand is light.' Ah, light! It took time to learn.

"Antonino would show me all the little things, including the bleeding. There is a way that you bleed people in the back in case they have a bad cold. You put a little piece of cotton inside a glass and you light it. You put in on the skin, and the flame goes out, but it makes a vacuum and it sucks the skin a little higher so you can make a few little cuts with a sharp razor. Then you light another piece of cotton and put the glass back, and it sucks the blood in, just like a leech would do, see? Only the leech would bite. This worm would bite you, but this is done professionally without the leech. If something had to be done, Antonino would say, 'Get the cotton. Get the match ready.' And he showed me not to cut too deep, just enough to nick the skin. He showed me how it's done, and he made me do it.

"One winter he must have caught a bad cold, poor fellow, and he died a few days later. Maybe he had pneumonia or some heart condition. He was over ninety years old. He loved me. He and his wife too. She was so glad that I was around and that he was teaching me. They thought I was their child. Maestro Antonino didn't have any children, but he thought I was just like his own boy. He talked to me just like I belonged to him."

III

Chris had always hoped to follow his brothers and sisters to the United States. On one occasion he had his picture taken with a cigarette in his hand "to make myself big." He sent it to his sister in St. Louis, and she made arrangements to sponsor him.

In 1918, at the age of thirteen, he left "to shake the money tree in America." He remembers the moment of departure. "It came the day in late fall, I left for Palermo with my father and mother and finally got on the ship. They called it a passenger ship, but I guess it was a cargo ship. It was not very big. We stayed a couple of hours waiting. I don't want to break down, but just think. You're on the boat and you're leaving your mother on the dock. The plank is still between the boat and the dock, and there's your mother. You stand and watch her for two or three hours. You don't think of drinking, you don't think of nothing, just the separation. Once in a while she would wipe some of the tears on her eyes, and my dad. . . . Oh, you couldn't describe the feelings of a son and the folks that you're leaving behind. I was happy in a way that I was coming here, but I was very unhappy leaving them behind me. It seems to me that while I was watching them I had a lump in my throat as big as my fist. I couldn't swallow, I couldn't . . . boy, what a feeling! And there they were, and finally came the time that they pulled the plank and they rang the bells, and the boat was pushed away from the dock, and we started going on the Mediterranean.

"I can remember everything during the trip. We were supposed to arrive in fifteen days, but it took longer, maybe eighteen, nineteen days. All the way to New York, the ship leaned on one side. I don't know whether the cargo moved or whether the wind was from the west, but on one side you couldn't see the ocean, and on one side you could see it. The working crew was French people. They didn't speak Italian, although some of them understood, and naturally they were feeding strange foods to me. They were not cooking like my mother, in other words. There was one guy, he used to sell liquor, *anisette*, and he would talk Italian real well. He would pass some information. 'Tomorrow we be in New York, Brooklyn, New York. *Domani arriviamo, arriviamo in America!*' And in the early morning when we arrived I had not slept all night because I wanted to see what the United States looked like. It was foggy, you know, we couldn't see very far. Finally, we went by the Statue of Liberty, and they told us, 'Look at the Statue of Liberty. *La liberta! Viva la liberta!*' And, oh, I watched this big statue there with the lights! I was tickled pink to be in the United States after that long trip. You know, you don't see nothing but the sky and the water, and the ship looks like a walnut shell in comparison with the bigness of everything else. So when I got there I was very, very happy."

From New York Chris went by train to St. Louis, a trip that lasted two days. He wanted to get off in East St. Louis, Illinois, but the conductor restrained him. Once across the Mississippi and into St. Louis, however, he still got off at the wrong station. Then, with an incredible bit of luck, he walked straight from the wrong station to his sister's front door.

At first, America was not the money tree Chris expected. He worked at his brother's fruit market but was unable to converse in English with customers. He got a job in an Italian barbershop, but no one would sit in his chair. In the spring he went to Illinois and worked for six months as a water boy on a railroad crew. Then he returned to St. Louis and took a job in a shoe factory. Two or three years later, he moved to Detroit to be with another sister. Chris packed soda ash for a year and then was introduced to an Italian who offered him $35 a week to work in his barbershop. The two became good friends and, when Chris was about twenty-one, his friend opened another shop and sold his share of the first to Chris for $1,500. The shop had a regular clientele that included doctors from a hospital next door.

In the meantime his parents had come from Italy, the last of the family to arrive in the United States. The trip was so terrible for his mother that she vowed never again to cross the ocean. Chris's father had other plans: he wanted to see that his seventh child, Chris, was married and return as soon as possible to Sicily.

Down the street from the rented house where Chris and his parents were living was a family Mr. Vitullo had known in Sicily. He told Chris, " 'Before I go in old country, I'm gonna see that you get engaged, and I'm gonna see that you marry this family. This girl is beautiful, and someday you gonna have beautiful kids because you're a nice young fellow. And this girl, she's very attractive and beautiful.' My dad, he knew what he was talking about!

"He didn't have to argue very much to convince them that I was his chip from the block, and, if he could have the honor, it was his intention that his son would marry their daughter. And so they agreed that they would meet with me. They lived two, three doors away from where I lived, and I didn't even know Gloria.

"So one Sunday we went over and they had a dinner for us. I had to have respect first. My dad said, 'This is my son Chris, and this is Mr. Sam Tumino and his wife.' We all ate together at the same table. Gloria was there and my mother and my dad and her mother and father and one of her sisters and brother-in-law. I met some of the boys, Gloria's brothers Phil and Sam. I knew the brother-in-law from the old country because I used to give him haircuts when I was a little boy. They all knew that Gloria was going to be engaged and someday was going to marry with me, and they were all glad. I was happy to be part of the family."

It was decided that the wedding would take place in June 1926. Once the plans were settled, Chris's father returned to Italy, never to see his wife or son again. Chris and Gloria's courtship was not unlike their parents'. "In those days, the Italian people, they didn't permit their daughter to go out all alone with a boy friend. So we obediently lived up to the rules of the family tradition. We didn't go out together. I used to do more talking to Gloria on the phone than I did in person. I would call her up and tell her what I thought of her—that she was a nice girl—and naturally one of us talked one day and another talked another day, and we arrived to many talks together. We had desire to be together some-day, but we wanted to be obedient to the father and mother. Gloria was a smart girl and she was a good, good girl and she wouldn't do anything that was disobeying the rules or tradition of the family.

"When we got married, we were very happy after that with an excep-tion that whatever comes along, you have to take, sickness or otherwise. We lived together forty-five years, Gloria and me. Yeah, we lived to-gether forty-five years. We had a lot of good times together and a lot of bad times together. We worked, we paid our bills honorably, and we dressed well. We bought a house, we paid for the house, we had a little bit of money, whatever God provided, but we did it all in a good faith and honestly, and we arrived to the point that probably if God wouldn't want Gloria to pass away, maybe Gloria and I, we would be together today. But that's the way it goes in life, and we have to take what's coming to us."

In a matter of minutes Chris's narrative had slowed to a crawl. His eyes were red and his mood weary and resigned. The man who had spoken with such relish about his youth was losing interest in his story. Then he made an allusion I did not yet understand to the story of the cup.

IV

"Maybe a couple of weeks after we got married Gloria got sick, and she had an operation. It was just like appendicitis, but the doctor discovered she had something wrong with her tubes. He came out of the operating room with his hands wrapped to talk to me. 'Chris,' he said, 'Gloria's got a little bit of spots on her tubes, and if I remove them you're not going to have any children.' 'Doctor,' I said, 'Don't waste no time. Forget about the children. Take care of my wife.' She was just eighteen, a young girl.

"Gloria wanted a child very bad. She didn't lose her hopes since the doctor thought he left a little bit of the nodule so the tube could function. Today they probably could have done it and she could have had chil-dren, but then she went through hell. We visited so many doctors, so many places. We spent a lot of time and money explaining this situation to other doctors throughout part of our life. And Gloria really wanted a child. She thought it would have been a miracle, a gift from heaven. For over ten years we went to a lot of doctors. But it was impossible to have any children."

Chris's mother lived with him and Gloria almost from the beginning of their marriage. "Don't forget, my mother lived with me for twenty-five years. She became just like my little girl. If I would have had a child, who knows, maybe I wouldn't have taken care of my mother the way she deserved to be taken care of. I just roughly guess and say God wanted me not to have any children, so I wouldn't fail to respect my mother." As hopes for a child waned, Chris and Gloria made plans to open a beauty shop together. But in 1936, just after Chris placed a deposit on one, Gloria became sick and was taken to Keller Hospital, the one next to his barbershop.

"That really knocked me to pieces. She had spinal meningitis, and I was very worried, believe me. I didn't sleep. I stayed at that hospital from morning till night. I didn't work or nothing. I had the barber shop, but somebody else was taking care of it.

"The doctors felt so bad. They felt bad for knowing me and knowing Gloria. In fact, as Gloria began to get a little better, one of the doctors told me, 'Chris, we're going to tell you something else. Gloria might be affected in her walking.' I said, 'What makes you think that way?' He said, 'Everything is all right except that she has no reflex in the bottom of her feet. She could be crippled.' I said, 'What do you mean reflex?' And he showed me. He put a little sharp thing at the bottom of her feet. The foot didn't move, neither foot. I said, 'You know, doctor, Gloria never was ticklish in her feet.' And he looked at me just like he heard some good news. 'My golly,' he said, 'maybe you got something, Chris.' He began to think a little different, and in time he scratched off that crippling situation and Gloria got better. She was in the hospital about two months. It took more than a year for a complete recovery.

"I had to change my plans about the beauty shop. I had about $7,500, which I spent it all on Gloria. And the doctors, they didn't charge me nothing. When she came out of being sick she was a very nervous person. She used to cry and scream. The doctor said, 'Gloria, you gotta go back to work. You gotta get yourself a job.' And so Gloria went to try again. She put an application in at Sears and they said, 'When do you want to start working, Gloria?' 'Well, I start right now.' 'Well, we haven't decided where we're going to put you, but since you're a beauty operator, we'll put you in cosmetics for today, and tomorrow we see what we're going to do.' So the next day they put her in furniture and she worked thirty years in furniture."

V

The years of coming to terms with Gloria's sterility and sickness were also the years of the Depression. Many businesses suffered, but Chris's barbershop stayed afloat. He was a "little" barber to some "big" people.

"I had the doctors from Keller Hospital. I had all the chemistry guys working for Parke-Davis that lived in the Sheridan Apartments. I had Frank Cavanaugh, which he was then a judge, and later he became mayor of the city and governor of the state. And some of the prosecuting attorneys that lived in the Sheridan, they would come over and get a haircut and shave. I had some bootleggers. I knew what they were talking about when they met sometimes in the barbershop.

"I had a lot of poor people. I used to tell them to come over even though they didn't have no money. 'Come over, let me take care of you. We don't have any books to put that you owe me. Keep on looking for a job.' I had several families that they came over to the barbershop and talked to me about the hospital next door. People that came in this country and didn't know how to speak well, I was able to introduce them to the doctor. I would translate from Italian to English the best I knew how. I'd say, 'Doctor, they haven't got no money.' 'Don't worry, we'll take care of them.' I was one of Dr. Keller's friends, just like a doctor over there, and I was only the little barber next door.

"People like John Crowley and Tony Tedesco and Frank Mueller used to come over and get a haircut. They belonged to the St. Vincent de Paul Society. John Crowley was Cadillac Stamping, Tony Tedesco was Huron Realty, and Frank Mueller, he owned every store on Monroe Avenue. They took me out a couple of times to show me what they were doing. They would visit poor people or bring something to poor people. They took me with them whenever there was a visit to make to an Italian family. They would come by the barbershop. 'Chris, you want to go with us about an hour?' 'Okay.' I would finish up my customer and excuse myself. I had a couple of barbers working for me, and I went and we visited families and we talked a little bit. If someone didn't have no shoes to go to school, well, we wrote a little check and ordered a pair of shoes for him right away. If they didn't have any food, many times we went to the store ourselves and got food—some meat, some spaghetti, some beans, or we gave them a little money to go buy their food. Those days were poor days. Even if people looked for a job day and night, they couldn't find one.

"All my friends there at St. Vincent de Paul, they were well-to-do people. I was very happy to be with them, although they were better than me, you know. I was grateful to do things for them because they did it to help me too. They came in and got a shave and a haircut from me. They never went no place else."

When World War II came, barbering was declared a nonessential business, so Chris, at the age of thirty-five, became a grocer. "I started with a nephew of mine. We put in $500 apiece and we worked real hard. I worked from maybe five in the morning to twelve at night. I did a lot of maneuvering around. I was getting things that were hard to get. I had people coming to me for miles. If they needed onions, I had maybe three, four hundred bags of onions in the back room. The farmers wouldn't sell potatoes for three dollars a hundred pounds, but they would sell them for ten dollars. I bought them for ten dollars, I would sell them for ten dollars. I progressed from a little store to a nice market, almost a supermarket. I was selling fourteen sides of beef a week. I was selling hundreds of pork butts and pork loins. I had three butchers. We worked real hard, but I was able to earn enough money to buy a house and to buy whatever Gloria or my mother needed."

When the war was over Chris looked for ways to do something with the money he was making. He nearly invested in Florida hotels but backed out at the last minute. Then came an offer of $150,000 for his store. Chris wanted to sell, but his partner refused. A few years later, the grocery chains moved in, and the value of Chris's market plummeted. In 1955 he sold his interest to his partner for a mere $5,000. Then he tried the wholesale meat business and later a restaurant. Friends offered to loan him money for a liquor license, but Dr. Keller talked him out of the idea. Finally, around 1957, Chris returned to barbering, which he did until his retirement in 1974.

"While I was a young man, I felt a lot of times, deep down in my heart, that I was capable of doing other things than being a barber. I felt that I could have done better, but I hesitated to make sure. Before I took a jump, I wanted to measure the distance. I wanted to make sure everything was all right, and that hesitation . . . sometimes you got to take a chance. But I'm happy though. I don't miss nothing. I miss a lot of money, but money isn't everything. It seems to me that where there is money there is some of those guys that say, 'Look, if you had another couple hundred thousand dollars, maybe you could do better business. Why can't we give it to you and be your silent partner?

"I could have been a multimillionaire today. That $150,000 could have done a great work, but I got left behind. I see many things like that little mouse, you know. You leave your own bread and butter because someone else is making it bigger. You leave your own living area for more. Sometimes it doesn't work out, just like the little mouse who left his onion fields for the cheese warehouse. I stayed with the wild onions, but I have seen and practically touched with my fingers. . . ."

VI

While Chris was still in the grocery business his mother died. He is not sure exactly what year she died but believes she lived to be eighty-four.

One evening she was sick with a cold and told Chris the story of how her own mother died. "She went into a coma and stayed quiet in bed. She began to breathe slowly and slowly until the last breath." Sometime around 1950 Chris's mother died the same peaceful way. She and her son had lived apart for only seven years.

In 1969, nearly two decades later, Gloria retired from Sears. "Toward the end of her working days, Gloria became a little sick. She had high blood pressure, and she was unable to control it. She was taking medication. She was a little overweight, and she started out taking medicine that the doctor was giving her for reducing. I think some of the medicine was making her sick.

"I saw her ankles swelling a little bit. In the hospital they suggested that she go on a salt-free diet, but Gloria wouldn't stand for it. In one instance we had some company and she cooked some food. I begged Gloria—this time I remember just like I remember you—I said, 'Honey, don't eat this food, please.' I begged her not to eat it, and she pushed my hand out of the way and said, 'Forget about it. I want to die full.'

"While Gloria was sick I must have lost thirty-five pounds because you don't eat no more. I was worried about Gloria. I didn't want to lose her, but there is only so much you can do. She didn't accept my advice easily. You know how it is dealing with your wife. Your wife becomes your second person, and there is always some debate between the two of you. 'Gloria, you got to go to bed.' 'That's all right, you go to sleep, I'm not sleepy.'

"Then there was an epidemic of flu, and Gloria contracted that flu. Her body was not properly balanced, and that flu put her in bad shape.

"I called Dr. Capilla and said, 'You better come and see my wife.' She said, 'You know, Mr. Vitullo, we don't make no home visits.' And I said, 'What kind of visits do you make? Your patient needs attention. Gloria doesn't talk like Gloria. You gotta come and see her and relieve me from thinking.'

"She said, 'It's going to cost you a hundred dollars for the visit.'

"I said, 'Don't worry about it. What is a hundred dollars? Come and see your patient.' She finally came over, and she touched her reflex and said, 'Gloria, what do you think you got, a stroke or something? You're all right. You got the flu. Why don't you give yourself a chance? Two or three days and you'll get better. You take your medication.' I think the doctor goof it up. I think the doctor kill her. I blame that doctor so much. If I could have done something dirty to that doctor I think I would have.

"Gloria went into a coma. They put her in intensive care and, boy oh boy, what they did to help her! She came out of the coma, but she was pretty sick, poor girl. I said, 'She looks a little better today,' but Dr.

Capilla told me, 'Yes, but she's not out of the woods yet.' She went back in a coma that evening, and I don't think she ever came out from then on.

"I used to talk to her while she was in the coma. I went close to her, and I talked to her. The nurses said that she would hear me. I told her, 'Gloria, you gotta think for the best. You remember when you were bad sick, I used to tell you that you got to live for me. Now I'm telling you again. You can't leave me all alone. You gotta be with me.' She nodded her head, you know, almost tears in her eyes because I had tears in my eyes. She didn't make it that time. She didn't make it.

"So Gloria died. When she was sick she told me to go to a lawyer and write up the will so that whatever she had would be mine. And to show her how much I cared about her and not the money, I said, 'Don't worry about it. We'll take care later. Let's start thinking of getting well. Let's not talk about that you're going to die.' But Gloria died, and everything went to hell. The relatives wanted the money. I stayed sad for a few months without doing anything, and then I realized that it had to be done. I went to a lawyer and disclosed the condition of the estate. I thought for sure that my wife's relations would say to me, 'We don't want no estate. We didn't work. You did the work with your wife. You should have it.' But they didn't do that. They wanted the money.

"I wrote a check for each one of them and paid them off. It cost me maybe hundred and ten, hundred and fifteen thousand dollars. In one instance I told the lawyer, 'This Mario Antonelli is a nephew. Before we write him a check, I want to see him. He owes me money.' And I seen Mario. Mario came over with another lawyer, and I said, 'Mario, I never bother you, but you owe me and your Aunt Gloria $1,500. I got the check right here to show you. It's over seven years, and I never bother you because you never had it, but now you're going to get some money from this estate and I think I deserve you to pay me back what you owe me.' And you know what he said to me? He said, 'You never give me no money. I don't owe you no money.' He denied it! He denied it completely! I could have burned up. I told Mario, I said, 'I want you to say that and look at me in the eyes.' He wouldn't even look at me. I felt at the moment I could have squeezed his head off, sincerely. I could have lost my temper, but the lawyer seen me, and he said, 'Don't get sick, Chris. You're too big for $1,500 to let that get you out of control. You're too good of a man. Forget it.'

"It was the principle. It was actually the principle. But I tell you, he is a poor individual. He hasn't got nobody. His wife left him. He's got more trouble that you could shake a stick at. Because what he put in that cup, it's nothing but dirt, and he gets dirt from all over. So you get back what you put in."

VII

For years after Gloria's death in 1971, Chris secluded himself in the house where he and his wife and his mother had been "three in one." To add to his grief, he was burglarized several times. He lost silver coins, watches, and rings, even Gloria's wedding ring. "All these losses and all the problems about Gloria's relations all focused toward me and I was alone to face them. I couldn't relax. It seems that I got awfully nervous thinking of all these problems. I could have lost my mind, thinking the same things. When it comes to thinking the same thing over and over and over and you don't forget the thing that you're thinking of, you don't forget the loss of Gloria, you don't forget the breaking and entering in my house. . . . Those few things were disturbing my life like you have no idea. That's why I got sick. I got sick because I was not going behind that disastrous thinking. I can't even explain how bad it was, but I saw the picture every minute as soon as I lay down in bed. I couldn't sleep. I would go to bed at ten or eleven o'clock and stay awake until eight o'clock in the morning. Sometimes I would doze off about half an hour.

"One day a cousin of mine called me and said, 'What are you doing? Are you gonna die home? Are you not going to go no place? You know she's never going to come back.' For a little while I was thinking Gloria was really coming back. I left everything the way it was, the way she left it. I never moved a thing. The moving was only by the robbers. This cousin of mine was begging me, 'You know, there are so many friends that you could visit with, so many girls that are situated the same as you, and we need one another. I go dancing. I have a good time. I got fifty girls. You come over. Even if you don't dance, you come over and see what's going on in the world.' So he was telling me that he was having a good time and there were so many people waiting to meet me, so many friends that I could have, and I didn't have to be in the house all alone and grieve and grieve about Gloria's death. I could start living, and it would be better for me and better for Gloria also. What are you gonna do? So I went with him a few times. One time he took me to the 'Y,' and there I met Ann."

Ann was a widow who had originally come from the Carolina hills. She had lost her husband years before Chris lost Gloria. She and Chris went out to dinner and slowly became good friends. In 1979, at Ann's urging, they decided to get married.

Chris was seventy-four at the time and sick. Having to sell his old house and move to Ann's upset him further. He threw out decades of accumulations, burning pictures and papers, even clothes and hundred-year-old letters to his mother. Today he regrets the destruction, but "no one was with me to tell me not to do it." Following his marriage, Ann nursed him through surgeries for hernia, prostate trouble, and hemorrhoids. He is better now but still grumbles about his stomach.

When I first visited Chris in the summer of 1981, Ann fussed over me, setting out lunch and keeping a cool drink in my hand. On several occasions, other old people were present, guests whom Ann had invited over or picked up. Sometimes Chris and Ann would squabble in my presence, he expecting her to be obedient, she maintaining a will of her own. Chris has no idea how he could have managed the last two years without her.

"Ann and I, we go over and see Gloria. We bring some flowers. We go and see her husband in the cemetery, and we work on the grave, and we bring him flowers. We have no jealousy. We know that they're gone and we do what we can toward them for respect. I don't care whether the relations go or not, but I go visit Gloria. I talk to her a little bit.

"I don't know why I had to marry again, but God wanted it that way. Being sick, I don't know what would have happened to me if I didn't have somebody to take care of me, so I guess God knows more about how to arrange things. I mean, why did Ann have to come in the picture? I didn't even know Ann, and just think. . . . But that reminds me what I was telling you about this story of what you put in, you take out."

Then he told me the story of the cup.

VIII

Our final meeting of the summer took place in the enclosed back porch of Chris and Ann's brick bungalow. Outside, a morning rain held off the day's heat. Sensing that this might be our last conversation, Chris was in a talkative mood. He brought out old mementos, pictures, and documents and alluded to all the things he had yet to say. My thoughts, however, were on the cup, and, as Chris sorted out keepsakes in search of a date or a place, I asked what had been placed in the cup for him.

"Today I'm capable of realizing that my mother fed me by breast. I was the youngest, and all my sisters were young women. They thought maybe I was their angel, you know? My grandmother, she had shriveled up after ninety years, but when I was a very little boy she would put me on her lap and hug me and kiss me just like her little precious. Everybody took care of me, so what better thing can a mother do for a son than to give her love? You and I, we realize how much the mother does for a son. Only a son doesn't know that the mother does so much for him, cleaning him, keeping him clothed, and feeding him. I got to tell you that in the old days the mother would chew the food and put it from mouth to mouth, just like the birds. This is not done anymore, but they used to do it in my time. This is a conception in my mind, that maybe my sisters and my mother, they chew the things and they put it in my mouth. So how much mother can do for son? My mother put a lot in the cup. She put more than a hundred lire in a cup for me. She gave me her blood, and she gave me her breast to feed on.

"My dad separated himself from us, you know, he went away. I felt disappointed that my dad's estate had to be mishandled by a relation, but my dad left me good thinking. He wanted me to be respectful of other people. There is a relation of ours, you've got to go to him. Don't wait for the other guy to say hello to you. You got to go to him and say hello first. This is important in life.

"I gotta leave in the cup for those that are dear to me. Eventually I'm gonna make papers for those that I want in my death to share the things that I had. I like to share with them my good thinking, but the bad stuff I like to forget. Whenever I get in contact with them, I tell them about obedience. I tell them they've got to be obedient to their father and mother. In the old ideas, obedience was something that had to be carried out. People obeyed the elderly people. I tell them about the Commandments. 'Love thy neighbor.' They have to learn that if you love others like you love yourself, then it's good material in the cup. In the cup you put the respect for your friends, the love for your mother and father, the love for your relatives and for your friends. If you haven't got that and you think you can do without, I think you're wrong. If you're doing anything wrong, your conscience will bother you, you don't sleep well, but if you're at peace with everybody you meet, everybody you meet is your friend, then you sleep well. You don't expect nothing in return but the same thing you put in.

"I tell young barbers to respect their trade. I tell them to be courteous, to ask the people, 'Do you want me to trim the hair from your ears or from your nose?' 'You have one eyebrow that sticks out. Should I cut it off?' Don't cut it! *Ask* the customer if he wants it cut, and if he tells you to cut it then you know he's going to be happy. Then you ask about the head. 'How do you like the hair? Longer? What does your wife think when you get home? Is she going to think that I cut it all off?' Kind of open up a conversation with the customer, and try to get his idea of what's best for himself.

"In the old country you learned the hard way. A barber over there worked for very little money, but a lot of people had the respect because he was just like . . . they called him professor. 'Hi, *professore*!' What kind of professor was he? Some barbers, they didn't even know how to write and read. Yet they knew the trade, and they were capable of giving a haircut to a man and pleasing him. My mother used to say that the person that doesn't have his hair cut by a barber, he'll have his head just like a stepladder. She said the money spent in the barbershop, it is blessed by the wife, because the wife, she is the first one to appreciate her husband's looks. When a barber finish shaving and cutting the hair for a man, and he goes home, his wife sees a different picture. Boy! You look beautiful, you know. And it's true today. You go in a barbershop and you get a haircut. I bet the minute you get up from that chair you feel better. I think the barber is a nice profession to follow. We have books of the barber profession, how it started, how it was done originally. The barber has been an honorable profession for a long, long time.

"I think I still owe the world something. I try to do some work for this Presbyterian church now. I think they need me very bad, and you should see the poor people! There was a little Mexican woman, oh, about sixty, and she always called me sweetheart. She looked at me just like if I was her inspiration for something. I know she needed clothes. When she came over to the church last Friday, I took her in the lot where I parked my car, opened up my trunk, and I showed her. I said, 'I got this for you.' There was some woman's clothes. She had tears coming out of her eyes. Isn't that satisfaction? Doesn't it mean anything? I did it for her and I was glad, and I know she appreciated it or she wouldn't have cried. Then she said, 'Can I have that purse?' There was a purse that I had it in my trunk. 'Sure, you can have it.' And I brought a hat, it looked like a coon hat, and I said, 'You think you wanna wear this hat for the wintertime?' She said, 'Yes, can I have it?' 'Sure.' And I put everything in a bag, and she said, 'You know, I need a pair of shoes.' 'I'll get you a pair of shoes.' We're gonna buy a pair of new shoes for her, some socks. . . .'

"I went and visited a girl yesterday, Ann will tell you. She's got four kids. I gave a haircut to the mother and the kids, all of them. We brought them some stuff we had at home. They were so happy. This girl, she couldn't be better than my daughter. She thinks I'm her father. She kisses me, she loves me, just like her father. I don't think there is any better respect."

Before I left that day Chris took me in the basement of his house and gave me a haircut. Then we went outside, and he showed me his vegetable garden, still dripping from the morning shower. "I never told my life story," he said, "because you acquire so little of it at a time. But I'm thankful to God that I'm still able to remember some of those things and bring it about to you—some of the sad things and some of the good things. My friends are not too many, but I share with them my friendship, and they have the respect for me, and I appreciate it, and it makes me happy. I'm the kind of a guy that likes to please. I like to be happy with the people I live with, and if they're not happy, it's not going to be my fault. Don't try to make this the last session between you and I. I like your friendship. Since you think I be that person to give you some kind of inspiration I be glad to talk to you, anytime. I'll tell you the truth, what I know. We could see if you can make up a nice, nice story."

INTERPRETATION: REMEMBERED ENCHANTMENT; LIVES MADE FABULOUS

I am pleased to conclude this collection of life stories with one as warm and engaging as Chris Vitullo's. Seeing "if you can make up a nice, nice story" was a serious matter to Chris and so was being "some kind of inspiration" to me. I loved his description of Maestro Antonino, a childless man who exemplified technical generativity and showed how culture is quietly transmitted when a skill is being taught. I appreciated the ease with which he spoke of the strong feminine influence in his life, and I admired the direct, physical caring he exhibited in his retirement. I was touched by the way he put his arm around me on one occasion and said I was like his own son. It was clear to me that though Chris had never had children—a serious disappointment in his life—he had nevertheless achieved a sense of generativity. In our conversations that sense was manifest in what I call the generative transference. When Chris retold the fables of "The Cup" and "The Two Mice," he wanted not only to entertain but also to impress important lessons upon me. These were not stories from long ago that he merely chanced to remember; they were the very stories with which his life was fused. They were alive because he was in them.

At seventy-six Chris is returning in his mind to the first culture he experienced. By being present in that culture's stories, he both ensures their propagation and gives himself a sense of living on. How he does so is the subject of this interpretation.

REMEMBERED ENCHANTMENT

In *The Uses of Enchantment* psychoanalyst Bruno Bettelheim identifies important messages that fairy tales carry "to the conscious, the preconscious, and the unconscious mind" of a child.[1] When Hansel and Gretel are abandoned in a dark, thick forest, the child's unconscious fears of desertion are given shape; and when the two of them outwit the witch and find their way back home, the child is assured in his depths that self-reliance is the answer to those fears. When Beauty is given over to a horrible Beast, a young girl's latent anxieties about intimacy are illuminated; and when Beauty transforms Beast into a prince, the girl learns that virtue is powerful and that the rewards of intimacy outweigh the terror. Because they often fail to express their inner dilemmas in words, children pour them into the animals and witches and godmothers and princes of a story and vicariously experience their resolution. Enchanted by the story, saying no more than "it was good" or "tell it again," children are given confidence and guidance as they set out in life.

Chris Vitullo's life story draws our attention to the other side of the exchange, to the benefits that accrue to one who, at the end of life, is a teller of tales. Chris delighted in entertaining me with the stories he had heard as a child, and I was engaged by his warmth and charm. But why, out of all the tales he must have heard, did he retell one about a cup and another about two mice?[2] And why did these tales occur to him at the moment they did in the rendering of his life story? Chris did not recite these stories, which are more fables than fairy tales,[3] merely for entertainment. In his mind he was passing on truths that had stood the test of a lifetime. What messages did the stories convey, not to me but to him? As Bettelheim explored the meaning of tales to the young generation who hears them, Chris Vitullo's life enables us to explore their meaning to the old generation who tells them. What are the generative uses of remembered enchantment?

Let us begin with the story of the cup.

Chris first alluded to this fable when he spoke of a minor incident in his life that I have omitted from the written record. In the first year of his marriage to Gloria he was required to live with her in her father's house. This meant that his mother would have to be taken in by his sister. The sister refused, and his mother suffered the disgrace of living for a year with strangers. Now, Chris told me, history had repeated itself. At the age of ninety-seven, the very sister who had closed the door on her mother was refused entry by all seven of her children and had to be put in a nursing home. Chris was saddened by the turn of events but noted, "What you put in, it's what you gonna get back. That's another story I have to tell you."

He told me the story a few minutes later.[4] Just after asking, "Why did it have to happen?" in reference to his aged sister's predicament, he asked of his own life, "Why did Ann have to come in the picture?" He had just said, "Being sick, I don't know what would have happened to

me if I didn't have somebody to take care of me." His spoken answer to
his query was, "I guess God knows more about how to arrange things."
But his unspoken answer was: "Because I put in twenty-five years of
care for my mother, I am cared for in my old age." In Chris's first
allusion to the story, God was cast as the godfather and Chris's sister as
the godson. In the actual telling of the story, Chris himself became the
godson, while God remained the godfather.

In his third use of the fable Chris became the godfather.[5] A nephew
who had borrowed $1,500 never paid it back and was brazen enough to
take even more from Gloria's estate. Like the godfather, Chris will place
no more in the cup for him, and the nephew will get what he deserves:
"What he put in that cup, it's nothing but dirt, and he gets dirt from all
over."

The final use of the story came at the end of our conversations when I
asked what the previous generation had placed in the cup for him and
what he had left in it for those to come. Though it was I who introduced
this variation, Chris was immediately able to work with it. It released a
good deal of feeling in him. On his mother's side, he said, life had given
him direct nourishment, which he envisioned as food passed from mouth
to mouth. On his father's side, life had given him the ideals of obedience
and respect. These are the very qualities he wants to return to life.
Obedience and respect are values he stresses to young people, and when
he said, "I still owe the world something," he was speaking in particular
of offering poor people the maternal care he himself received. In this
usage of the fable, Chris saw himself first as the godson and then as the
godfather.

In each of his four references to the story, then, Chris identifies with
its characters in a different way. In the first, he is neither the godfather
nor the godson; in the second, he is the godson; in the third, he is the
godfather; in the fourth, he is both. With each new meaning he infuses
into the story, it appears wiser to him. In his hands, the story itself
becomes a cup. It has a structure firm enough to contain the meanings
Chris wants to place in it, and it has a space open enough to hold a
variety of those meanings. "You get back what you put in" is a moral at
once definite and open-ended.

Chris projects himself into the empty spaces of the fable just as
children project themselves into fairy tales. But Chris is at the opposite
end of life than they. Whereas children need to build confidence and
self-reliance as they look to the future, he needs to find order and
coherence as he looks to the past. He has to see large segments of his
life in a single glance, to affirm the choices he has made, and to "set
things right." He has to say to himself that in moments of crisis he

honored cultural ideals and that those ideals are worth passing on to the next generation. Chris is an old man undergoing a life-review[6]—a process my presence intensified—and seeking senses of generativity and ego-integrity.

The story of the cup assists the work of Chris's life review by giving him a scenario into which he can condense major themes in his life. Through his varied applications of the characters and plot of the fable, Chris summarizes motifs spanning anywhere from a decade to a lifetime. The story is also a medium for Chris's assertion that things have come out right. His sister, his dishonest nephew, the next generation, and he himself have all gotten what they deserve. Chris's life becomes a testimony to the belief that life is ultimately just, that "you get back what you put in." Chris can now teach the next generation that someone who works hard and treats others with respect and takes care of his parents will not come to a lonely, bitter end. This, the deepest meaning of the story for Chris, is the only one he does not explicitly connect to the story. The connection can be ascertained only indirectly, from the context and timing of the story's telling.

Chris's story of the two mice condenses and confirms other aspects of his life. "While I was a young man," he said, "I felt a lot of times, deep down in my heart, that I was capable of doing other things than being a barber." Though a large man, Chris referred to himself as a "little" barber who cut the hair of some "big" people. When he left barbering, his chance came to make it big as they had. Whether because of his partner's or his own lack of nerve, Chris failed to make his fortune and returned to the humble profession of barbering. The assertion that he came within a whisker of millions gives him stature and self-respect. And the story of the mouse who returned to the country to eat wild onions tells Chris the grass is greener on his side of the fence. The fable helps him affirm what had to be in his working life and alleviate regret over what he missed. In some ways, it is an apologia for a little man who never made it big.

Among the countless stories Chris heard, the fable of the two mice comes back now because its structure can sustain the meanings emerging from his life review. So fundamental are these meanings that Chris remembers the story as the "first" his mother ever told him. In a way, he has matters backward. He believes that all the meanings in the story were present when he first heard it and that only now, at the end of his life, has he finally discovered them. But if he had made his million (and, perhaps, exploited people in the process) the story of the humble country mouse would not now be running through his mind. Nor, if Ann had not come into his life, would he be seeing such wisdom in the story of the cup. Chris does not find the meaning that existed in the stories back then. Rather, he imbues the stories with the meaning that exists in his life now.

Chris was not the only subject in my research to take advantage of the empty spaces of favorite stories to insert the psychological content of one's station in life. One woman remembered being enthralled at the age of ten by the story of Bluebeard. The story is about a man who has murdered a number of wives and is about to butcher the innocent Fatima when she is rescued by her brothers. It is a cautionary tale about the allure and danger of what happens in the darkest rooms of the castles of men. Its moral is, don't give in to your sexual curiosity. The girl who was so powerfully attracted to the story was unaware that she had undergone a humiliating experience of sexual abuse at the age of three. When she read the story of Bluebeard, some of her repressed experience was allowed into consciousness, but only because she saw it as Fatima's, not her own. The story illuminated hidden aspects of herself, and she felt understood by it. It was what Freud might have called a "screen" story.[7]

At fifty-five, however, the woman used the story in a different way. Her life had turned out to be a series of "butcherings" at the hands of various men and women with whom she had been sexually involved. After an attempted suicide at forty-six, she received therapy at the hands of a competent clinician and "started over" in a new area of the country. When I interviewed her, she referred to the story of Bluebeard as the "script" of her life—a different use than she made of it at ten. Like Chris Vitullo's tales, hers summarized for her a constant theme in her life. Unlike Chris's, however, "Bluebeard" did not affirm that theme as right for her. Instead, it gathered all her experience into one place, so she could decisively turn her back on it. At fifty-five, she was not affirming the script but getting a new one.

Similarly, the messages Chris heard in "The Cup" and "The Two Mice" when he was a boy were no doubt different from the messages they carry in his old age. He may have heard his father's account of the cup as an admonition to be obedient and respectful: if you are not, the cup will give you dirt. His mother's story of the mice may have meant, stay close to home and close to me. But now, at the other end of life and with his unique history, the stories are filled with meanings that clarify and affirm the course of his life.

The ambiguity of folktales and fairy tales thus allows teller and listener, who are at different stages in life, to fill them simultaneously with different meanings. I know a great-nephew of Chris's who feels closer to Chris than to his own father. When Chris told him the story of the cup, the nephew took its lesson to be, if you work hard, it will pay off in the end. When he was told about the mice, he heard something else: you cannot let work take over your life, you have to stop and concern yourself with people. The nephew used one story to fuel his extraordinary ambition and another to control it. The messages he heard were compatible with Chris's but different from them. The marvelous thing about tales passed from one generation to the next is that they can carry different but related meanings at the same time, enriching the telling for the older generation, enriching the listening for the younger, making both appreciate how "wise" the story is.

LIVES MADE FABULOUS

And so we come by way of the simple telling of tales to a final channel of generativity. When the end of life comes close, some individuals blend their lives with the mythic elements of culture. Like Prospero in *The Tempest*, they find themselves on an enchanted isle where the real and the fabulous are mixed and where they can magically regain what is theirs and bring their enemies to justice. In *The Tempest* Prospero sets everything right (he even marries off his daughter!), releases his spirit, and then enters his tent to spend the night telling the story of his life.

In rendering his life, Chris Vitullo returned to the stories he had heard as a child and with their help brought order and coherence to his life. When he introduced the fables of "The Cup" and "The Two Mice," he did explicitly what other subjects did implicitly. Everyone, and older narrators in particular, brought in the mythic elements of a culture and made their lives fabulous.

Although I did all I could to ensure historical accuracy in my recording, my presence no doubt stimulated the injection of the mythical into the historical. I was, after all, converting lives into stories and in that sense making them fablelike. I was not merely setting down facts but looking for meaning. In doing so, I am sure I subconsciously began to call for myth and see lives as instances of archetypal dramas.

When a life is made fabulous, both in its telling and in its writing, it is not divorced from historical truth, but it is moved a few steps in the direction of myth. Events appear more marvelous than when they happened. Characters come out a bit taller, a bit more powerful and loving, a bit more exemplary. The particular life story seems to be the retelling of a collectivity's ancient stories. If there is value in this telling for the elder whose life is mythologized, there is greater value for the young who hear of the life. The young need myth, they need heroes and heroines to activate dreams of who to be. Were Chris's life not blended with a meaning system, his nephew would never have pictured him as someone worth emulating. Had Chris not possessed integrity, his nephew would have lacked "some kind of inspiration" to strive for the ideal. A life made fabulous speaks to the preconscious and unconscious of the young, offering them empty spaces for their projections, providing them with models for identification, and giving them hope.

In most discussions of the life review of the elderly, this aspect is overlooked: how, as a life is gone over, it is returned to and cleansed in a culture, how it acquires generativity and integrity from the accretion of mythic elements. We have seen how Sister Josette Biondi affixed herself to a culture by "standing for" certain of its principles and how Hannah Gordon did the same by envisaging her life as a piece of Russian literature. Ali Birri shaped his life story so that it followed the Twelve Steps of Alcoholics Anonymous, and Sarkis Hashoian dwelt on the seven years of his life that constituted a prototypical story of deliverance. One way or another, all connected their lives to the mythic substratum of an enduring culture, and all derived therefrom the benefits of generativity and integrity.

Chris Vitullo believed his life exemplified the lessons of stories he had heard long ago. He identified with those stories, saying in effect that although his life would not endure, the truths it taught would endure. Blending his life with two fables, he gave it wholeness and extension and made it accessible to the next generation.

If Chris had matters backward about finding meaning in his parents' stories, in a far more important way he had matters just right. He was not consciously striving for integrity or fusing his life with a culture. He wanted no more than to delight and to teach. All else that he did, all that has been the subject of this interpretation, he did indirectly, and it was the indirection that made it effective. Like Prospero, Chris placed his life on an enchanted isle and let the island's spirits do the rest.

PART · IV

Conclusion

12 · *The Culture Connection*

Sometime between the beginning and end of my research on generativity the public concern over "meism" and "narcissism" passed
quietly away. Our various strains of cultural individualism and egocentrism were allowed to live once again in the shadows they prefer. What
did not pass, however, were the conditions giving rise to a preoccupation
with the solitary self and the conditions requiring an understanding of
the many ways human beings move beyond Me and pass life on to
others. The contraceptive revolution was not reversed; available data
indicate that its hold was solidified.[1] And the demographic revolution
continued its slow, inexorable reshaping of the human life cycle. The
lives seen in profile in this book have been lived in the middle of these
revolutions, and now it is time to take stock of what has been learned
from them and where the learnings fit on the wider map of psychological
theory and method.

GENERATIVITY IN ITS NEW SETTING

I introduced a typology at the beginning of the book to serve as as guide
for identifying varieties of generative experience. In the life stories that
followed, *biological generativity*, the first type, was never observed directly.
Although narrators and I touched on meanings associated with the physical transmission of life, we did not become biologists and pursue that
transmission in itself. Rather, we were interested in its footprints in the
realm of emotion—in the numbing conviction that one had caused a
child's ugliness or death, in the repugnance and joy of giving birth, in the
guilt surrounding an abortion. Although biological processes are out of
bounds for social scientists, the meanings attached to them are not, and
many researchers are now investigating the dilemmas posed by physical
fertility and sterility.

Parental generativity proved to be fully accessible to life-historical investigation. Indeed, more leads opened up in this area than I could possibly follow. I was able to describe the lingering consciousness of *damage* suffered at the hands of parents and of damage inflicted on children. I saw how individuals tried to make up for earlier harm by taking advantage of the *second chances* tendered by the greater overlap of generations and by *reworking the heritage* received from the past. Rectifying damage in some realistic way (what I term *redoing*) was a strong motif in midlife generativity.

I was also able to sample a shift in the timing of *agency and communion in parenthood*. As families shrink in size and women turn toward continuous employment, a growing number of men are becoming involved in the care of children. For them communal impulses are being released, not suppressed, by the arrival of children. Paucity of subjects prevented me from drawing conclusions about the role of masculinity and femininity across the broad spectrum of generativity, but the interplay of masculine and feminine in the stories I did collect was worth watching. Men appeared in women's stories at one extreme as usurpers of their wombs and at the other as guides into nurturant cultures—malevolence on the one hand and benevolence on the other, but both from positions of power. The power of women was not as evident in the stories of the men, with the important exception of a mother's power. All four men remembered their mothers as strong, all had developed special bonds with them, and all had a discernible and in some cases prominent "feminine" component to their personalities. These incipient patterns suggest questions for further research. If more men continue to be involved in parenting, will more women move in the opposite direction, assuming roles of cultural stewardship filled predominantly by men? If so, how will they affect the balance of masculinity and femininity in the lives of those they guide? And will there continue to be a link between feminine influence and communal modes of generativity, masculine influence and agentic modes?

Certain to grow is the number of grandparents who are able to exert on their grandchildren the extensive influence that Hannah Gordon and her husband did on theirs. Many of these grandparents will know their grandchildren for forty or more years, and some will head four- or five-generation families. The grandchildren will be able to question their forebears with the perspective of adults and to identify positively or negatively with living figures whose experience stretches far into the past. There will, of course, be more people living in retirement, a period of life that is lasting longer than in the past. Though three of the eight persons whose stories appear in this book were retired, only one alluded to opportunities opened up by their new-found leisure. Saying, "I think I still owe the world something," Chris Vitullo spoke of volunteer work he was now able to do with poor people and young barbers. But none of the stories addressed in any substantial way the generative possibilities—the second and third chances—for the newly retired "young-old." Nor did any explore the psychological transition to retirement as an entry into a new culture. The young-old are relatively healthy, secure economically, and active politically. Before the onset of physical decline (before they will have to be cared for rather than care), they have the freedom and time for contributions ranging from being good grandparents, and not just to their own grandchildren, to fashioning institutional legacies.

A wide path of inquiry I did not have time to follow concerns stepparenting. Some experts predict that by 1990 more spouses will be living in second marriages than in first marriages and that one out of every five children will be living with a stepparent.[2] In the past stepparenting was occasioned by death rather than divorce. Now both old and new sets of parents remain alive, and children are shared by two households and have a double set of relatives—as many as eight grandparents. For those who live in stepfamilies, the "relative explosion" will reshape the expression of parenting. How will stepmothers and fathers, stepgrandmothers and grandfathers discipline and care for children who are not their biological descendants?

Nor did any story explore in depth a case of *technical generativity*. The passing on of skills was constantly touched on, but it was the focus of no life in this collection. There are of course numerous studies of educational technique, but most do not bring out what I hoped some story would: the meaning of a skill against the large background of culture. Chris Vitullo's idealized recollection of Maestro Antonino, brief though it was, came close to target. Through the medium of barbering Antonino taught his apprentice an ethos of courtesy, respect, and obedience.

In retrospect, the greatest contribution of these stories was in the domain of *cultural generativity*, the site of most "generative ingenuity" and the one most ignored by previous research. This locale was hospitable to the life-historical method and willingly yielded up its wealth through the particularities of the lives I studied.

In these lives I observed key moments in the relationship between individual and culture that may now be arranged in a model scenario. The first moment is that of conscious entry into a society. This moment occurs when one becomes aware of and identifies with the symbols of one's culture of birth or when one discovers a new culture in adult life. A specific kind of *nourishment*, conscious and unconscious, becomes available at this moment: a map of existence for the intellect, heroic figures and great deeds for the imagination, guidance for the will, and a people to belong to. The individual is sensitized to the unique stream of nourishment that will continue to come from this culture. But the culture has to be "good enough" for the sensitization to take effect and for the individual's latent energies to be activated. The internal representation of cultural entry is an experience of identity, the founding event that leads later on to cultural fertility.

When entry involves a new culture discovered in adult life, the individual acquires a "new" self that seems uncannily "old." She or he gains a new interpretation of personal history from a mediator of the culture. If the culture is precisely right for the initiate, it *transforms defects* into virtues and *validates the new self* by giving it a reproductive outlet. Entry constitutes another variant of the second chance. The stage is set for one who has failed at parental generativity to be fertile in an entirely different way.

A second key moment in the relationship between the individual and culture comes when the prospect of *death* enters a life. Existing research suggests that this often happens at midlife; therefore for some it may coincide with the discovery of a new community. According to Daniel Levinson, this is the time for deillusionment, for letting go of the myths and beliefs about life that have proven false.[3] But Levinson also claims it is the time for creating a legacy, and in that connection I have witnessed certain individuals at midlife not stripping themselves of myth but realigning themselves with it so as to make a better match. Having let go of illusions that flew in the face of reality, they go on to amplify those aspects of the self that are truly present, that have outlets in reality, that are idealized by their culture and valued by its young. They begin to stand in tangible ways for the culture's beliefs and principles and prescriptions for action and even begin to *care for the culture* itself. They become concrete and very real symbols of an abstract element in a shared meaning system.

During a life review in old age—another moment in this composite sketch—the process is carried a step further. Pressed by a need for integrity, some individuals cleanse their lives in the culture's symbols and fuse them more completely with the ideal. Historical accuracy is not forgotten as they tell their stories to others, but myth enters in the service of narrative truth. If a life is unattached to myth it will nourish no one, but if it does not stand up to a realistic gaze, it will appear hypocritical and collapse under the burden of its mythical accretions. In *lives that are made fabulous* heroes are ordinary men and women who are somehow different from the rest of us. They are actual persons and yet exemplars.

A final moment in the scenario comes at death, when meaning is extracted from the individual's life by his or her successors. In the rituals surrounding death the bereaved make explicit which elements of culture the deceased stood for. In an effort to maintain continuity with the deceased they "take in" these elements. As the years pass, they remember and retell stories from his or her life that match a valued archetype. These recollections become the *good stories with generative power*.

This scenario of moments in the transmission of culture through exemplary lives is no more than a template against which personal histories can be gauged and understood. Parts of it can be traversed by one person in a matter of years, by another in decades. In one adult's life it can be a dominant theme, in another's an obscure one. No one I studied experienced it in its entirety. This is not surprising, for I think the most common manifestation of fertility will continue to be forms of parenting within families. Only a few among us—a small number of creators, conservators, and renovators—will live lives characterized by significant expressions of cultural generativity.

Implied in what I have said throughout this book is a model of a culture that is "good enough." To make explicit the characteristics of such a culture, let me gather into one place the scattered references I have made to them. From the standpoint of the individual, a good enough culture possesses the following characteristics: elders who are able to serve as guides to a mythic center, initiates who validate the elders' path by following it, and ritual to regulate movement along the way. It contains a collection of heroic lives and great deeds from the past and present, idealized to the point that they inspire adherence to shared values yet realistic enough that the ideal appears both credible and possible. It has enough tradition, prescriptions for action, and control to provide a wrap for individuals who could not otherwise be held together, but not so much that the individual is smothered and cultural change prevented. Culture consists of more than these elements, but they are the ones that nourished the individuals studied here. A culture that is good enough makes demands on individuals and inevitably brings about repressions, but its benefits to old and young prove greater than its costs.

"MOMENTS," NOT "STAGES"

When I set forth a theory of generativity at the outset of this book, I referred to problems in considering it a stage. For one thing, ongoing changes in the structure of the life cycle made matters difficult for any fixed-stage theory of development, especially one tied closely to age norms. Then there was a scheduling dilemma: Erikson defines childbearing as a prime component of generativity, and yet he assigns generativity to middle adulthood. The fact is that childbearing begins for the vast majority of women not in middle adulthood but in very early adulthood. (In the United States, the median age of a mother at the birth of her first child has been near twenty-three since the turn of the century.[4]) Another problem was that generativity is chronologically the longest of Erikson's stages, spanning several decades of middle adulthood in which it is the "ascendant" motive and/or defines the "nuclear" conflict. But I am aware of no evidence that generativity is dominant for so long in more than a handful of adults; it appears, rather, to be only intermittently ascendant. Finally, Erikson holds that the tasks of earlier stages must be mastered before those of later stages can be successfully completed. Thus only individuals who have achieved identity and intimacy are in a position to resolve favorably the crisis of generativity and realize its virtue: care. Elegant and compelling though stage theory is, it has fit poorly any life I have studied. Nor is it especially well tailored to those studied by Erikson.[5]

A way beyond these problems is to think of generativity not as a stage but as an impulse released at various times between the late teens and old, old age. Different types of generativity, having their own schedules, will be released at different moments. The task of the life-historical researcher is to identify such moments, note their cultural context, observe their aftermath in episodes of fertility, and interpret them.

The idea of *moment* is not foreign to Erikson, and in his studies of concrete lives he has been exquisitely sensitive to features of timing. *Young Man Luther* and *Gandhi's Truth* were about the precise instants when a society activated a leader's inner conflicts and turned them to collective gain. According to Erikson, Luther and Gandhi were able to solve on a large scale difficulties they could not work out in their personal lives because they happened to arrive at the same junction that a church and a nation were reaching. Comfortable as he is with the word *moment*, however, Erikson limits its application to historical development. It is history that has moments, but individuals that have stages.

To describe moments and episodes in lives has certain advantages over describing stages. Moments imply nothing about the proper age for the appearance of a motive, nor about its duration or ascendancy, nor about its foundation in the successful completion of previous tasks. Moments make room for accidents in what Klaus Riegel calls the outer-physical dimension of life and for chance encounters that dramatically alter a life's direction—in other words, for surprise.[6] A vocabulary of moments and episodes keeps one from the developmental determinism that has been the occupational hazard of life-span psychologists from Freud on down and from behaviorists' unwarranted expectations of prediction and control. The vocabulary is also compatible with the "life course" perspective of sociologists who pay particular attention to how the experience of historical cohorts (the Depression generation, for example) affects individual development. These sociologists are far more inclined to speak of timing in a life than they are of stages.[7]

In the lives in this volume, an assignment as a teacher, an invitation to run a concert series, the birth of a child, even a request to tell a story were all moments that initiated episodes of activity in which generativity was featured, not always as the dominant or ascendant motive but certainly as a principal one. The moments did not result from favorable resolutions of prior crises of identity and intimacy but from a fortuitous match of individual and society that occasionally came about by chance. Individuals propagated themselves in spite of problems with identity and intimacy or even had those problems animate their creativity from below in a phenomenon I call the transformation of defect. The energy released during generative episodes was intrinsically fertile. As one man said, you could not *not* give it away. The flow of energy came from others and was returned to them: it was social in character. And it was culture-specific. That is, it had a strong impact on those who shared one's interpretation of existence but little on those who did not.

In retrospect, the presence of this energy explains why I was referred to many of my subjects. Had I come upon the scene during a different episode in their lives, I might not have been put in touch with them. This is part of the natural selection for stories that I spoke about previously: in periods of sterility people do not want to tell their stories, nor does their "energy" flow to those who might provide referrals. Only Hannah Gordon seemed devoid of vitality when I spoke with her, but even she recaptured it when recounting her life. My presence created a brief moment.

Like a vocabulary of stages, a vocabulary of moments reflects a descriptive and explanatory strategy, not a definitive rendition of reality. Its bias, which can easily become a distortion, is to overdramatize single events in a life and see them as the cause of too much. But because moment claims less than stage, the researcher is freer to observe the enormous variation in lives, taking what they give rather than forcing them into ill-fitting molds. Moments permit an examination of the synchrony between various dimensions in life, for example, between technical and cultural fertility. Nor, by giving up the language of stages, does the researcher lose the ability to generalize and to construct theory. Scenarios of typical moments and episodes can be written and used as frames of reference against which individual differences can be appreciated. When an episode is sufficiently long, when it builds on previous inner developments and becomes the foundation for later ones, when it occurs at an appropriate age, then—and only then—can it be called a stage.[8]

To argue for moments instead of stages is to fight the tendency of some theoreticians to absolutize findings from small samples of subjects by predicating them of all people. It also counteracts the laypersons' desire, which often becomes a desperate need, for a psychological road map to guide them through life's anxieties with the conviction that they are getting somewhere. But the major reason for recommending such a vocabulary is that it is truer to the complexity of actual lives. Generativity appears on and off in different guises through fifty or sixty years of adult life, and a case could even be made for its antecedents in children. Only on rare occasions does it merit the term *stage*.

TOWARD A NARRATIVE PSYCHOLOGY

The language of moments, episodes, and scenarios brings us to the larger perspective of story, and while we have that perspective let us pause to see how it overlooks the psychological study of lives. For me the history of story in psychology goes back to my first day as a graduate student at the University of Chicago and an incident in which an eminent professor dismissed a piece of evidence as "merely anecdotal." On that occasion I learned very quickly the place of narrative in scientific psychology, and I must admit that, coming first, the professor's pronouncement carried a great deal of weight. It took me many years to realize that the indisputable benefits of scientific psychology came at a cost: a blindness to whatever could not be apprehended by its method. If a human experience would not give up its secret to science, it was not worth studying or, worse still, it was not there.

Now I am aware that story has always had a place, albeit an obscure one, in the history of psychology. And I am proposing a term, *narrative psychology*, to give that place more visibility and to attract to it a number of widely scattered interests. By narrative psychology I mean both a content and a method, both the study of stories themselves and the use of the story form to capture phenomena overlooked or only partially apprehended by science.

As a content, narrative psychology would concern itself with the personal and social dynamics of stories—with the process of their creation and retention, with the preferred themes of individuals at various points in life, with the positive and negative identifications that readers make with characters and plots. Some study of stories has already been done, much of it under other names. Thus we know a little about memory for stories,[9] and a great deal more about the creation of stories in response to TAT pictures.[10] There has been a continuing stream of research on the effect of violence in televised stories upon the behavior of viewers. Milton Erickson has made explicit use of "teaching tales" in therapy, and both Roy Schafer and Donald Spence have interpreted the psychoanalytic interchange as an attempt to fabricate coherent narrative.[11] Yet these very diverse areas of inquiry have not been linked by their common thread: the story form.

As a method, narrative psychology would be used in investigations that judge the meaning of a behavior to be as important as the behavior itself. Use of narrative to discover meaning would require a sophisticated understanding of what happens when a story is told and how the story is shaped by its social setting. A practitioner must know, for example, *how memories speak* and have a feel for special cases such as *the telling of trauma* and *remembering enchantment*. To use the narrative method well requires a special set of skills: clinical sensitivity, a strong theoretical bent, the ability to read critically in several disciplines, and literary power that will bring findings not only to scholars but beyond them to the general public.

If narrative psychology has a place, it is on the margins of psychology, sharing borders with anthropology, sociology, history, and education— disciplines that have been more hospitable to first-person accounts than has psychology itself. Anthropology's tradition of ethnography, its study of folklore, and its guiding concept of culture have much to offer scholars interested in narrative. Through the field-work tradition begun by Bronislaw Malinowski during World War I, anthropology influenced the Chicago school of sociology, which thrived on qualitative methods in the 1920s and 1930s and established a lasting place for biography. That place is being kept today by sociologists interested in the social determinants of the life course. Since the middle of the century historians too have been using oral accounts not only to construct the biographies of individuals but to document a community's interpretation of significant events. Although education has always had a tradition of similar research, much of its early work was undertaken by scholars trained in anthropology and sociology. Beginning in the 1960s, however, as federal agencies began to fund qualitative studies, educational researchers have undertaken more of them.[12] Ironically, it is psychology, the natural home of the in-depth interview, that has proved most stubborn about granting it legitimacy anywhere but in the clinic.

Within its borders narrative psychology would contain accounts and interpretations of experience ranging from the portraits of such writers as Robert Coles and Thomas Cottle, for whom the building of psychological theory is a remote concern, to the studies of researchers such as Daniel Levinson, whose age-related theory of stages dominates the biographies he presents. In the former, the individual stands out; in the latter, the general does. Beyond these extremes are pure story on the one hand (and that is not psychology) and pure theory on the other (which views an actual life as nothing more than a launching pad). Narrative psychology means story plus. A narrative psychologist would rarely speak of a life story without telling one, but he or she would not tell one without drawing out its implications for theory. Once again, Clifford Geertz's method of thick description comes close to what I have in mind.

There are philosophical underpinnings for narrative psychology within the phenomenological tradition and a practical model of operation within the clinical. The clinic is the place where questions were first asked about the truth of a life story and how it may be verified or disconfirmed. As a preliminary guide beyond the clinic, John Dollard's criteria for the life history have much to recommend them. Because of their origin in a seminar on culture and personality, the criteria stress the individual in relation to culture, an emphasis that is often lacking in the interpretations of case histories done in psychoanalysis. In addition, the methodological expertise of Henry Murray and students of personology such as Robert White ought to be consulted.[13] Murray had an abiding and influential concern with understanding fully the individual, non-clinical case. A great deal of life-storytelling takes place in natural settings, and what is known of the narrative method from therapy ought to be complemented with knowledge gathered from these settings.

Psychologists who use first-person renditions of experience in their research are notoriously inconsistent in naming what they do. In particular they are careless with the words *narrative* and *story*. I want to insist on protecting the meaning of these words. Literary theorist Barbara Smith defines narration as "verbal acts consisting of *someone telling someone else that something happened.*"[14] In a story what happened is woven into an account with conflict and resolution, uncertainty and clarity, an account that goes somewhere. And yet, psychoanalysts such as Roy Schafer and Donald Spence, who have been important voices for the narrative perspective in psychoanalysis, dilute the meaning of *story*. Schafer, for example, writes that to theorize is to adopt a particular "narrative strategy" and that to think or feel is to "act."[15] One can appreciate Schafer's reasons for advocating an action-language but not his overextension of the word *narrative*. Difficult as it may be to draw and maintain conceptual boundaries, explanation is not narration, nor are thoughts and emotions behaviors, nor are all first-person accounts stories. Psychologists would do well to adopt the conceptual rigor regarding the meaning of story that has characterized the work of individuals such as anthropologist Oscar Lewis and French sociologist Daniel Bertaux. William Runyan's recent *Life Histories and Psychobiography* is another source of historical and conceptual clarity.[16]

I do not propose that narrative psychology merely do spadework for mainstream psychological study of the life span or mine hypotheses that can be "conclusively" tested by science, as if a scientific study in psychology ever provided the last word on a subject. Nor should it be regarded simply as a source of color to bring to life some quantitative finding that might otherwise be too drab. Narrative psychology can play these roles, but it is at its best when it stands at the center of a research project and addresses questions that experimental, survey, or longitudinal research cannot. Then its strengths can be exploited: its predilection for the individual rather than the aggregate, its sensitivity to timing and its openness to chance happenings, its ability to probe the meaning with which people imbue major life events, the accessibility of its findings to laypersons. If narrative psychology is done well, it will be read.

In the case of generativity, the narrative method turned out to be well suited to the research content. I found that stories were a natural vehicle for carrying the meaning of a life from one generation to the next, and I found that both stories and generativity could be understood only in relation to an abiding culture. These findings return us for a final word to our main avenue of exposition.

THE CULTURE CONNECTION

That avenue takes us to two very different schools of psychology that share a common view of culture. The first is classical psychoanalysis, in which culture appears as the repressive might of civilization. Internalized in the superego, it wars incessantly with the id and creates false consciousness in the ego. The second is humanistic psychology, which construes culture as a cocoon from which the individual must escape, autonomous, self-fulfilled, and free. Psychoanalysis says that individual and culture ideally reach the truce of sublimation, but in humanistic psychology the illusion is created that culture will simply go away.

These positions are based on implicit life-cycle perspectives. Though as therapies both schools work with adults, psychoanalysis relentlessly pushes its interpretations back to the beginning of life, and humanistic psychology takes the adolescent view that life's paramount task is to establish a separate sense of self. Because both perspectives are taken from the first half of life, psychoanalysis and humanistic psychology end up in agreement on the role of culture: it is your adversary.

But if one picks up the other end of the stick and takes the end of life as a vantage point, culture turns out to be an ally, and so it appeared in these stories of generativity. Newly discovered in middle age, cultures gave the subjects of the stories order, direction, and community at a time when they badly needed them. The cultures "contained" these individuals, who could not otherwise be held together, gave them nourishment, and provided them with generative outlets. For older subjects, culture was the enduring apparatus of meaning to which they affixed their lives. One way or another everyone collaborated with culture and partook of its ability to transcend the finiteness of his or her own existence.

Some narrators, of course, had lived in cultures that damaged them and had to be escaped. And cultures did demand repressions that introduced deception into consciousness. (The repressions I focused on were *intergenerational silences* that led to *hidden legacies*.) Though one culture was left for another, however, culture itself was never escaped. Individuals kept improving the fit between themselves and their cultures by entering new ones, renovating existing ones, or changing themselves. During their generative episodes, they maintained a culture connection, by which I mean an inner link to a collective symbol system.

The culture connection was often unconscious. Narrators remembered only those incidents from their childhood that fit an existing archetype, or they used a culture's fables to tell themselves that their lives had come out right. Some felt themselves standing for a culture's principles; some used their life stories to propagate its prescriptions for living. Rarely were narrators aware of these connections, and rarely did they tell their stories as if they "owned" them. Rarely did they sense that the subjective meaning they infused into their accounts was actually shared meaning.

Ordinarily it would be a truism to say that culture is never escaped or that it may actually be of benefit to individuals, but humanistic psychology and psychoanalysis have a blind spot in this regard. And their blind spot—particularly that of humanistic psychology—has become the public's: in 1981 pollster Daniel Yankelovich estimated that 80 percent of adult Americans who work for pay were engaged in the search for self-fulfillment. According to Yankelovich, an essential belief of these Americans was that the ideal self is unfettered by culture. This and other contradictions in their quest, he suggested, were dooming them to failure.[17]

The reasons for the blindness go beyond two schools of psychology that happened to pick up a certain end of the life-span stick. The road winds back further: first to a well-documented tradition of individualism in the United States, the most recent outgrowth of which was the psychology of self-fulfillment that spread so rapidly in the 1970s,[18] and,

second, to an older world view that characterizes Western thought generally. In his study of Japanese models of maturity, anthropologist David
Plath was able to reflect on contrasting models that characterize the
West. The Japanese concept, he wrote, centers on "the cultivation of
personal capacities for relatedness," on a "self trying to vibrate sympa-
thetically in a convoy of others." But the Western archetype of growth is
aimed at "cultivating a self that feels secure in its uniqueness in the
cosmos. . . . We enter into a social contract out of animal weakness and
practical need. But social participation can only diminish us: Our highest
self is realized in peak experiences . . . that take us out of the social ruck.
All life long we struggle to defend this uniqueness from the downdrafts
of collective conformity."[19]

It is not that the subjects of my research (and, presumably, many of
Yankelovich's 80 percent) failed to establish connections to culture; it is
that they failed to see them. When we tell our stories, to ourselves if to
no other, we are much more likely to own the breaks we make from
existing communities and existing systems of meaning than we are to
own the links we forge to them. Those of us who come to psychotherapy
when we are between meaningful attachments are much more likely to
be encouraged in this direction than we are to be dissuaded from it. And
so, in the name of personal growth, we try to secure our sense of being
"unique in the cosmos." In the process we unconsciously make the most
profound cultural connection of all: to the archetypal Western myth of
self-discovery and freedom.

If there is a single impression I might leave with the reader of this
book it is this: there is no such thing as a culture-free self, and there is no
way to outlive the self without the vehicle of culture. Whether one looks
at the stories we tell about ourselves or whether one looks at the marks
we leave when we die, culture inevitably appears. In the chill of death,
dew forms on the web of significance on which we collectively live our
lives and for a time reveals its outline.

NOTES

INTRODUCTION

1. David Riesman set the narcissism of the 1970s in the context of longstanding American individualism in "Egocentrism," *Character*, 1 (1980):3–9.

2. Christopher Lasch, "The Narcissist Society," *New York Review of Books*, September 30, 1976, p. 5.

3. Herbert Hendin, "The Revolt against Love," *Harper's*, August 1975, pp. 20 and 22. Hendin adapted this article from *The Age of Sensation* (New York: Norton, 1975).

4. Erik H. Erikson, *Insight and Responsibility* (New York: Norton, 1964), pp. 130–31; *Childhood and Society*, 2d ed. (New York: Norton, 1963), pp. 266–68; *Dimensions of a New Identity* (New York: Norton, 1974), p. 124.

5. Peter Marin, "The New Narcissism," *Harper's*, October 1975, pp. 45–56.

6. Francis Hearn, "Adaptive Narcissism and the Crisis of Legitimacy," *Contemporary Crises* 4 (1980):117–40.

7. Richard Sennett, *The Fall of Public Man* (New York: Vintage, 1976).

8. In 1981, survey researcher Daniel Yankelovich estimated that 80 percent of adult Americans who work for pay were engaged in the search for self-fulfillment, 17 percent intensely and 63 percent less so. See "New Rules for American Life," *Psychology Today* 15, no. 4 (1981):35–91.

CHAPTER 1: A THEORY OF GENERATIVITY

1. Erikson, *Childhood and Society*, pp. 266–68; *Insight and Responsibility*, pp. 130–32; *Identity: Youth and Crisis* (New York: Norton, 1968), p. 138.

2. Erikson, *Dimensions of a New Identity*, p. 124.

3. Erik H. Erikson, *Childhood and Society* (New York: Norton, 1950), p. 232.

4. Erik H. Erikson, "Dr. Borg's Life Cycle," *Daedalus* 105, no. 2 (1976):24.

5. Matilda White Riley, "Aging, Social Change, and the Power of Ideas," *Daedalus* 107, no. 4 (1978):45. A more sympathetic critic is George Vaillant, whose longitudinal studies of male development have led him to insert additional developmental tasks into Erikson's model and to picture the progression through these tasks as climbing a spiral staircase. Vaillant has found that the Eriksonian tasks must be mastered sequentially, but that there is enormous variation in the ages at which mastery occurs. See Vaillant, and Eva Milofsky, "Natural History of Male Psychological Health: IX. Empirical Evidence for Erikson's Model of the Life Cycle," *American Journal of Psychiatry* 137 (1980):1348–59.

6. Writers with ethical and theological interests have been more receptive to the concept than psychologists. See, for example, Don S. Browning, *Generative Man* (Philadelphia: Westminster, 1973); John N. Kotre, "Generative Humanity," *America* 133 (1975): 434–37; Evelyn E. Whitehead and James D. Whitehead, *Christian Life Patterns* (Garden City, N. Y.: Doubleday, 1979).

7. Daniel J. Levinson, *The Seasons of a Man's Life* (New York: Ballantine, 1978), pp. 222–23.

8. Erik H. Erikson, *Young Man Luther* (New York: Norton, 1958); *Gandhi's Truth* (New York: Norton, 1969).

9. Several studies have found that middle-aged adults are more likely to report a fear of death than are older adults. See Richard A. Kalish, "Death and Dying in a Social Context," in Robert H. Binstock and Ethel Shanas, eds., *Handbook of Aging and the Social Sciences* (New York: Van Nostrand, Reinhold, 1976); Vern L. Bengtson, José B. Cuellar, and Pauline K. Ragan, "Stratum Contrasts and Similarities in Attitudes toward Death," *Journal of Gerontology* 32 (1977):76–88.

10. Robert J. Lifton, "The Sense of Immortality: On Death and the Continuity of Life," in Robert J. Lifton, ed., *Explorations in Psychohistory* (New York: Simon and Schuster, 1974), pp. 275–76.

11. Levinson, *Seasons of a Man's Life*, pp. 209–21.

12. This analysis of timing features in generative expression borrows from Klaus F. Riegel, "The Dialectics of Human Development," *American Psychologist* 31 (1976):689–700.

13. Clifford Geertz, *The Interpretation of Cultures* (New York: Basic Books, 1973), p. 5.

14. Margaret Mead, "Long Living in Cross-Cultural Perspective," paper presented at the meeting of the Gerontological Society, San Juan, Puerto Rico, 1972.

15. Harvey C. Lehman, "The Creative Production Rates of Present versus Past Generations of Scientists," *Journal of Gerontology* 17 (1962):409–17; Wayne Dennis, "Creative Productivity between the Ages of 20 and 80 Years," *Journal of Gerontology* 21 (1966):1–8.

16. Vaillant and Milofsky, "National History of Male Psychological Health," p. 1350.

17. My thinking along these lines was aided by an unpublished paper of David Gutmann, "Transformations of Narcissism across the Life Cycle."

18. David Bakan, *The Duality of Human Existence* (Chicago: Rand McNally, 1966).

19. Erikson, "Dr. Borg's Life Cycle," p. 19.

CHAPTER 2: THE CHANGING CONTEXT OF GENERATIVITY

1. Charles F. Westoff and Norman B. Ryder, *The Contraceptive Revolution* (Princeton: Princeton University Press, 1977).

2. Charles F. Westoff and Elise F. Jones, "Contraception and Sterilization in the United States, 1965–1975," *Family Planning Perspectives* 9 (1977):153–57. The theoretical maximum allows for nonusers who are nonsurgically sterile, subfecund, trying to get pregnant, pregnant, or in the postpartum period.

3. Charles F. Westoff, "Trends in Contraceptive Practice: 1965–1975," *Family Planning Perspectives* 8 (1976):57.

4. Ibid., pp. 54–55; Westoff and Jones, "Contraception and Sterilization"; Kathleen Ford, "Contraceptive Utilization in the United States: 1973 and 1976," *Advanced Data* (HEW), August 18, 1978, No. 36.

5. George Masnick and Mary Jo Bane, *The Nation's Families: 1960–1990* (Cambridge, Mass.: Joint Center for Urban Studies, 1980), pp. 7 and 43. Essentially the same projection was made three years later by David E. Bloom and James Trussell. Their study was reported in *Family Planning Perspectives* 15 (1983):224–25.

6. Edward Pohlman, *The Psychology of Birth-Planning* (Cambridge, Mass.: Schenkman, 1969).

7. Jessie Bernard, *The Future of Motherhood* (New York: Penguin, 1975), pp. 22–24.

8. David Gutmann, Jerome Grunes, and Brian Griffin, "The Clinical Psychology of Later Life: Developmental Paradigms," paper presented at the meeting of the American Gerontological Society, Washington, D.C., 1979.

9. U.S. Bureau of the Census, *Historical Statistics of the United States: Colonial Times to 1970* (Washington, D.C.: U.S. Government Printing Office, 1975), Part I, B116–125; U.S. Bureau of the Census, *Statistical Abstract of the United States: 1979* (Washington, D.C.: U.S. Government Printing Office, 1979), No. 102.

10. Morris Rockstein, Jeffrey Chesky, and Marvin Sussman, "Comparative Biology and the Evolution of Aging," in Caleb E. Finch and Leonard Hayflick, eds., *Handbook of the Biology of Aging* (New York: Van Nostrand, Reinhold, 1977), pp. 6–8.

11. Levinson, *Seasons of a Man's Life,* pp. 218–21.

12. Douglas C. Kimmel, *Adulthood and Aging,* 2d ed. (New York: Wiley, 1980), pp. 202–3; Riley, "Aging, Social Change, and the Power of Ideas," p. 49.

13. Mary Jo Bane, *Here to Stay* (New York: Basic Books, 1976), p. 25.

14. The data are such that some researchers caution against fixed-stage theories of the life cycle, noting that activities that once defined stages (e.g., education, parenthood, work, retirement) are increasingly being spread in smaller bits over an entire life.

15. Masnick and Bane, *The Nation's Families,* p. 9.

16. Riley, "Aging, Social Change, and the Power of Ideas," p. 48.

17. Bane, *Here to Stay,* p. 25.

18. Masnick and Bane, *The Nation's Families,* p. 28.

19. Ibid., p. 21; Frances E. Kobrin, "The Fall in Household Size and the Rise of the Primary Individual in the United States," *Demography* 13 (1976): 127–38.

20. Ethel Shanas, "Social Myth as Hypothesis: The Case of the Family Relations of Old People," *Gerontologist* 19 (1979):4. The percentages given are of those over sixty-five who have living children—about 80 percent of the total in 1975.

21. Kimmel, *Adulthood and Aging,* p. 23.

22. Bane, *Here to Stay,* p. 5.

CHAPTER 3: LIFE-STORYTELLING

1. Sigmund Freud, *The Interpretation of Dreams,* in James Strachey, ed., *The Standard Edition of the Complete Psychological Works,* vols. 4 and 5 (London: Hogarth, 1953); W. I. Thomas and Florian Znaniecki, *The Polish Peasant in Europe and America* (New York: Knopf, 1927), vol. 2, p. 1832; Oscar Lewis, *The Children of Sanchez* (New York: Random House, 1961); Robert Coles, *Children of Crisis* (Boston: Atlantic–Little, Brown, 1967). A succinct historical overview of first-person accounts in the social sciences is contained in the first chapter of Robert C. Bogdan and Sari K. Biklen, *Qualitative Research for Education* (Boston: Allyn and Bacon, 1982). An international perspective is offered in Daniel Bertaux, ed., *Biography and Society* (Beverly Hills: Sage, 1981). Historical background for the study of life histories, which incorporate personal documents other than first-person

accounts, is provided in William M. Runyan, *Life Histories and Psychobiography* (New York: Oxford University Press, 1982).

2. Sigmund Freud, *The Psychopathology of Everyday Life,* in Strachey, ed., *Standard Edition,* vol. 6.

3. Alan Watts, *Beyond Theology* (New York: Pantheon, 1964), p. 29.

4. Hence the relationship of analytical to narrative ability is analogous to that of formal to concrete operations in the developmental theory of Jean Piaget.

5. Robert N. Butler, "The Life Review: An Interpretation of Reminiscence in the Aged," *Psychiatry* 26 (1963):65–76. A review of Coleman's and Meacham's work is found in Sharan Merriam, "The Concept and Function of Reminiscence: A Review of the Research," *Gerontologist* 20 (1980):604–9. In general, researchers have contended that reminiscing and the life review function positively for individuals, though, according to Merriam, the evidence is still inconclusive.

6. Daniel Bertaux, "Histories de vies—ou récits de pratiques? Méthodologie de l'approche biographique en sociologie," unpublished report (Paris: Centre d'Etudes des Mouvements Sociaux, 1976); "The Life Course Approach as a Challenge to the Social Sciences," in Tamara K. Hareven and Kathleen J. Adams, eds., *Aging and Life Course Transitions* (New York: Guilford, 1982), pp. 138–39.

7. The enormous effect made by an altered definition of the interview situation is illustrated in a brief report of work with torture victims, who were able to speak of their victimization only when "therapy" became "testimony." See Ana J. Cienfuegos and Cristina Monelli, "The Testimony of Political Repression as a Therapeutic Instrument," *American Journal of Orthopsychiatry* 53 (1983):43–51.

8. John Dollard, *Criteria for the Life History* (New Haven: Yale University Press, 1935; reprint, New York: Peter Smith, 1949), p. 15.

9. John N. Kotre, *The Best of Times, the Worst of Times: Andrew Greeley and American Catholicism, 1950–1975* (Chicago: Nelson-Hall, 1978).

10. Greeley, "More Useful Life," Universal Press Syndicate, copyright 1979.

11. John N. Kotre, *Simple Gifts: The Lives of Pat and Patty Crowley* (New York: Andrews and McMeel, 1979).

12. Robert Langs, *The Technique of Psychoanalytic Psychotherapy* (New York: Aronson, 1974), vol. 2, pp. 33–87..

13. Juxtaposing intersecting stories was the strategy adopted by Oscar Lewis in *The Children of Sanchez.*

14. Bertaux, ed., *Biography and Society,* pp. 7–9. Bertaux's predecessors in sociology faced the question of the truth of life stories as early as the days of the Chicago school. See, for example, pp. 187–90 of Clifford R. Shaw, *The Jack-Roller* (Chicago: University of Chicago Press, 1930; reprint, 1966).

15. Donald P. Spence, *Narrative Truth and Historical Truth* (New York: Norton, 1982), pp. 31, 166–68.

16. Gordon W. Allport, *Personality: A Psychological Interpretation* (New York: Holt, 1937). An excellent review of the idiographic-nomothetic debate in psychology, along with a judicious examination of the place of idiographic methods, appears in Chapter 9 of Runyan, *Life Histories and Psychobiography.*

17. Geertz, *Interpretation of Cultures,* pp. 3–30. My method calls for more generalizations across cases, however, than does the model proposed by Geertz.

18. Barney G. Glaser and Anselm L. Strauss, *The Discovery of Grounded Theory* (Chicago: Aldine, 1967).

CHAPTER 4: MIRROR, MIRROR

1. J. Robert Oppenheimer quoting the *Bhagavad Gita* when the bomb was first detonated in 1945.

2. William James describes religious conversion as a change in the "hot place" of consciousness. A dimly perceived region of awareness is suddenly activated and becomes a center of personal energy. When it becomes a center, a "new" soul or self is felt to have arisen there. The truth is that this "new" self was in the background of awareness—dormant—all along. See *The Varieties of Religious Experience* (New York: Collier, 1961), pp. 164–65.

3. Robert J. Lifton, *Thought Reform and the Psychology of Totalism* (New York: Norton, 1961).

CHAPTER 5: JOURNEY INTO THE LIE

1. I use the word *Dream* as Daniel Levinson used it in *The Seasons of a Man's Life* to refer not to a sleeping dream or a daydream but to a vision of what one hopes to be and to have in the future, to "a vague sense of self-in-adult-world . . . an imagined possibility that generates excitement and vitality." See *Seasons of a Man's Life,* p. 91.

2. Bernice L. Neugarten, "Adult Personality: Toward a Psychology of the Life Cycle," in Bernice L. Neugarten, ed., *Middle Age and Aging* (Chicago: University of Chicago Press, 1968); Bernice L. Neugarten and Gunhild O. Hagestad, "Age and the Life Course," in Binstock and Shanas, eds., *Handbook of Aging and the Social Sciences.*

3. Bane, *Here to Stay,* p. 25.

CHAPTER 6: A CHOSEN LIFE

1. Peter Marris, *Loss and Change* (New York: Pantheon, 1974).

2. Erikson, *Gandhi's Truth,* p. 130.

3. Richard A. Kalish, "Death and Dying in a Social Context," in Binstock and Shanas, eds., *Handbook of Aging and the Social Sciences;* Bengtson, Cuellar, and Ragan, "Stratum Contrasts and Similarities in Attitudes toward Death"; Lifton, "Sense of Immortality"; Levinson, *Seasons of a Man's Life,* pp. 209–21.

4. Vaillant and Milofsky, "Natural History of Male Psychological Health," p. 1350.

CHAPTER 7: IN A DREAM CASTLE

1. Elizabeth Loftus, *Eyewitness Testimony* (Cambridge, Mass.: Harvard University Press, 1979).

2. Ulric Neisser, *Memory Observed* (San Francisco: Freeman, 1982), p. 47.

3. Neisser's study of John Dean's testimony in the Watergate hearings led him to conclude that single recollections often have as their basis a sequence of repeated experiences (ibid., p. 158).

4. Charles H. Long, *Alpha: The Myths of Creation* (New York: Braziller, 1963).

5. Alfred Adler, *What Life Should Mean to You* (Boston: Little, Brown, 1931), p. 19.

6. Ibid., p. 74.

CHAPTER 8: BEING A DADDY

1. "A New Kind of Life with Father," *Newsweek,* November 30, 1981, pp. 93ff.
2. Bakan, *Duality of Human Existence.*
3. David Gutmann, "Men, Women, and the Parental Imperative," *Commentary* 56, no. 6 (1973): p. 62.
4. Marjorie Lowenthal, "Toward a Sociopsychological Theory of Change in Adulthood and Old Age," in James E. Birren and K. Warner Schaie, eds., *Handbook of the Psychology of Aging* (New York: Van Nostrand, Reinhold, 1977).
5. Levinson, *Seasons of a Man's Life,* pp. 228–36.
6. Carl Jung, "The Stages of Life," in Joseph Campbell, ed., *The Portable Jung* (New York: Viking, 1971), p. 16.
7. In a 1981 survey of fifteen hundred American families, eight out of ten men agreed that when both parents work, "mothers and fathers should play an equal role in caring for children" ("A New Kind of Life with Father," p. 93).

CHAPTER 9: THE MESSAGE

1. Dollard, *Criteria for the Life History,* p. 4.
2. Martin E. P. Seligman, *Helplessness* (San Francisco: Freeman, 1975).
3. Leon Festinger, Henry W. Riecken, and Stanley Schachter, *When Prophecy Fails* (Minneapolis: University of Minnesota Press, 1956).

CHAPTER 10: WHEN THE WHEAT WAS GREEN

1. Henry M. Greenspan, "Awe Is Not Enough," unpublished paper, 1982.
2. Anthony G. Greenwald, "The Totalitarian Ego," *American Psychologist* 35 (1980):603–18.
3. I suspect that a linear narrative structure also facilitates memory, but laboratory studies lack the ecological validity to be of much help in this regard. See Neisser, *Memory Observed,* p. 4.
4. David W. Plath, "Resistance at Forty-Eight: Old Age Brinkmanship and Japanese Life Course Pathways," in Hareven and Adams, eds., *Aging and Life Course Transitions,* p. 116.
5. This is an element that Donald Spence misses in his treatment of narrative truth. In my view, life stories in psychoanalysis are judged true not only if they possess coherence and aesthetic finality (criteria that Spence points out) but also if they match the stories of Oedipus or Wolf Man or any of the other psychoanalytic classics. See Spence, *Narrative Truth and Historical Truth.*

CHAPTER 11: THE CUP

1. Bruno Bettelheim, *The Uses of Enchantment* (New York: Alfred A. Knopf, 1976), p. 6.
2. Actually, Chris told three stories in our sessions together. The third, which he related after the story of the cup because it was also told by his father, was about gullibility. Its moral was "you can't believe everything you hear." Unlike the other two stories, however, this one was never referred to again. Hence I omitted it from the written life history.
3. Chris's stories lacked the fantastic, supernatural events that fairy tales are full of,

and they were explicit about the truths they wanted to teach, which is a characteristic of fables.

4. In the written version of his life story, Chris tells the story of the cup at the end of Part VII, which was later than in the spoken version. I relocated the story in the written version to maintain chronological sequence.

5. The third use appears at the end of Part VI of the written version.

6. Butler, "The Life Review."

7. Sigmund Freud, "Screen Memories," in Strachey, ed., *Standard Edition,* vol. 3, pp. 303–22.

CHAPTER 12: THE CULTURE CONNECTION

1. Although detailed results from the 1982 National Survey of Family Growth will not be available until October 1984, other data show that in 1982 sterilization, followed by the pill, was America's most common method of contraception. See Jacqueline D. Forrest and Stanley K. Henshaw, "What U.S. Women Think and Do about Contraception," *Family Planning Perspectives* 15 (1983):157–66.

2. Claudia Dowling, "The Relative Explosion," *Psychology Today* 17, no. 4 (1983):54–59.

3. Levinson, *Seasons of a Man's Life,* pp. 192–93.

4. Paul C. Glick, "Updating the Life Cycle of the Family," *Journal of Marriage and the Family* 39 (1977):6.

5. For example, when Erikson explicitly made the attempt to apply his stage theory to the life of Luther, he could not separate the stages of identity and generativity. See the epilogue of *Young Man Luther.*

6. Riegel, "Dialectics of Human Development"; Albert Bandura, "The Psychology of Chance Encounters and Life Paths," *American Psychologist* 37 (1982):747–55.

7. A succinct account of the premises of the "life course" approach may be found in the preface of Hareven and Adams, eds., *Aging and Life Course Transitions.*

8. I am willing to concede that generative moments, at least of the nonbiological kind, may accumulate in the third quarter of life and so provide the basis for belief in a stage. Carol Ryff and Susanne Heincke recently completed a study showing that individuals perceive the tasks of generativity to characterize middle age (40–45) rather than young adulthood (20–30) or old age (60 plus). Though their study did not address the critical question of what constitutes a stage, it did suggest that the generative impulse is triggered more frequently in middle adulthood than in other periods of life. See Carol D. Ryff and Susanne G. Heincke, "Subjective Organization of Personality in Adulthood and Aging," *Journal of Personality and Social Psychology* 44 (1983):807–16.

9. John D. Bransford and Marcia K. Johnson, "Consideration of Some Problems of Comprehension," in William G. Chase, ed., *Visual Information Processing* (New York: Academic, 1973); Jean M. Mandler and Nancy S. Johnson, "Remembrance of Things Parsed: Story, Structure and Recall," *Cognitive Psychology* 9 (1977):111–51.

10. The literature on the TAT is extensive; use of it in life-span research is typified by Bernice L. Neugarten and David L. Gutmann, "Age-Sex Roles and Personality in Middle Age: A Thematic Apperception Study," *Psychological Monographs* 72, no. 17 (1958), Whole No. 470.

11. Sidney Rosen, ed., *My Voice Will Go with You: The Teaching Tales of Milton H. Erickson* (New York: Norton, 1982); Roy Schafer, *Narrative Actions in Psychoanalysis* (Worcester, Mass.: Clark University Press, 1981); Spence, *Narrative Truth and Historical Truth.*

12. Bogdan and Biklen, *Qualitative Research for Education,* pp. 1–26.

13. Henry A. Murray, *Explorations in Personality* (New York: Oxford University Press, 1938); Robert W. White, *Lives in Progress* (New York: Holt, Rinehart, and Winston, 1952).

14. Barbara H. Smith, "Narrative Versions, Narrative Theories," *Critical Inquiry* 7 (1980):232. This entire issue of *Critical Inquiry* is germane to narrative psychology, as is the work of literary scholars who study autobiography.

15. Roy Schafer, *A New Language for Psychoanalysis* (New Haven: Yale University Press, 1976); *Narrative Actions in Psychoanalysis.*

16. Runyan, *Life Histories and Psychobiography.* Another excellent treatment of narrative appears in Bertram J. Cohler, "Personal Narrative and Life Course," in Paul B. Baltes and Orville G. Brim, Jr., eds., *Life-Span Development and Behavior* (New York: Academic 1982), pp. 205–41.

17. Yankelovich, "New Rules for American Life."

18. Riesman, "Egocentrism"; Yankelovich, "New Rules for American Life."

19. Plath, "Resistance at Forty-Eight," pp. 118–20, 123.

INDEX

ABOUT THE AUTHOR

JOHN KOTRE is professor of psychology at the University of Michi-
gan, Dearborn. He is also the author of *Simple Gifts: The Lives of
Pat and Patty Crowley; The Best of Times, the Worst of Times: Andrew
Greeley and American Catholicism;* and *The View from the Border: A
Social Psychological Study of Current Catholicism.*

THE JOHNS HOPKINS UNIVERSITY PRESS

Outliving the Self

*This book was composed in
Linotron Fournier text and display type
by Huron Valley Graphics, Ann Arbor, Michigan,
from a design by Cynthia W. Hotvedt.*

*It was printed on 50-lb. MV Eggshell paper
and bound in Joanna Arrestox book cloth
by The Maple Press Co., York, Pennsylvania.*